Working with Evidence 2

The Modern World

Peter & Mary Speed

Oxford University Press

Oxford University Press, Walton Street, Oxford OX2 6DP

Oxford London
New York Toronto Melbourne Auckland
Petaling Jaya Singapore Hong Kong Tokyo
Delhi Bombay Calcutta Madras Karachi
Nairobi Dar es Salaam Cape Town

and associated companies in
Beirut Berlin Ibadan Mexico City Nicosia

Oxford is a trade mark of Oxford University Press

© Peter & Mary Speed 1985
First published 1985
Reprinted 1986

ISBN 0 19 917068 1

Typeset by MS Filmsetting Ltd, Frome, Somerset
Printed in Great Britain by Butler & Tanner Ltd, Frome

Acknowledgements

The publishers would like to thank the following for permission to reproduce the illustrations;

Anglo-Chinese Educational Institute, pp 79, 84, 87, 88 and pp 77, 80 from *Rent Collection Courtyard*, Foreign Languages Press, Peking 1970; Associated Press, p 117; John Batchelor, p 25; BBC Hulton Picture Library, pp 53, 64, 70, 76, 96, 118, 120, 123, 125, 126, 130, 131, 134, 136; BBC Hulton Picture Library and The Bettmann Archive, pp 103, 107, 108, 110; Barnabys Picture Library, p 6 (Sara Ellis), p 56; Camera Press, pp 40 (Tony McGrath), 46 (James Pickerell), 68 (Imperial War Museum), 81 (Chinque), 85, 86, 91 (Alfred Gregory), 98 (R. J. Chinwalla); © The City of Oakland, The Oakland Museum, p 104; County Record Office, Huntingdon, p 121; Earthscan, p 92 (Mark Edwards); Mark Edwards Picture Library, p 100; Stewart E. Fraser *One Hundred Great Chinese Posters* © 1977 Images Graphiques Inc, cover & p 82; John Frost and Trade Union Congress, p 133; Imperial War Museum, pp 2, 3, 4, 7, 8, 10, 12, 14, 20, 23, 31, 33, 35, 129; Library of Congress, p 106; Ministry of Defence, p 28; Maggie Murray/Format, p 90; Museum of London, p 127; New York Public Library, p 101, Mrs Roy Nockolds and the RAF Club for the painting by Roy Nockolds, p 26; Novosti Press Agency, p 63; The Photo Source, pp 27, 29, 30, 34, 36, 38, 39, 47, 50, 52, 59, 65, 67, 73, 74, 75, 93, 94, 97; Popperfoto, pp 32, 69, 95, 114; The Press Association, pp 138, 140, 142; RAF Museum, pp 13, 15, 16; Rex Features, pp 41, 42, 48; Franklin D Roosevelt Library, Public Domain, p 102; Society for Cultural Relations with the USSR, p 72; Topham, pp 44, 45, 112, 116, 119; Ullstein Bilderdienst, West Berlin, pp 18, 19, 51, 54, 55, 57, 60; Wurtt Landesbibliothek Stuttgart, p 58 from NSDAP *Trust No Fox and No Jew*

The objects on the front cover were provided by the Ashmolean Museum, Oxford and the copy of the *Little Red Book of Mao Tse-tung* by the Anglo-Chinese Educational Institute, London.

To the Teacher

Almost every good history course is written for children that are average – average in their ability, the interest they show, and the effort that they are prepared to make. This is as it should be, but it does make problems for enthusiastic pupils. While they can gain much from a general course, they will master it quickly and easily, and then demand more. *Working with Evidence* fills that need. It is a collection of sources for the young student to interpret, with the help of questions. There are exercises to challenge the more able, but at the same time, most of the tasks are within the grasp of anyone of sound ability.

The books have a number of aims. The first is to encourage the enthusiasm for history which we hope is already present. To that end, we have avoided anything dour, like Acts of Parliament, but have chosen sources which are interesting, and some even amusing. However, no source has been included just because it is entertaining; each one makes a serious contribution.

Secondly, we want to encourage study in depth. This should not be at the expense of study in breadth, but once pupils have covered a general history course, they will gain far more if they then look at a few topics in detail.

Our third aim is to give some idea of the nature of historical evidence. Pupils often ask how we know what happened in the past and using the sources is the best way for them to find the answer. They should soon learn that sources support, complement or contradict each other and can, indeed, do all of these things at the same time.

Finally, we hope our readers will develop a number of skills, useful not only in history, but elsewhere. They will be asked to do the following:

1 Understand thoroughly each of the sources.
2 Evaluate the sources, compare them, and, where necessary, decide between them.
3 Extract from the sources what seem to be the most useful ideas and facts.
4 Synthesise the information so gained in a piece of writing.
5 Follow this work with further research and study.

The two books in this series were written to complement the *Oxford Junior History*, Books 4–6, but they could be used alongside any similar course. They are meant for children aged from about 10–13, but those preparing for external examinations will find them a useful introduction to the study of documents.

Contents

Chapter 1 *The First World War*
The Trenches   2
Trench Warfare   7
The War in the Air   12

Chapter 2 *The Second World War*
The German Victory in the West, 1940   18
The Battle of Britain   24
The War in the Desert   30

Chapter 3 *Two Problem Areas:
              The Middle East and South-East Asia*
The Fall of the Bar-Lev Line, October 1973   36
The War in Vietnam   44

Chapter 4 *Hitler's Germany*
The Nazis   51
Anti-Semitism   57

Chapter 5 *Russia*
The Communist Revolution in Petrograd, November 1917   63
Communists and Peasants   68

Chapter 6 *China*
China Before the Communist Revolution   73
The Peasants in Communist China   79
The Cultural Revolution   84

Chapter 7 *India*
Caste in India   90
Sacred Cows in India   95

Chapter 8 *The United States of America*
The Great Depression   101
President Roosevelt and the New Deal   107
The Black Americans   112

Chapter 9 *Britain*
Lloyd George and the Beginnings of the Welfare State   118
Votes for Women   125
The General Strike   131
The Falklands   138

Chapter 1 *The First World War*

The Trenches

At the start of the First World War the Germans quickly overran most of Belgium, and much of northern France. The French and British just managed to stop them before they took Paris. This was at the Battle of the Marne. Both sides had deadly weapons, especially machine guns and artillery, and now that the armies had halted, the men tried to protect themselves by digging trenches. Soon, these ran in an unbroken line from the Belgian coast to the Swiss frontier.

The first trenches were dug in a hurry, and without much planning, but before long they became complicated defensive systems.

In this section, you are going to read what it was like to be in the trenches.

An English officer, Robert Graves, describes his first night on duty in the front line:

Dunn showed me around the line. He introduced me to the platoon sergeants, then went back to sleep. I found myself in charge of the line. The men of the working party, whose job was to repair the trenches, looked curiously at me. They were filling sandbags with earth, piling them up bricklayer fashion, then patting them flat with spades. The sentries stood on the fire-step, stamping their feet, and blowing on their fingers. Every now and then they peered over the top for a few seconds. Two parties, each of an N.C.O. and two men, were out in the company listening posts, connected with the front trench by a sap about fifty yards long. The German front line stretched some three hundred yards beyond. From the berths hollowed in the sides of the trench came the grunt of sleeping men.

I jumped on the fire-step beside the sentry and cautiously raised my head, staring over the parapet. I could see nothing except the wooden pickets supporting our barbed wire, and a dark patch on two of the bushes beyond. The darkness seemed to move and shake about as I looked at it: the bushes started moving singly at first, then both together. The pickets did the same. I was glad of the sentry beside me.

I said: "It's funny how those bushes seem to move!"

"Aye, they do play queer tricks. Is this your first spell in the trenches, sir?"

A German flare shot up, broke into bright flame,

Soldiers in trench How are these men spending their time?

dropped slowly and went hissing into the grass behind our trench. Instinctively I moved.

"It's bad to do that, sir," said the sentry, as a rifle bullet cracked and seemed to pass right between us.

Goodbye to All That

1 What were the troops on duty doing during the night?
2 How far away were the Germans?
3 What could Robert Graves see in no-man's land? What strange sensations did he have?
4 What made Robert Graves jump? What happened when he did? What should he have done?

Keeping watch

Whenever the ground would let them, both sides dug mines under each other. Robert Graves wrote:

> Constant mining went on in this Cambrin-Cuinchy sector. We were likely to be blown up at any moment. An officer of the Royal Engineers tunnelling company won the Victoria Cross while we were there. A duel of mining and counter-mining had been going on. When the Germans began to undermine his original boring, he rapidly tunnelled beneath them. It was touch and go who would get ready first. He won. But when he detonated his mine from the trench by an electric lead, nothing happened. So he ran down again, retamped the charge, and got back just in time to set it off before the Germans. I had visited the upper boring on the previous day. It ran about twenty feet under the German lines. At the end of the gallery I found a Welsh miner on listening duty. He cautioned me to silence. I could distinctly hear the Germans working somewhere below us. He whispered: "So long as they work, I don't mind. It's when they bloody stop!"
>
> *Goodbye to All That*

1. What was the reason for digging mines?
2. Draw a diagram to show the "duel of mining and counter-mining" which Robert Graves describes.
3. How did the Royal Engineers officer win his V.C.?
4. Whom did Robert Graves find when he visited a mine?
5. What was the man doing? What worried him most? Why do you suppose this was?

One important duty was to patrol no-man's land at night. Robert Graves describes his first patrol:

> My orders for this patrol were to see whether a certain German sap-head was occupied by night or not.
>
> Sergeant Townsend and I went out at about ten o'clock, both carrying revolvers. We went ten yards at a time, slowly, not on all fours, but wriggling flat along the ground. After each movement we lay and watched for about ten minutes. We crawled through our own wire entanglements and along a dry ditch: ripping our clothes on more barbed wire, glaring into the darkness until it began turning round and round. Once I snatched my fingers in horror from where I had planted them on the slimy body of an old corpse. We nudged each other with rapidly beating hearts at the slightest noise or suspicion: crawling, watching, crawling, shamming dead under the blinding light of enemy flares, and again crawling, watching, crawling.
>
> We found the gap in the German wire and at last came within five yards of the sap-head. We waited quite twenty minutes listening for any signs of its occupation. Then I nudged Sergeant Townsend and, revolver in hand, we wriggled quietly forward and slid into it. It was unoccupied. On the floor was a wicker basket containing something large and smooth and round, twice the size of a football. Eventually I dared to lift it out and carry it

back, suspecting it might be one of the German gas-cylinders we had heard so much about.

We got home after making a journey of perhaps two hundred yards in rather more than two hours. The sentries passed along the word that we were in again. Our prize proved to be a large glass container quarter-filled with some pale yellow liquid. Everybody seemed greatly interested in it. The theory was that the vessel contained a chemical for re-damping gas masks. I never heard the official report.

Goodbye to All That

Note: the sap-head would have been a small section of trench, in front of the main line.

1 What was the purpose of the patrol?
2 What weapons did the two men carry? Why did they take these rather than rifles, do you suppose?
3 How did they move?
4 In what ways was it unpleasant to be in no-man's land?
5 How did the two men make sure there were no Germans in the sap head?
6 What did Robert Graves bring back with him? What did he think it might be? What was the general opinion when he returned?
7 How long was the journey back? How long did it take?
8 Why did sentries need to know when patrols were out and when they came in, do you suppose?

A French sergeant, Jacques Péricard, has given us this account:

To fortify the places which were in sight of the enemy, we could only work at night.

Almost always we had snow or rain, as uninvited guests. Then we used to work in our capes, looking like monks who were digging their own graves.

From our dug-outs to our places of work, the distance, made longer by the winding of the communication trenches, was all of two kilometres. Those who have been at the front will know what it means to walk at night along two kilometres of communication trenches. You hit your shoulder on the sides, you are caught by roots, you stumble over a stone, or sink in a puddle, you dent your forehead at every turning.

Here and there a shell has struck the parapet and filled the trench with earth; a tree, cut down by the blast of an explosion has landed right in the middle of the path.

Sometimes you run into troops carrying planks, stakes, boxes of grenades or cartridges. You then have to hoist yourself on top of the parapet to clear the way, and when it is raining, and you do the same thing several times,

Communications trench Troops and supplies had to move regularly along this trench. In what ways would mud like this make an army less efficient?

you soon find yourself so caked in mud that it is impossible to see any of your clothes.

Face à Face

1 Why do the troops have to work at night?
2 What often made their work unpleasant?
3 How far did the men have to go to reach their place of work? (How far is that, roughly, in miles?)
4 List the ways in which it was difficult to walk along a communications trench.

A French officer, Louis Mairet wrote:

We go through the mud and the rain to Ville-en-Woevre.

I arrive with one shoe in my hand, a shoe that I had great difficulty in pulling out of the mire. It is the least important and most amusing of the things that happened on the journey. Cost: one pair of socks. We sink in the mud up to our knees: you have to see it to believe it. The mud is indeed the other enemy: glutinous and terrible. From now on we are going to live in the mud, or rather, fight against it with all our strength. We sleep in makeshift shelters, without camp beds to lie on, or rubber sheets to keep off the rain. And it rains, it rains wickedly every night. In spite of everything we do, we sleep, as I put it, 'backs to the mud, and faces to the rain.' So we live, in the heart of a wood, hardly able to move because the mud is above our ankles, buried alive, and badly fed because the fatigue parties are in danger of getting lost or being drowned.

Le Carnet d'un Combattant

1 What problems do the rain and the mud make for the troops?
2 What equipment do they lack?

Another problem was the cold. The winter of 1916–1917 was especially bitter. Louis Mairet wrote:

In the trench, when I go my rounds during the night, warm air comes from the dug-outs. And like the tramps who pause outside the kitchens of rich houses to smell the cooking, I stop at the entrance of the saps. The gusts of air stink, but they are deliciously warm on my face which is blue with the biting cold of the dawn. Sometimes I go inside. On the stairs an acrid smoke chokes me, blinds me, makes my eyes run. At the bottom, I sit on the ground, to find some air that is fit to breathe. I open my eyes; I can see nothing but fog and a red dot. They always have a stove, with no chimney, or a brazier, on which they burn wood. You have a little warmth at the risk of being suffocated. My eyes become used to the darkness. I can make out a dirty table, some broken beds, a circle of shadowy figures around a fire. It is a brazier, where the pieces of a grenade box are burning. Two men and a corporal are stretching their chapped, trembling hands towards it. I cannot see their faces which are buried in their balaclava helmets, but there are icicles on their bristling moustaches, and their entire bodies are steaming like oxen back from ploughing. They say nothing. They have just come off guard duty. They are still wearing their sheepskin jackets, frozen into folds.

Opposite me, sitting on a box, a grey-haired old man is looking after the brazier. It is a tricky job. He takes the wet boards and lays them side by side above the flames: then, when they are dry, he plunges them into the heart of the fire. He stays seated, without saying a word. 'Does he never go to sleep?' I ask the corporal. The corporal takes out his pipe and says, 'That man has nowhere to go. He has his own place, but it's over there at the back where the smoke collects, and it's impossible to sleep. So he looks after the fire, because without a fire you can't sleep either. And he sleeps there, on his box.' I look at the old man again, and, indeed, he has dozed off. He will wake up soon, when something tells him that his fire needs wood. And so it is every night, for nights and nights on end. He is asleep now, his head on his chest. But I can only see his hands, his poor, worn, black hands, clasped together as if in prayer.

Le Carnet d'un Combattant

1 What is unpleasant about the entrances to the dug-outs? Why does Louis Mairet stop by them?
2 How do the men heat their dug-outs? Why is this unpleasant?
3 What shows that the corporal and the two men are very cold? What have they been doing?
4 Why has the old man chosen to look after the fire?
5 How does he sleep?

There were times, even in the trenches, when the men could relax. Robert Graves wrote:

In the interval between stand-to and breakfast, the men who were not getting in a bit of extra sleep sat about talking and smoking, writing letters home, cleaning their rifles, running their thumbnails up the seams of their shirts to kill lice, gambling. Lice were a standing joke. Young Bumford handed me one: 'We was just having an argument as to whether it's best to kill the old ones or the young ones, sir. Morgan here says that if you kill the old ones, the young ones die of grief: but Parry here, sir, he says that the young ones are easier to kill and you can catch the old ones when they go to the funeral.'

Goodbye to All That

1 How do the men pass their time?
2 What jokes do they make about lice?
3 What do you suppose they really felt about lice?

Jacques Péricard wrote about his men:

Each one did as he pleased.

Some who were determined to sleep flung themselves on beds of dried leaves as soon as they had finished their coffee and slept like logs, snoring until the next day.

Card players gathered round a candle which had been stuck on a stake driven into the ground.

The happy owner of a daily paper, something rare in the trenches, settled down to his feast with a greedy eye and devoured the four pages from the first line of the title to the last line of the advertisements. He was quite indifferent to the hungry glances of the others who were waiting their turn, and thinking he would go on reading for ever.

Discharge certificate What men were given these certificates? Why did they need them, do you suppose?

The other men talked. The conversation was sometimes light-hearted, but more often serious. War makes people solemn. We want to know why we allowed our country to be invaded; why the enemy was unable to follow up his victories; why we felt sure we were going to win; what punishment would be meted out to the aggressors for their horrible crime; what changes the war would make to France. But our favourite topic was our families. The war drew together as never before children and parents, wives and husbands, engaged couples. A twin torrent of letters goes every day from the rear to the front, from the front to the rear, torrents of fire, burning with malice, disappointment, anger and unhappy memories.

Face à Face

1. How did Péricard's troops spend their time?
2. What questions did they ask themselves?
3. What did they talk about most?
4. How had the war affected family feelings?
5. What were their letters like? Why do you suppose this was?

Here are some verses from a poem by Wilfred Owen, who was a soldier in the First World War. He was killed a week before it ended.

The poem describes twenty-four hours in the trenches.

Exposure

Our brains ache, in the merciless iced east winds that knive us . . .
Wearied we keep awake because the night is silent . . .
Low, drooping flares confuse our memory of the salient . . .
Worried by silence, sentries whisper, curious, nervous,
  But nothing happens.

Watching, we hear the mad gusts tugging on the wire,
Like twitching agonies of men among its brambles,
Northward incessantly, the flickering gunnery rumbles,
Far off, like a dull rumble of some other war.
  What are we doing here?

The poignant misery of dawn begins to grow . . .
We only know war lasts, rain soaks, and clouds sag stormy.
Dawn massing in the east her melancholy army
Attacks once more in ranks on shivery ranks of grey,
  But nothing happens.

Sudden successive flights of bullets streak the silence.
Less deathly than the air that shudders black with snow,
With sidelong flowing flakes that flock, pause and renew;
We watch them wandering up and down the wind's nonchalance,
  But nothing happens.

Pale flakes with fingering stealth come feeling for our faces . . .
We cringe in holes, back on forgotten dreams, and stare, snow-dazed,
Deep into grassier ditches. So we drowse, sun-dozed,
Littered with blossoms trickling where the blackbird fusses.
  Is it that we are dying?

To-night, His frost will fasten on this mud and us,
Shrivelling many hands, puckering foreheads crisp.
The burying-party, picks and shovels in their shaking grasp,
Pause over half-known faces. All their eyes are ice,
  But nothing happens.

1. What does the soldier see and hear, during the night and during the day?
2. What does he do?
3. What are his feelings?
4. What questions does he ask himself?
5. How does he feel about the coming of the dawn?
6. What impressions of life in the trenches does this poem give you?

Written Work
You are a soldier in the First World War. Write a diary of your life in the trenches.

Research
1. Read books by men who were in the First World War. Your local library will almost certainly have some.
2. Find out about the weapons used in the First World War.
3. Find out what it was like to drive and fight in tanks.

Trench Warfare

As you saw in the last section, the First World War began as a war of movement, with the Germans sweeping forward hundreds of miles. In little more than a month, though, the French and British had fought them to a standstill and the rival armies dug trenches. It was now the ambition of the generals on both sides to break through the enemy lines and start the war of movement again, with their foes on the run. It did not happen, and the front hardly moved until 1918. In this section you will see some of the reasons why.

Early in the war, Jacques Péricard took part in one of the many attacks that the French made against the Germans. This is what he wrote afterwards:

Our commanding officer passes along the ranks: 'We are going to have the honour of charging. I am counting on you.'

The charge! a magic word, and such a French word, recalling glorious names which make us feel brave: Bouvines, Fontenoy, Valmy, Reichshoffen.

Now we can see the horizon in the first light of dawn.

The officers explain the plan of attack:

'The trench which we are going to take is there, beyond that big oak tree, about a hundred yards from us. Between it and us, there is this very thick wood which you can see.'

The order comes. Silently we slip out of the trench. We are in the wood. So that we can stay out of sight as long as possible we fall flat on our faces.

Flat on our faces! So this was the charge I had been dreaming about!

We go forward twenty yards without trouble: then, suddenly, from the enemy trench there is a murderous fire. The bullets whistle over our heads, to the right, to the left. They thud into the tree trunks and snap the branches.

A moment's hesitation and we go on our way. Behind us a terrible cry, drawn out, like the howl of a dog, baying at the moon. My heart misses a beat at the thought of a wounded friend.

The corporal in front of me stops in his tracks without making a sound. A bullet has gone right through his head. As I crawl past him I see the dreadful wound and look away.

Bzz, bzz, bzz go the bullets.

Over the top How is this charge different from the one Péricard describes?

The enemy is now quite near. I have to climb over heaps of dead and wounded. The snow has become black mud, streaked with red. My hands are sticky with blood.

Oh, Fontenoy! Oh Valmy!

Here, surrounded by friends, but only 50 yards from the enemy, I feel quite alone, more alone than in a desert. I have no hope of help or comfort from anyone. I have to find within myself the strength to go on. I am still crawling, the bullets fall like hail, and more and more of our men are killed.

I say to myself, 'Shall I reach that tree stump alive?'

Bzz, bzz, bzz, go the bullets.

At last I leave the wood. In my group there is not a single man of my company. Six of us dive into a shell hole, hardly seven or eight yards from the enemy trench. Above our heads the machine guns pour out a deadly fire. What can we do? To retreat is almost certain death; to advance gives us a chance. Let's take our part of the trench and our friends will rush to our help. We group together, rifles in hand, and at a signal from one of us, we leap up. Before we take a single step, four of us fall.

Now there is only one man left with me, obviously a new recruit. We look at each other. It is impossible to speak in the noise of the firing. I make a signal of despair: there is nothing we can do. But the boy doesn't agree with me, and he waves at the enemy trench as if to say 'Come on!' Oh, the brave young man! What happened to him? I never saw him again, though afterwards I looked at every regiment that marched past me, hoping to find him.

I shake my head, and fall back to the ground. Suddenly I feel dreadfully tired, overcome by the horrors I have seen, and the disappointment at our failure. I cannot find the strength to go back.

But I can't stay there for ever. The Germans might take me prisoner, and I don't want that at any price. I slide out of the hole and start crawling once more. The hail of bullets has not slackened. Every moment I am expecting the one which is bound to hit me. It will be before I reach the bush. I pass the bush. It will be between those two bodies. Then my worries change. I ask myself where the bullet will strike me. Will it be in the neck, like the corporal? Or in the forehead like this captain? Or in the heart like that soldier?

However, I make my way, little at a time. I am already on the edge of the forest. There I stop, worn out. I can go no further, I am sure. I close my eyes, almost hoping that a bullet will put me out of my misery.

Our trench isn't far away, though; only ten yards. Supposing I tried? I stiffen and collapse: I stiffen again and at last I reach the trench after an effort which I think is going to kill me. I drag myself over the parapet and fall flat on my face. I have only one thought, one need, one wish: to sleep, sleep, sleep until the end of the world.

Face à Face

1 What does the word 'charge' mean to Péricard?
2 How, in fact, is the 'charge' made?
3 How far away are the German trenches? What is there between them and the French lines?
4 What happens while Péricard is going forward?
5 How close does Péricard get to the German lines?

Field gun Why is the ground in this condition? (See page 10).

6 Where does he take shelter? How many men are with him?
7 Why do the men decide to attack?
8 What happens as soon as they try?
9 What does the young man with Péricard want to do?
10 Why does Péricard decide to return?
11 What does he think about as he crawls back?
12 Why does he have great difficulty in reaching his own trench?
13 What does he do as soon as he arrives?
14 What would you say was the main reason the French attack failed?

It was not long before generals decided to try blasting the way clear with artillery. They hoped their guns would destroy the enemy trenches and blow up his machine-gun nests. The infantry could then go forward without much danger. The British tried this several times, as, for example, at Passchendaele in 1917. To prepare for their attack they fired $4\frac{1}{2}$ million shells in nineteen days.

We shall see the battle through the eyes of a young artillery officer, P. J. Campbell, who wrote a book about it called *In the Cannon's Mouth*. He had charge of a battery of field guns. They were quite light and were supposed to follow close behind the infantry, giving them support.

The day before the infantry attack, Campbell and his friend Jack went to their colonel for orders:

> The Colonel began talking to Jack. It would be perfectly straightforward, he said. The Boche had been given such a hammering that he would not know whether it was last night or tomorrow morning, when the attack started. It would be just like the last show over again. Jack would simply have to follow the infantry, unrolling telephone wire as he went, and stopping every now and then to let them know at headquarters how far the advance had gone.
>
> 'Just like going for a country walk.' Captain Cherry said.

Note: By the 'last show' the Colonel meant the capture of Messines Ridge earlier that year.

In the Cannon's Mouth

1 What was to be Jack's job on the day of the attack?
2 How did the colonel say the Germans would be feeling? Why?
3 How did the colonel and Captain Cherry think the attack would go?

Campbell describes what happened next morning:

> It was still very quiet: the quietness gave a sense of unreality to the morning. But I could feel my heart beating.
>
> One gun behind us on the other side of the canal fired a second too soon. Then Frank blew a loud blast on his whistle, but I only heard the first note. The bombardment began as he was blowing. All the guns in the Ypres Salient opened fire and the roar of artillery drowned every other sound. All the guns in the Salient! It sounded like all the guns in the world. It sounded as though the sky was falling, as though the thunder of the guns had cracked it, as though the world itself was breaking into pieces. Our shells were breaking it. Low down, all along the eastern horizon, I saw their red flashes as they burst, spurts of fire in the darkness. And now the German rockets were going up, their S.O.S. signals, the call for artillery support: red, green and yellow lights, and showers of beautiful golden rain. A few German shells came back at us, but for the most part they were falling a long way in front, on the infantry, on the trenches from which the attack was now being made. We should get it later probably, I thought: but we had no casualties at this time.

In the Cannon's Mouth

1 What did the bombardment sound like to Campbell?
2 What did the Germans do in reply?
3 Why did Campbell think so few enemy shells were falling on the British guns?

After a while, the British field guns moved forward as planned, but then things began to go wrong.

> Cherry rang up again. He did not sound so optimistic this time. Some enemy strong points were still holding out and our advance had been held up for the moment.
>
> 'Look at the road!' Josh said to me.
>
> It was packed with guns and waggons and other transport, all the way up to the top of the ridge in front of us, and for some way behind it. But it was not moving. Nothing was going over the crest. What was wrong? 'I can put two and two together as well as anyone else.' Josh said. 'They're not going on because they can't, because the Boche is still there and would see them if they went over the crest.'
>
> I waited. Surely the line would start moving soon. Cherry had said it was only in one or two places that we had been held up. Surely the next attack would be successful. But the long line on the road did not move.

In the Cannon's Mouth

1 Why, according to Captain Cherry, had the British advance been halted?
2 What was there on the road?
3 Why was the column not moving, did Josh say?

Wounded men Why was rescuing the wounded particularly difficult and dangerous? What did P. J. Campbell do when he was asked to help? (See page 11.)

This is what happened in the afternoon.

Some time later Frank and the Major returned. 'It's utter lunacy,' the Major was saying. 'We shell the place for a month until there isn't a yard of ground left that isn't a shell-hole, and then they expect the infantry to be able to advance, and they tell us to move our guns up there.'

There was no road, he said, there was nothing at all. It would have been utterly impossible to take guns up there even if the German positions had been captured. 'Why don't they go and look at the place and see it for themselves?' he said.

We had our tea. Edward had come up from the wagon lines to find out the latest news and when the limbers would be wanted for the advance. 'There won't be any advance,' the Major said. 'I'm telling you, it was as much as a man could do to walk about. Guns! Why, you couldn't push a bicycle up there, or a ruddy pram.'

In the Cannon's Mouth

Note: A limber was an ammunition box on wheels, drawn by horses. The gun was hitched behind it.

1 What had the British guns done to the ground?
2 What was the Major's opinion of what had happened?
3 Whom do you suppose he meant by 'they'? What did he say 'they' should do?

Later, Campbell himself went forward and took shelter in what, at first, he called a 'dug-out'.

It was not a dug-out in the ordinary sense of the word. In Flanders you could not dig down to a depth of more than one or two feet because you came to water. But you could strengthen houses or farm buildings by reinforcing the walls and the roof with sandbags or blocks of concrete. The Germans were better at this than we were, probably because they could employ forced Belgian labour. Every building behind their line was converted into a small fort, with slits through which machine guns could be fired. These were the pill-boxes as they came to be called later. Almost indestructible by shellfire, they were extremely difficult to capture, and time after time during the fighting of 1917 our attacking infantry overran a line of pill-boxes only to be shot at from behind and forced to retire by unwounded enemy soldiers who had come out of the forts.

In the Cannon's Mouth

1 Why was it impossible to make a proper dug-out in Flanders?
2 What could be done instead?
3 What were the buildings called?
4 How did they stop an attack?

Even where there were no pill-boxes a few machine gun nests usually survived the bombardment. They held up the enemy until reinforcements arrived.

Campbell met some infantry who had been in the attack:

We saw some men coming down the slope in front of us. They didn't seem to be walking properly; they looked as though they were walking in their sleep. I saw Tommy's colonel going out to see them. 'Come on lads!' I heard him say. 'I'll take you up there.' They took no notice of him. They just walked past him. He called some of them by name. 'Come back with me: I'll lead you there myself: don't let the Regiment down!' He was an oldish man, his voice was pleading, not commanding. They went on walking. Some of them stopped when they reached the trench at Bank Farm. Others crossed it and went on up the hill. It was the first time I had seen men who were finished.

The attack had failed. Our men were back where they had started.

In the Cannon's Mouth

1. How did the troops seem?
2. What did their colonel want them to do?
3. What, in fact, did they do?

Campbell was close to the front line, gathering information, when the Germans answered the British attack with a bombardment of their own. He dived into a shallow trench with some other officers. Close by was a pill-box which the British were using as a dressing station, that is, a place where doctors attended the wounded:

I hoped it would only last for five or ten minutes. Heavy shelling was usually over in a short time. But it went on. Some of the shells fell very close, and they were big ones. I flattened myself against the earth. The dressing station was about twenty yards from me; I was the nearest one to it. There was not room inside for all the wounded men who had been brought there. Some had to be left outside, or were taken outside if they were hopeless cases. They were a long time dying. Their crying rose to a scream as they heard the sound of a shell coming, then fell away to a moan after the shell had burst.

I lost all count of the shells and all count of time. There was no past to remember or future to think about. Only the present. The present agony of waiting, waiting for the shell that was coming to destroy us, waiting to die. I did not speak to Vernon. Vernon did not speak to me. I had shut my eyes, I saw nothing. But I could not shut my ears. I heard everything, the screaming of the shells, the screams of pain, the terrifying explosions, the vicious fragments of iron rushing downwards, biting deeply into the earth all round us.

I could not move. I had lost all power over my limbs. My heart throbbed, my face was burning, my throat was parched. I wanted a drink. There was lime juice in my water bottle on my back, but I could not move my arm to pull it towards me. I could think of nothing but my own suffering. Still the cruel shells screamed in their fiendish joy, still the sun beat down on us.

It stopped. I did not realise that it had stopped. I do not know how long I lay there, thinking that it still went on, but I heard a voice and I opened my eyes. A newcomer had joined us, an officer of the Engineers. To my surprise I recognised him. It was someone who had been at school with me five or six years before. I had not liked him. There was a smear of dried blood down one of his cheeks. He kept on touching the wound with his finger and then looking at his finger to see whether the bleeding had stopped.

'Lot of wounded up at the top,' he was saying. 'Any of you fellows coming up with me?'

None of us spoke.

'They're crying,' he said. 'I've heard them.'

Still no one spoke.

'We can get a stretcher,' he said.

One of the others spoke for us all. 'We've got our own job to do,' he said.

He waited for another minute. None of us moved. 'No one coming?' he said. Then he went away. I did not see where he went: I never saw him again.

In the Cannon's Mouth

1. Why did Campbell think the shelling would soon end?
2. What, in fact, happened?
3. What was happening to many of the wounded at the dressing station?
4. What was Campbell expecting to happen to him at any moment?
5. Why was he unable to drink?
6. Who appeared when the shelling stopped?
7. What did he want the officers in the trench to do?
8. What was their excuse for refusing?
9. What do you suppose was their real reason?

Written Work

You are a newspaper reporter who has visited the front line. Write a report for your paper. In it describe an attack that has taken place and explain why it failed.

Research

1. Read about some of the battles which took place before 1917, especially the Somme offensive of 1916.
2. Find out more about the Passchendaele offensive. (It is sometimes called the Third Battle of Ypres).
3. How was the Battle of Cambrai, 1917, different from Passchendaele? Why did the British fail?
4. Why were the German offensives of 1918 successful to start with? Why did they fail in the end?
5. Why were the British offensives of 1918 successful?

The War in the Air

When the First World War began, aeroplanes were still quite primitive. Generals thought they might go scouting, just as cavalry did on the ground. Indeed, the most famous German airman of the war, Manfred von Richthofen, began his career in the cavalry. Apart from gathering information, though, there was little that the aircraft of 1914 could do. The war soon forced changes. By 1918 the Germans alone had designed 140 different types of aeroplane and had built nearly 50,000 machines.

In this section you are going to see what it was like to fly and fight in various kinds of aircraft.

In 1914 it seemed that airships were better than aeroplanes. It was a German, Count von Zeppelin, who had pioneered them, and it was the Germans who used them most. At first, they only had 13 military airships, but they soon built a lot more. All the time they improved them so that they would fly faster and higher, and carry heavier loads. They were able to make long distance bombing raids long before aeroplanes could.

In the first extract the navigator of a Zeppelin, Franz Lampel, describes a raid on London:

Over England at last! Our hands are drawn to the bomb release lever like iron to a magnet; but the time has not yet come. London is our objective and there still remains a good two hours' flight before we arrive at our journey's end. We lean out of the portholes, and pick out landmarks and locate them on the map as well as we can from that height. Below us everything is still as death, and the country is perfectly darkened.

Far, far away, we see a light, and soon afterwards a second. They lie on our course. A short calculation follows. We must be right over London. Shadows cover the entire city, yet even so the various districts and the main streets can be recognised in the moonlight.

Damaged airship

At high speed we steer for the city, the Commander standing ready on the bombing platform. 'Let go!' he cries. The first bomb has fallen on London! We lean over the side. What a cursed long time it takes between release and impact when the bomb travels those thousands of feet! We fear that it is a 'dud' – until we hear the explosion. Already we have frightened them: away goes the second, an incendiary bomb. It blazes up underneath and sets fire to something. Now a second incendiary hit is seen. Its flames have scarcely leapt upwards in a shower of sparks before we hear an explosion so loud it can be heard above the roar of the propellers. At the same time on come the searchlights, reaching after us like gigantic spiders' legs: right, left and all around. In a moment the bright body of the ship lies in the beams.

'Hard aport!' The steersman spins his wheel, and in a moment we are out of the dazzling rays. But it is no longer pitch dark. The countless beams of searchlights fill the sky with a vivid light. They have lost us – strike wildly past us, catch us once again, go on over us. This mad frolic continues for hours on end.

We lose all idea of time as we fly on, every half minute releasing another bomb. Every explosion is observed, and its position pin-pricked on the map.

It is difficult to understand how we manage to survive the storm of shell and shrapnel, for, according to the chronometer, we have spent a good hour under that furious fire. When London lies far behind us, the searchlights are still stabbing the darkness – more than sixty of them – looking for the bird that has already flown.

The German Air Force in the Great War, Georg Neumann

1 How long does it take to reach London from the coast? (The entire trip lasted 12 hours.)
2 How does the navigator find his way?
3 What precautions have the English taken against air raids?
4 How do the Germans know they are over London?
5 What are the two types of bomb which they drop?
6 What defences do the English have?
7 How do the crew of the Zeppelin protect themselves?
8 What do they do as they drop their bombs?
9 How long do they spend over London?
10 Where does Lampel contradict himself?

The oldest types of military aircraft were observation balloons, which had been in use for over a hundred years. They were common in the First World War. A famous American airman, Eddie Rickenbacker describes them:

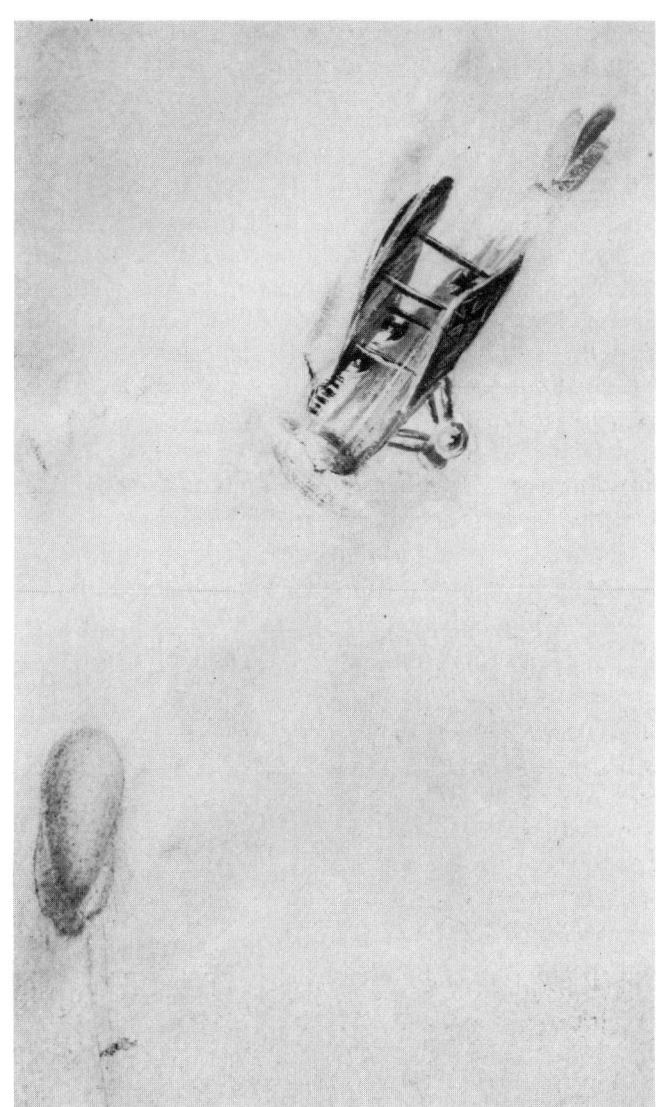

German fighter attacking observation balloon

Observation balloons are a most valuable way of spying on the enemy. They are huge in size, forming a sausage some two hundred feet in length and perhaps fifty feet in diameter.

These balloons are placed along the lines some two miles behind the front-line trenches. From his perch two thousand feet above the ground, the observer can study the ground and pick up every detail over a radius of ten miles on every side. Clamped over his ears are telephone receivers. With his telescope to his eye he observes and talks to the officers on the truck below him. They in turn inform him of any special object about which information is wanted. If our battery is firing upon a certain enemy position, the observer watches for the bursts and corrects the faults in aim. If a certain roadway is being blown up by our artillery, the observer tells the battery when enough damage has been done to make the road useless. Observation balloons are thus a constant menace to ground forces.

It naturally occurs to every airplane pilot that such a huge and unwieldy target must be easy to destroy from the air. They cannot fight back with any hope of success. All that seems to be needed is a sudden dash by a fighting airplane, a few shots with incendiary bullets – and the big gas bag bursts into flames. What could be more simple?

Fighting the Flying Circus

1. How big are balloons?
2. Where are they placed? How high do they fly?
3. How far can the observer see?
4. How does he talk to the men on the ground?
5. Give two examples of the ways in which an observer in a balloon can help artillery.
6. How does Rickenbacker think a balloon can be destroyed?
7. Why does he think it will be easy?

Later, Rickenbacker and four other American airmen went to attack German balloons. They left early in the morning so that they could fly well behind the German lines and steal up on their targets before it was too light. This is what happened when Rickenbacker reached his balloon:

I headed directly for the swinging target. There facing me in the middle of the balloon was a huge Maltese Cross, the emblem of the German air force. I shifted my rudder a bit and pointed my sights exactly at the centre of the

Aerial photograph and map Aircraft were important for reconnaissance right from the start of the war. Soon, their pilots were taking photographs. From these photographs it was possible to draw maps, like the one on the right. Use the map to recognise as many things as you can from the photograph. T.M. stands for Trench Mortar. What does M.G. mean, do you suppose? Note the shell craters on the photograph.

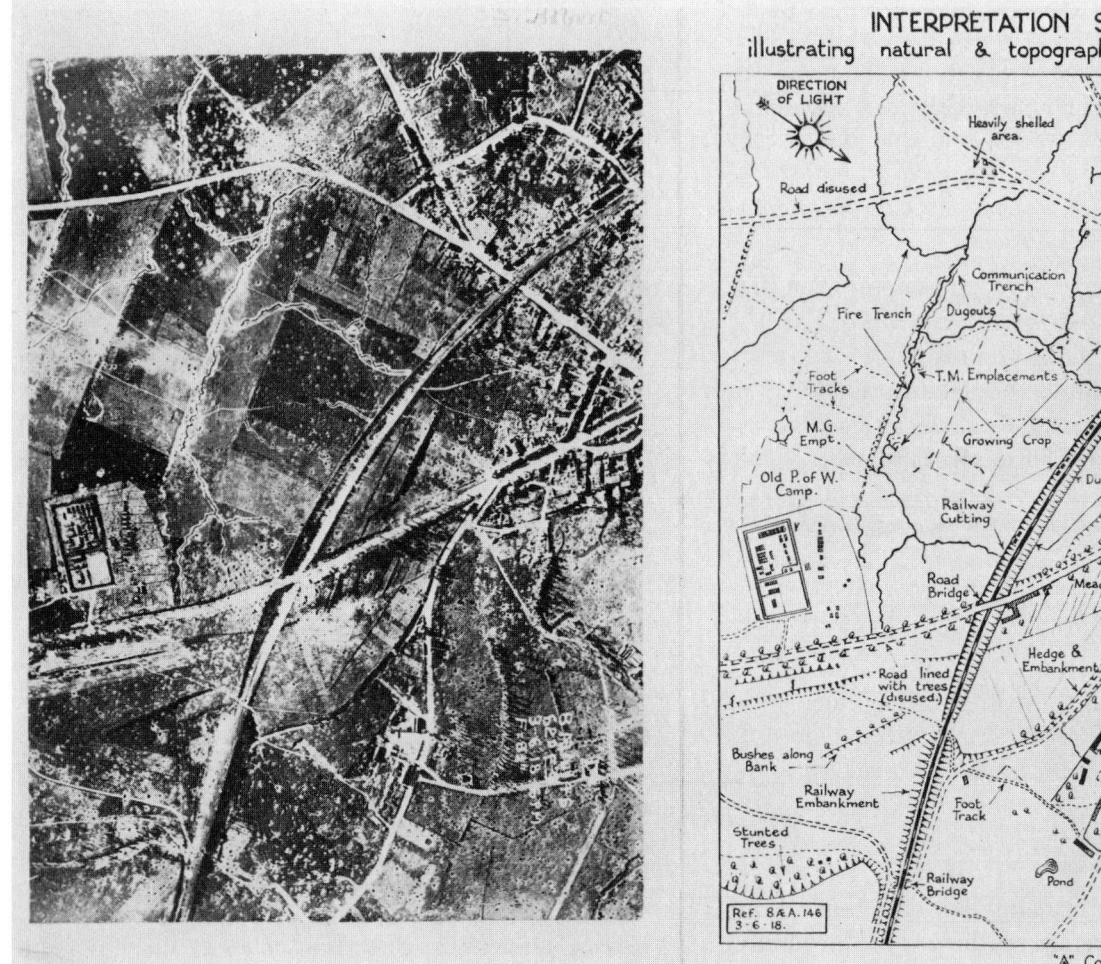

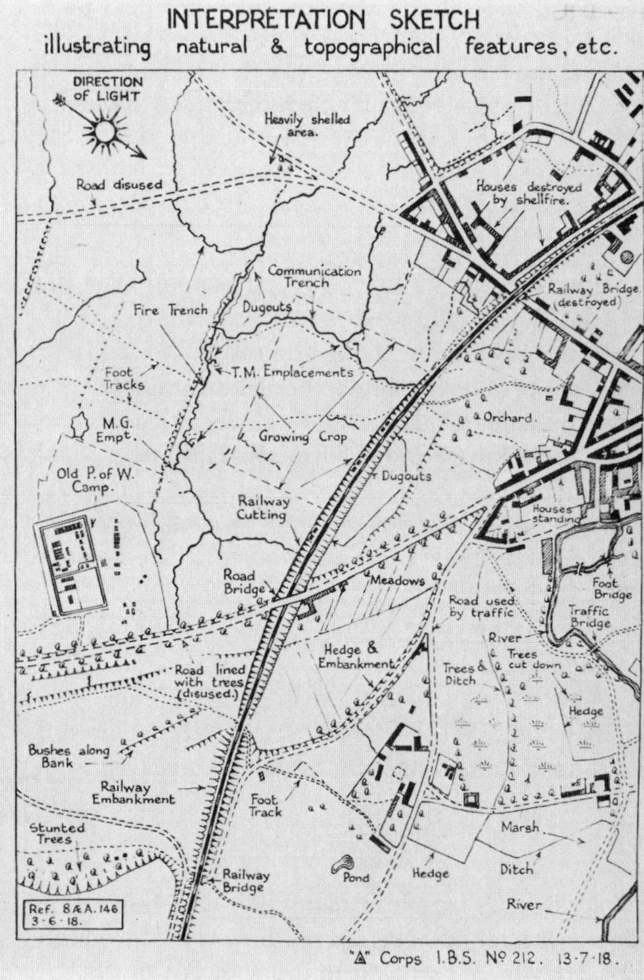

cross. Then I pressed both triggers with my right hand. I saw three or four streaks of flame flash ahead of me and enter the huge bulk of the balloon. Then the flame abruptly ceased. With the largest target in the world before me, I had failed because of a stupid jamming of my guns. But some three or four bullets had entered the sides of the balloon – of this I was certain. Why had they failed to set fire to it?

Later on I was to discover that flaming bullets often puncture balloons without producing the expected blaze. The very speed of their flight leaves no time for the ignition of the gas. Often in the early dawn the dews and moisture in the air dampen the balloon's envelope and hundreds of incendiary bullets penetrate it without doing more damage than can be repaired with a few strips of adhesive plaster.

I flew through a fiery curtain of German bullets and set my course for home. Then I began to laugh at something that had happened. As I began firing at the sausage the German observer who had been standing in his basket with his eyes glued to his binoculars had obviously been taken entirely by surprise. The first warning he had of my approach, was my bullets. He instantly dropped his glasses and dived headlong over the side of his basket with his parachute. I caught the merest glimpse of him as I swept past and there was a look of terror and surprise on his face which almost made up for my disappointment.

Arriving at the aerodrome I found that I was the last of my little party to land. The other four were standing together – looking rather sheepishly in my direction.

'Well, what luck?' I asked. Nobody spoke. 'I thought I saw a big blaze in your direction Jimmy,' I went on. 'Did you get him?' 'No,' replied Jimmy, disgustedly. 'The balloon was not up in the air at all. I didn't even see where they had hidden it.'

'Did you get yours, Reed,' I asked, turning to Chambers.

'Hell, no,' retorted Lieutenant Chambers. 'I shot the thing full of holes, but she wouldn't drop.'

The other two pilots had much the same stories.

'I supposed you burned yours all right Rick?' said Reed Chambers, rather enviously. 'What do you think of us fellows anyway?'

'I think, Reed,' I replied, 'that we are the rottenest lot of balloonatical fakers that ever got up at two-thirty in the morning.'

Fighting the Flying Circus

1 Why did Rickenbacker only hit the balloon with a few shots?
2 Give two possible reasons why the balloon did not catch fire.
3 What danger was Rickenbacker in?

Observation balloon Why was it important to destroy these balloons? Why was it difficult to do so?

4 What did the German observer do when he saw Rickenbacker?
5 How successful had the other airmen been?

At first, the only bombing an airman could do was to throw hand grenades out of his cockpit. Soon, though, both sides were building aircraft especially for bombing. The next extract is by a British pilot, C.P.O. Bartlett, who flew a De Havilland bomber. It was written in March 1918 when the Germans were making one of their last great attacks of the war. The British were having trouble holding them:

We bombed long lines of transport on the road to Fontaine with great effect. We then shot up troops, transport and kite balloons for all we were worth. I got several bursts into a balloon which was hauled down, and others into troops and transport from 800 feet. Naylor fired 800 rounds with his back guns, getting a long burst into a grey and green Albatross just below us,

15

and saw him crash into a field. He also dispersed a machine gun crew which was firing at us. Only after circling and diving low for fifteen minutes and exhausting our ammunition did we turn for home. Altogether a priceless stunt and a thrill to see the war from close range.

We left again at 1.30 p.m. with similar objectives and had equally good results. I observed movements of all sorts: gun limbers tearing about, ammunition being hurried up, men and horses on the run, ambulances and transport of all kinds in continuous streams on every road, troops resting in the fields a mile or two behind the lines. Also countless fires, ammunition dumps going up in colossal explosions and much else of interest.

Bomber Pilot

1. What did the British airmen bomb?
2. What did Bartlett shoot with his machine guns?
3. Who was Naylor, do you suppose? What did he shoot at?
4. Why did Bartlett come home?
5. How did he feel about his raid?
6. What did Bartlett see on his afternoon flight?
7. What do you learn from this extract about De Havilland bombers? (Crew and armament)

A particularly important type of aeroplane was the 'scout' which, today, we would call the 'fighter'. You have already seen scouts in action, attacking balloons. Their main tasks were to protect their own bombers and observation planes, and to destroy those of the enemy. In this extract C.P.O. Bartlett says what happened when a German scout attacked his De Havilland:

Violent signals from Sambrook indicated danger below and, banking sharply, I saw a small, vicious aircraft hurtling up at us at great speed. Realising I had no chance of out-manoeuvring him I headed for home leaving the shooting to Sambrook and weaving so as to give him the best zone of fire. On his first dive he got a burst through my dashboard, shattering much of it, the bullets passing just over my left shoulder: while another bullet went through the feed of my Vickers gun, (the other was already jammed). With tracers passing all round and through us, but with Sambrook fortunately untouched and blazing away with his twin Lewis guns, we were making very slow progress against the strong west wind. I could see our tracers passing all round and apparently through the V-Strutter Albatross. He nevertheless dived on us three times, closing to point-blank range on each dive, and I could see his head clearly and almost his expression as he turned away. I felt this could not go on and one or other of us must go down within the next minute or so. At last, after his third dive he sheered off. I fancy he had had more than enough of Sambrook's Lewis guns and may well have been wounded. Although the first, he was certainly one of the most persistent and daring fighters I met during the war.

Bomber Pilot

1. How did Bartlett learn he was about to be attacked?
2. Why could the bomber not outmanoeuvre the scout, do you suppose?
3. What did Bartlett do instead?
4. What damage did the German do on his first attack?
5. How many times did he attack?
6. How close did he come?
7. Why, possibly, did the German stop attacking?
8. What did Bartlett think of the German pilot?

Dog fight The British fighter is in the ideal position, behind his enemy and above him.

R.A.F. ACTIVITIES

HORNETS OF THE AIR.

The most lively air battles were between scouts. Eddie Rickenbacker describes one of his. He was flying behind the German lines when he saw three of their scouts take off. He flew after them, and for a time, they did not notice him:

A single black blast from the anti-aircraft battery below caused the German airmen to turn about and look behind them. They had not expected any attack from this quarter.

When the leader made the first swerve aside I was less than two hundred yards from the rear Albatross. I was descending at a furious pace, regardless of everything but my target ahead. Fully two hundred miles an hour my Nieuport was flying. Without checking her speed, I kept her nose pointing at the tail of the rear Albatross, which was now darting steeply downwards to escape me. As the distance closed to fifty yards I saw my tracer bullets piercing the back of the pilot's seat. I had been firing for perhaps ten seconds from first to last. The scared Boche had made the mistake of trying to outdive me instead of out-manoeuvering me. He paid for his blunder with his life.

These thoughts flashed through my mind in the fraction of a moment. All the time my finger was pressing the trigger, I was aware of the danger of my position. Either or both of the other enemy machines were undoubtedly on my tail, exactly as I had been on their unfortunate companion's.

I believe I would have followed my first target all the way to the ground so desperate I was to get him. So I perhaps prolonged my terrific speed a trifle too long. As the enemy airplane fell off and began to flutter I pulled my stick back close into my lap and began a sharp climb. A frightening crash that sounded like the crack of doom told me that the sudden strain had collapsed my right wing. The entire spread of canvas over the top wing was torn off by the wind and disappeared behind me. The Nieuport turned over on her right side, and the tail was forced up. Slowly at first, then faster and faster the tail began revolving around and around. Swifter and swifter became my downward speed.

Fighting the Flying Circus

1 What warned the Germans that Rickenbacker was behind them?
2 How far away was he at that moment?
3 How fast did he dive on his target?
4 At what range did he open fire?
5 What mistake did the German make?
6 What danger was Rickenbacker in?
7 What mistake did he make?
8 What happened when he started to climb?
9 How does Rickenbacker's attack compare with the one the German scout made on C.P.O. Bartlett's De Havilland? (See page 16.)

Rickenbacker describes how he saved himself:

Although I had been experimenting constantly with rudder, joystick and even with the weight of my body I found I was totally unable to change in the slightest the stubborn spin of the airplane. Fully ten thousand feet I had fallen since my wing had collapsed. It was scarcely three thousand feet more – and then the crash! I could see men standing on the road in front of a line of trucks. All were gazing at me.

With a vicious disregard for what might happen, I pulled open the throttle. The sudden extra speed from the engine was too much for the perpendicular tail and before I realised it the whole aircraft was quite horizontal. The pull of the propellor kept her straight. If only I could keep her so I might make the lines. They seemed to beckon to me only two miles or so ahead.

Fighting the Flying Circus

1 How did Rickenbacker try to stop his aircraft spinning?
2 How far did he fall? How much further did he have to go?
3 Why was it daring to open the throttle, do you suppose?
4 What happened when Rickenbacker did open it?

Eddie Rickenbacker was just able to fly over the German lines and crash land on his own airfield.

Written Work
List the different kinds of airmen you have met in this section. Describe their work, difficulties, and dangers.

Research
1 Read about the development of aircraft **a** before the First World War, and **b** during the war.
2 Find out more about the American ace pilot, Eddie Rickenbacker.
3 Read about famous airmen from other countries, especially Manfred von Richthofen.

Chapter 2 *The Second World War*

The German Victory in the West, 1940

The Second World War began on September 1st 1939 when the Germans invaded Poland. Britain and France declared war on Germany as they had promised to help Poland. However, they did little to save their ally. Within eighteen days Hitler's armies had taken Warsaw, and soon afterwards the Poles surrendered.

There was now a delay while the Germans prepared their attack in the west. Then, on May 10th 1940, they invaded Holland, Belgium and France. Holland and Belgium were quickly overrun, the British fled home from Dunkirk and, on June 22nd, France surrendered. In just over six weeks the Germans had defeated four countries, two of them among the most powerful in Europe.

If attacking troops are to be successful they must usually outnumber the defenders by three to one. But study this table:

	Germans	Allies
Men	2,760,000	3,740,000
Guns	7,700	11,500
Tanks	2,600	3,600

Draw a bar diagram to compare the two sides.

Why did the Germans not only defeat their enemies, but do so very quickly? One reason was that the Germans used a new method of warfare, the blitzkrieg. But there were other reasons as well, and in this section we will look at a few of them.

German Panzer Division in France It is a mixed force with tanks, guns and motorised infantry.

German advance into Russia The blitzkrieg followed the same pattern here, as in France (see page 18). Why was air superiority essential, if it was to succeed?

In 1940, an American news correspondent called William Shirer was in Germany. America did not enter the war until 1941, so Shirer was able to follow the German armies as they advanced. Here is an extract from his diary:

> We were off shortly after dawn from Aachen across the Dutch province of Limburg to Maastricht. Little evidence that the Dutch did much fighting here. The houses whole, the windows unshattered. An occasional Dutch pill-box showed signs of having been hit by machine gun fire, but nothing heavier. Apparently the Dutch made no attempt to slow up the Germans by blowing up the road to Maastricht. One bridge over a creek had been damaged. That was all.
>
> We crossed over the Maas at Maastricht. The river is broad here and was a natural line of defence, though the Dutch did not take much advantage of it. They had done a half-hearted job of blowing up the bridges. Blown up one out of seven or eight spans on the two bridges I saw. The Germans had steel frames waiting in the rear, and within a few hours of bringing them up had the bridges as good as new. German supply columns were thundering over both bridges when we arrived.
>
> *Berlin Diary*

1. What signs of fighting did Shirer find in Holland?
2. What did he say the Dutch failed to do?
3. What proves that the Germans were well-prepared?

The Belgians had hoped to remain neutral so they had done nothing to upset the Germans. They would not even discuss plans for their own defence with the French and British. The Germans invaded Belgium none the less and soon overran most of the country. On June 4th the British Prime Minister, Winston Churchill, made this statement to the House of Commons:

> At the last moment when Belgium was already invaded, King Leopold called upon us to come to his aid, and even at the last moment we came. He and his brave, efficient Army, nearly half a million strong, guarded our left flank, and thus kept open our only line of retreat to the sea. Suddenly, without consulting us, with the least possible notice, without the advice of his Ministers and upon his own personal act, he sent a plenipotentiary to the German Command, surrendered his Army and exposed our whole flank and means of retreat.
>
> *The Second World War*, Vol. 2

Note: A plenipotentiary is a messenger who has full powers to make an agreement.

1 When did King Leopold of the Belgians finally call for help?
2 How important was the Belgian army for the British?
3 What did King Leopold do?
4 What does Churchill say about the way the King acted?

William Shirer watched the Germans advancing and wrote:

Allied bombers have completely failed to disturb German lines of communications by day-time attacks. One of the sights that overwhelms you at the front is the vast scale on which the Germans bring up men, guns and supplies unhindered. All day long you find unending mechanized columns. They stretch clear across Belgium, unbroken. And they move fast – thirty or forty miles an hour. You wonder how they are kept fed with petrol and oil. But they are. Petrol supplies come forward with everything else. Every driver knows where he can tank up when he runs short.

What magnificent targets these endless columns would make if the Allies had any planes!

Berlin Diary

1 Describe in your own words what Shirer saw.
2 What does he say the allies should have done?

When the fighting was over, Shirer wrote:

From what I've seen in Belgium and France and from talks I've had with Germans and French in both countries, and with French, Belgian and British prisoners along the roads it seems fairly clear to me that:

France did not fight.

If she did, there is little evidence of it. Not only I, but several of my friends have driven from the German border to Paris and back, along all the main roads. None of us saw any evidence of serious fighting.

The fields of France are undisturbed. The German army hurled itself forward along the roads. Even on the roads there is little sign that the French did any more than harry their enemy. And even this was done only in

Refugees How are these people travelling? How far could they go in a day, do you suppose? Why were refugees a great nuisance to their own armies?

the towns and villages. But it was only harrying, delaying. There was no attempt to come to a halt on a line and strike back in a well organised attack.

But since the Germans chose to fight the war on the roads, why didn't the French stop them? Roads make ideal targets for artillery. And yet I have not seen one yard of road in northern France which shows the effect of artillery fire. Driving to Paris an officer from the German High Command kept mumbling that he could not understand it. There, on that height, dominating the road, and providing wonderful artillery cover with its dense woods, the French must have had the sense to plant a few guns. Just a few would have made the road impassable, he kept repeating. But there had been no guns on those wooded heights and there were no shell-holes on or near the road. The Germans had passed along here with their mighty army, hardly firing a shot.

Berlin Diary

1 Where did Shirer go and with whom did he speak?
2 What conclusion did he draw?
3 How did the Germans advance? What were the only places the French tried to stop them?
4 How does Shirer suggest the French might have stopped the Germans?
5 What puzzled the German officer?

On June 3rd an important R.A.F. officer, Sholto Douglas, flew to the airfield of Villacoublay, near Paris. As he arrived the Germans began bombing. Later, Douglas wrote:

There were some fifty or sixty fighters of the French air force standing parked around the aerodrome and we saw a number of them blown up in the raid. Just as we were landing I had seen three of the French fighters take off, but so far as I could discover these were the only fighters to go into action from Villacoublay that day. There could be no excuse for such a lack of interest in trying to get at the enemy because our Air Staff had obtained reports through our own Secret Service only a day or two before that the Germans were planning a big raid on Paris, and that information had been passed on to the French.

After the raid was over we made our way to the Officers' Mess, and there we found all the French pilots – with the exception of the three who were airborne – sitting down quietly having their lunch, and so far as we could make out they were not at all interested in what had just happened. I could not help thinking what a contrast there was between their attitude and that of the gallant French pilots whom I had known in the First World War.

Years of Command

1 How many French fighters were there at Villacoublay?
2 How many took off to attack the Germans?
3 According to Douglas, why was there no excuse for the way the French behaved?
4 What did Douglas find most of the French pilots doing after the raid?
5 What was his opinion of them?

Here is a story William Shirer told:

The Germans say that in one tank battle they were attacked by a large fleet of French tanks after they had themselves run out of ammunition. The German commander ordered a retreat. After the German tanks had retired some distance to the rear, with the French following them only very cautiously, the Germans received orders to turn about and pretend to attack, firing automatic pistols or anything they had out of their tanks, and making complicated manoeuvres. This they did, and the French, seeing an armada of tanks descend upon them, though these were without ammunition, turned and fled.

One German officer told me: 'French tanks in some ways were superior to ours. They had heavier armour. And at times – for a few hours say – the French tank corps fought bravely and well. But soon we got a definite feeling their heart wasn't in it. When we learned that, and acted on the belief, it was all over.'

Berlin Diary

1 Why did the German tanks retreat, at first?
2 How, in the end, did they drive away the French?
3 What did the German officer say about the French tanks?
4 Why did he think the German tanks were able to win?

The one place from which the French were not expecting an attack was the Forest of the Ardennes. Accordingly, it was in this sector that they put some of their worst troops. They made up the French Ninth Army under General Corap. A British general, Lord Alanbrooke, went to see Corap in December 1939. Later he wrote:

Corap asked me to stand alongside him whilst the guard of honour consisting of cavalry, artillery and infantry marched past. Seldom have I seen anything more slovenly and badly turned out. Men unshaven, horses ungroomed, clothes and saddles that did not fit, vehicles dirty, and a complete lack of pride in themselves or their units. What shook me most, however, was the look in the men's faces, disgruntled and insubordinate looks, and

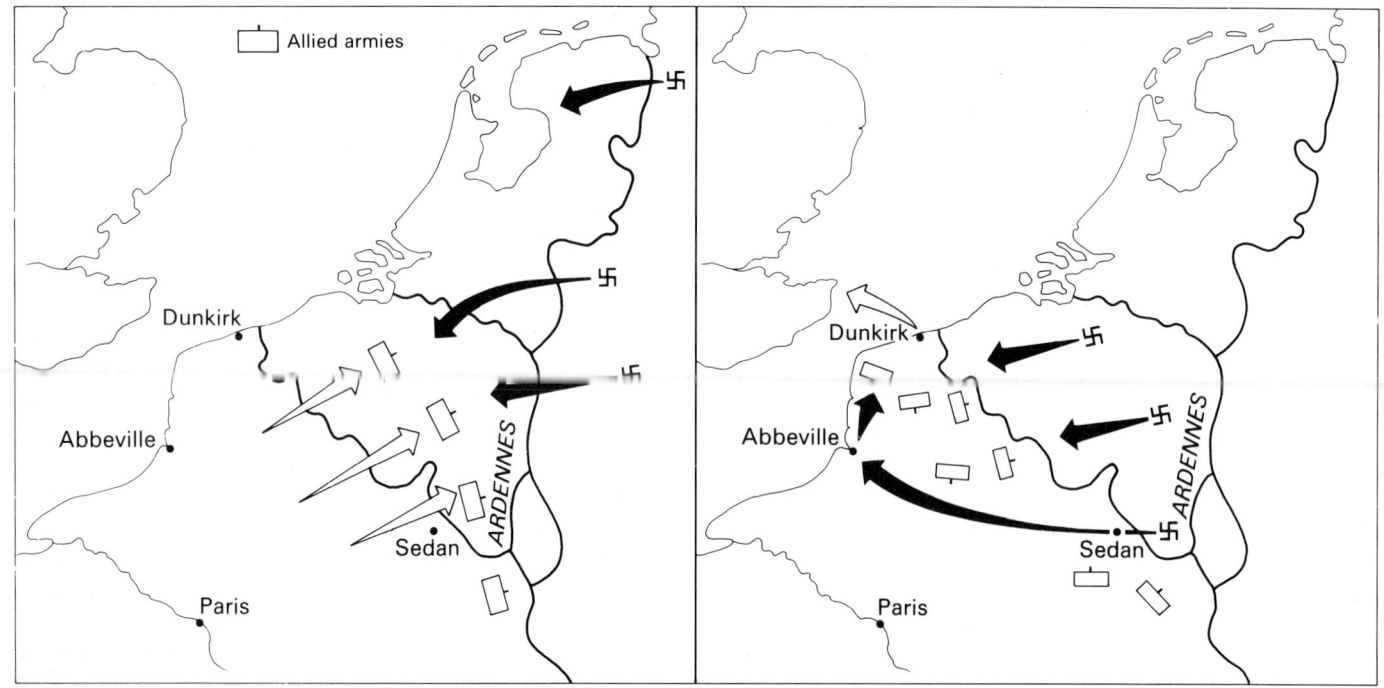

Victory in the West 1940

May 10th Germans attack. They overrun Holland and invade Belgium and Luxembourg.
British Army and best troops in French army go to help Belgians.
May 14th Panzer divisions under Guderian burst out of Ardennes where they have been hiding, and break through at Sedan.
May 20th Guderian reaches the sea at Abbeville. He cuts off allied armies in Belgium from the rest of France.
May 27th Belgian army surrenders.
Late May–Early June British army and some French troops escape through Dunkirk.
Many French troops are captured.

although ordered to give 'eyes left', hardly a man bothered to do so.

Note: When marching past, troops salute their officer by turning their heads toward him. 'Eyes left' is therefore an order to salute.

1 What did Alanbrooke say about the appearance of Corap's troops?
2 What was it about them which bothered Alanbrooke most?
3 What did most of them refuse to do?

To the surprise and dismay of the French, the Germans made their main attack from the Ardennes. They destroyed Corap's army very quickly.

On June 15th 1940 Churchill had a telephone call from Paul Reynaud, the French Prime Minister. Reynaud said the French armies had been defeated. Churchill flew at once to Paris and there was a meeting with the French Commander-in-Chief, General Gamelin. Churchill describes the meeting:

> The Commander-in-Chief briefly explained what had happened. North and south of Sedan, on a front of fifty or sixty miles, the Germans had broken through. The French army in front of them was destroyed or scattered. A heavy onrush of armoured vehicles was advancing with unheard-of speed towards Amiens and Arras, with the intention, apparently, of reaching the coast at Abbeville, or thereabouts. Alternatively they might make for Paris. Behind the armour, he said, eight or ten German divisions, all motorised, were driving onwards. The General talked perhaps five minutes without anyone saying a word. When he stopped, there was a considerable silence. I then asked, 'Where is the strategic reserve?' and, breaking into French, 'Où est la masse de manoeuvre?' General Gamelin turned to me, and with a shake of the head and a shrug, said: 'Aucune.' (There is none.)
>
> I was dumbfounded. What were we to think of the great French Army and its highest chiefs? It had never occurred to me that any commanders having to defend five hundred miles of front would have left themselves without a mass of manoeuvre. No one can defend with certainty so wide a front: but when the enemy has made a major thrust which breaks the line one can always have, one *must* always have, a mass of divisions which marches up in vigorous counter attack.

The Second World War, Vol. 2

1 What did Gamelin say the Germans were doing?
2 What question did Churchill ask? What was Gamelin's answer?
3 What does Churchill say the French should have done?

Gamelin went on to say that the allies might attack the German flanks but he did not sound hopeful. Churchill wrote:

> Presently I asked General Gamelin when and where he proposed to attack the flanks of the Bulge. His reply was 'Inferiority of numbers, inferiority of equipment, inferiority of method' – and then a hopeless shrug of the shoulders. There was no argument: there was no need of argument. And where were we British anyway, having regard to our tiny contribution – ten divisions after eight months of war, and not even one modern tank division in action?
>
> *The Second World War*, Vol. 2

Note: The French army was 88 divisions strong.

French town after bombardment After the first few days of the campaign it was only in the towns and villages that the French made much resistance.

1 What three reasons did Gamelin give for the defeat of the allies?
2 Which of these reasons do you think were wrong, and which was right?
3 What did Churchill say about the British?

Here is what William Shirer said about the allied generals:

> The great trouble with the Allied command was that it was dominated by old men who made the fatal mistake of thinking that this war would be fought on the same general lines as the last war. Their thinking was fixed somewhere between 1914 and 1918 and never changed. I think this helps to explain why, when confronted by the Germans with a new type of war, the French were unable to counter it.
>
> It wasn't that these tired old men had to adapt themselves to a revolutionary kind of warfare overnight. One of the mysteries of the war in the west is that the Allied generals seem never to have learned the lesson of the Polish war. For in Poland the German army showed the tactics it would use in Holland, Belgium and France – parachutists and Stukas to disrupt communications in the rear, and swift, needle-like thrusts with Panzer divisions down the main roads through the enemy lines, pushing them ever deeper and then closing them like great steel claws, striking far into the enemy's rear before he could make a stand. Eight months passed between the Polish war and the attack in the west, and yet the generals of Britain and France failed to use this precious time to organise a new system of defence to cope with the tactics they watched the Germans use in Poland.
>
> *Berlin Diary*

1 According to Shirer, what kind of war were the British and French generals expecting in 1940?
2 How, in fact, did the Germans attack? Describe this in your own words.
3 Why did the French and British generals have no excuse for failing to change their ideas?
4 Do you agree with Shirer's criticisms of the French and British generals?

Written Work
You are a German general who has fought against the French and their allies. What weaknesses did you find in your enemies, and what mistakes did they make?

Further Work
1 Find out about the German blitzkrieg tactics.
2 What were the main war events in Holland, France and Belgium in May and June 1940?

The Battle of Britain

At the very start of the Second World War in 1939, the Germans conquered Poland. Then, in 1940, they overran Denmark, Norway, Holland and Belgium. France, their most powerful enemy in the west, surrendered on June 17th. Hitler was sure that Britain would now give in, rather than fight alone.

However, the British Prime Minister, Winston Churchill, had already said:

> We shall go on to the end, we shall fight in France, we shall fight on the seas and oceans, we shall fight with growing confidence and growing strength in the air, we shall defend our island, whatever the cost may be, we shall fight on the beaches, we shall fight on the landing grounds, we shall fight in the fields and in the streets, we shall fight in the hills: we shall never surrender.
>
> *Speech to the House of Commons,* June 4th, 1940

The day after France surrendered, Churchill made another speech in which he said:

> What General Weygand called the Battle of France is over. I expect that the Battle of Britain is about to begin. Upon this battle depends the survival of Christian civilisation. Upon it depends our own British life, and the long continuity of our institutions and our Empire. The whole fury and might of the enemy must very soon be turned on us. Hitler knows that he will have to break us in this island or lose the war. If we can stand up to him, all Europe may be free and the life of the world may move forward into broad, sunlit uplands. But if we fail, then the whole world, including the United States, including all that we have known and cared for, will sink into the abyss of a new dark age: made more sinister, and perhaps more protracted, by the lights of perverted science. Let us therefore so brace ourselves that, if the British Empire and its Commonwealth last for a thousand years, men will still say, 'This was their finest hour'.
>
> *Broadcast* June 8th, 1940

Battle of Britain

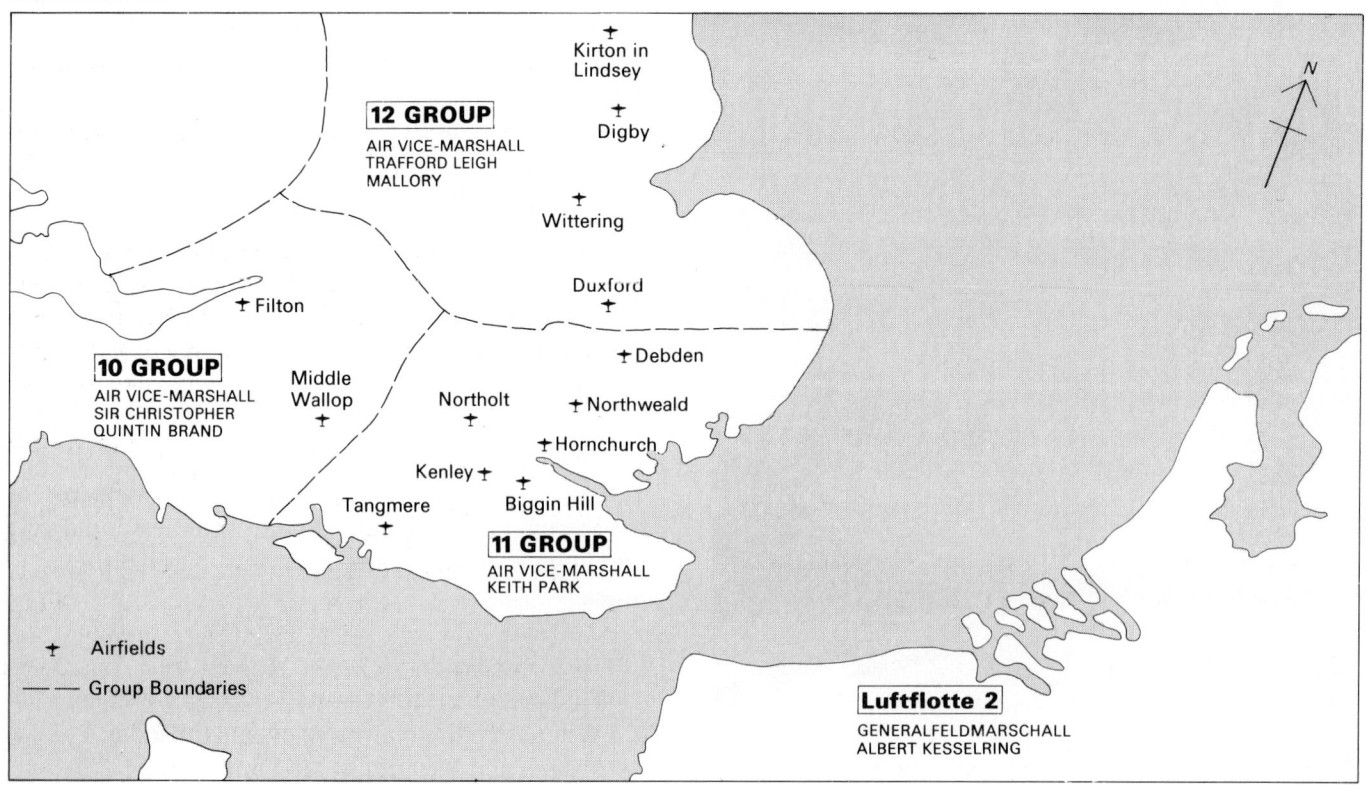

Hurricane (above) **and Spitfire** Though similar to look at, the two aircraft had important differences. What were they? (See foot of next column).

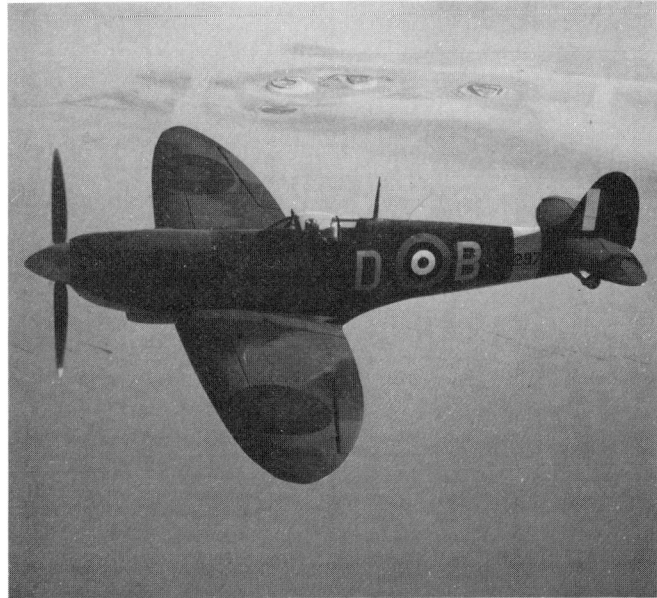

1. What battle is over?
2. What battle does Churchill say is about to begin?
3. Why, according to Churchill, does Hitler need to defeat Britain?
4. What will happen if Britain wins?
5. What will happen if Germany wins?
6. What does Churchill hope people of the future will say about this time in the history of the British people?
7. Why do you suppose Churchill was making speeches like this? (If you had been alive at the time, how would you have felt, listening to him?)

When Hitler realised Britain was not going to ask for peace, he made plans to invade. His problem was that he could not just send his troops across the Channel. He only had a few warships, while the Royal Navy had many. But this did not worry the Commander-in-Chief of the German airforce, Reichsmarschall Hermann Goering. He was sure his aeroplanes could destroy Britain on their own. Many people would have agreed with him. In 1925 a British military expert, Basil Liddell Hart, had written:

> A modern state is so complex that it offers a target highly sensitive to a sudden and overwhelming blow from the air. Imagine for a moment, London, Manchester, Birmingham and half a dozen other great centres attacked, the business areas and Fleet Street wrecked, Whitehall a heap of ruins, the people of the slum districts maddened to break loose and plunder, the railways cut, factories destroyed. Would not the general will to resist vanish?
> *Paris, or the Future of War*

1. What places does Liddell Hart think will be attacked?
2. What damage does he say will be done?
3. How does he say the poor people will behave?
4. What does he believe people in general will want to do?

The German aircraft which were meant to do the real damage were, of course, the bombers. To protect them the Germans had long range fighters, the Messerschmitt Bf 110s. However, as they were rather heavy and slow to manouevre, they, in turn, needed some protection. This came from some of the best single-seater fighters of the time, the Messerschmitt Bf 109s.

Fortunately for the British, they had two excellent fighter aircraft, the Hurricane and the Spitfire. A pilot tells us about them:

> Having flown both the Hurricane and the Spitfire, I feel it is true to say that one could not have had two better aeroplanes for their respective roles. The Hurricane was a slightly sturdier aeroplane and a more stable gun-platform whose role was to attack the bombers: the Spitfire was a dog-fighter that would get as high as possible as quickly as possible to keep the German fighters from attacking the Hurricane lower down.
>
> The Bf 109 was slightly faster than the Spitfire, especially in a dive. To counterbalance this, the Spitfire had the better turning circle and once in a dogfight, the Spitfire could get 'inside' the Bf 109. In fact, the first Bf 109 I shot down was when we were both upside down over St. Paul's Cathedral. In that situation I discovered that I had much more control than the man ahead of me, and I'm fully certain he went down as a 'flamer'.
> Group Captain J. H. Hill, 1940

1 What were the good points about the Hurricane?
2 What was its main task?
3 What was the Spitfire's task?
4 What advantages did the Bf 109 have over the Spitfire?
5 What advantage did the Spitfire have over the Bf 109?
6 In what circumstances did Group Captain Hill shoot down his first Bf 109?

Much, then, depended on the battle between the Spitfires and the Bf 109s. If the Spitfires won, the Hurricanes would have the Bf 110s and the German bombers at their mercy: if the Bf 109s won, they could escort the bombers to their targets.

Study this table which shows the numbers of fighters in the two airforces:

German Fighters		British Fighters	
Bf 109 (Single engine)	809	Spitfire (Single engine)	286
Bf 110 (Twin engine)	246	Hurricane (Single engine)	463
		Defiant (Single engine)	37
		Blenheim (Twin engine)	114

Note: Neither the 'Defiant' nor the 'Blenheim' was any use in the Battle of Britain.

1 How many more fighters did the Germans have than the British?
2 Counting only single engine fighters, how did the two sides compare?
3 How many times, roughly, did the Bf 109s outnumber the Spitfires?

Here is a German pilot's account of a battle:

> In comparison with my combats in France, I was very calm. I didn't fire, but tried again and again to get into a good position. But every time I got there the Tommy would break away.
>
> Finally my chance came. I saw a 109, and 200 metres behind him a Spitfire. I peeled off and dived, turning in behind him. Now it was I who sat 200 metres behind the Tommy. Be calm; don't fire yet! I applied full power and closed the gap, as the Tommy did with his own target. Now, at 100 metres, the wing-span filled the Revi gunsight. Suddenly, the Tommy opened fire, and the Messerschmitt in front broke away. I had pressed the gun button at the same instant. My first shot hit. The Spit streamed a long, grey smoke train and dived steeply into the sea, just off the coast. A great column of water marked the impact. At once I called my victory over the radio, and had enough witnesses to confirm the crash. My first Tommy was down.
>
> Max-Hellmuth Ostermann, August 12th, 1940

Spitfire in action What has the Spitfire just done? What movement must it make now?

1 How had Ostermann felt during his battles in France?
2 How did he feel this time?
3 What was the Spitfire doing when he attacked it?
4 From which direction did Ostermann attack?
5 At what range did he open fire?

Here is a Spitfire pilot's account of a battle:

> I saw a Bf 110 below me and dived down on him going very fast indeed. Unfortunately I was going too fast, and in the heat of the moment forgot to throttle back, with the result that I came up behind him at terrific speed and overshot him badly. I had a good burst of fire at practically point blank range as he flashed by and then I had to turn away very violently or I should have collided with him. His rear gunner took advantage of my mistake and fired a short burst at me, and put several bullets through my wing, very close to the fuselage and only a few inches from my leg. When I turned round to look for

the Hun he had disappeared. Though there was a lot of fighting in progress and machines were turning and diving all over the sky, I had dived below them all and couldn't do much about it. I returned to base absolutely furious with myself for having missed that Bf 110. He was right in front of me, and if only I had not gone at him so wildly I should have had him easily.

Anyway, it taught me to be a little more cool in future. One lives and one learns – if lucky.

David Crook, 609 Squadron, August 25th, 1940

1 Why did David Crook miss the Bf 110?
2 What two disasters did he nearly have?
3 Why did he leave the battle?
4 What did he say he had learnt?
5 By comparing this extract with the last one, you can discover an important advantage the German pilots had at the start of the Battle of Britain. What was it?

(David Crook was killed later in the Battle of Britain.)

Early in September 1940, a Squadron Leader wrote:

Two further pilots have come to us straight from a Lysander squadron with no experience whatsoever on fighter aircraft. Apparently demand has now outstripped supply and there are no trained pilots available in the Training Units, which means that we will just have to train them ourselves. However, it remains to be seen whether we can spare the hours, as we are already short of aircraft for our own operational needs. It seems a funny way to run a war.

Sandy Johnstone, 602 Squadron, September 3rd, 1940

1 Why was Sandy Johnstone unhappy about the two new pilots?
2 What does he say will have to be done for them?
3 Why will this be difficult?

People on the ground were able to watch the air battles. Years later one of these spectators wrote:

One Sunday morning I was standing at the top of our garden by the dug-out shelter which my father had sweated to excavate in time. We were watching a dog-fight between two fighters high above the Bickley area. They twisted and plummeted, rose and writhed, until finally one dropped in the familiar falling-leaf fashion. I jumped up and down with excitement and shouted, 'We've got one! We've got one!' My father was surprisingly quiet. Then as no parachute came out and the plane went into a vertical dive, he said softly, 'It's one of ours.' For an eight-year old, besotted by Buck Jones who always shot the Injun, or the guy in the black hat, I was stunned. Goodies could get killed as well as baddies.

Michael Salvard

1 Why was the little boy pleased and excited?
2 What, in fact, had happened?
3 What did Michael Salvard say he had learnt that day?

At the height of the battle Churchill said:

The gratitude of every home in our island, in our Empire, and indeed throughout the world, except in the abodes of the guilty, goes out to the British airmen who, undaunted by odds, unwearied in their constant challenge and mortal danger, are turning the tide of the world war by their prowess and by their devotion. Never in the field of human conflict was so much owed by so many to so few.

Speech to the House of Commons, August 20th, 1940

1 Who does Churchill say should be grateful to the British airmen?
2 What does he mean by the 'abodes of the guilty'?
3 What does he say the British airmen are succeeding in doing?

Here now is what Sandy Johnstone saw when he visited an airfield in Sussex, several weeks after the Battle of Britain had begun:

I drove over to Tangmere in the evening and found the place in an utter shambles, with wisps of smoke still rising from shattered buildings. Little knots of people were wandering about with dazed looks on their faces, obviously deeply affected by the events of the day. I eventually tracked down the Station Commander standing on the lawn in front of the Officers' Mess with a parrot sitting on his shoulder. Jack was covered with grime and the wretched bird was screeching its imitation of a Stuka at the height of the attack. The once immaculate grass was littered with personal belongings which had been blasted from the wing which had received a direct hit. Shirts, towels, socks, a portable gramophone – a little private world exposed for all to see. Rubble was everywhere and all three hangars had been wrecked.

Sandy Johnstone, August 16th, 1940

1 What had happened to this airfield?
2 What serious damage had been done?
3 Why do you suppose the Germans were attacking British airfields?

Fighter aircraft destroyed on runway

The Germans came close to destroying Fighter Command's airfields in the South-East, but on August 23rd there was an accident which changed the course of the war. Some German bombers lost their way and dropped their loads on London. Churchill ordered a raid on Berlin as revenge. Hitler was furious and ordered his own airforce to concentrate its raids on London.

Early in September the commander of 11 Group, responsible for the defence of South-East England, flew over London. Later, he wrote:

It was burning all down the river. It was a horrid sight. But I looked down and said, 'Thank God for that', because I knew that the Nazis had switched their attack from the fighter stations, thinking they were knocked out. They weren't, but they were pretty groggy.

Air Vice-Marshall Keith Park, September 8th, 1940

1 What did Keith Park see from his aeroplane?
2 What did he say about it? Why?
3 How did he misunderstand the Germans?

There were several attacks on London, the heaviest being on September 15th, 1940. We now call this Battle of Britain Day. The British lost 26 fighters: they claimed they had shot down 185 Germans. We now know the figure was 56, but even so, the Germans could not go on losing aircraft at that rate.

London burning Why was it a big mistake for the Germans to raid London? (See opposite).

Their attacks did not end at once, but they died away during the autumn.

As for the British, they had been able to build aircraft faster than they had lost them. The Royal Air Force was stronger at the end of the Battle of Britain than at the beginning.

Meanwhile, what had been the results of the bombing? The Germans had hoped to defeat Britain from the air. Perhaps they had thought heavy bombing of the big cities would make the British people surrender. However, in a speech in October 1940 Churchill said:

> It is the practice of many of my colleagues and many Members of the House to visit the scenes of destruction as promptly as possible, and I go myself from time to time. In all my life I have never been treated with so much kindness as by the people who have suffered most. One would think one had brought some great benefit to them, instead of the blood and tears, the toil and sweat, which is all I ever promised. On every side, there is the cry, 'We can take it', but with it, there is also the cry, 'Give it 'em back.'

Speech to the House of Commons, October 8th, 1940

1 What does Churchill often do after an air raid?
2 How do the people greet him?
3 What is their reaction to being bombed?
4 Look back to page 25 and see what Liddell Hart thought would happen.

Written Work

Write the story of the Battle of Britain from the point of view of a British pilot.

Now write it again, from the point of view of a German pilot.

Research

1 The Commander in Chief of Fighter Command was Air Chief Marshal Sir Hugh Dowding. Find out what you can about him, especially the way he fought the Battle of Britain, and what happened to him as soon as it was over.
2 Read about the part Lord Beaverbrook played in the Battle of Britain.
3 Read about some of the ace pilots of the Battle of Britain, like A. G. Malan and Peter Townsend of the R.A.F. and Adolph Galland and Ernst Udet of the Luftwaffe.

What qualities made an ace pilot?

The War in the Desert

By June 1940 the Germans had soundly beaten the French, so the Italian dictator, Mussolini, thought it was safe for him to declare war. He hoped to drive the British out of North Africa, so he ordered Marshal Graziani to invade Egypt. Graziani had 200,000 troops while General O'Connor, who was trying to stop him, had only 35,000. In fact, O'Connor's force routed Graziani's and would almost certainly have overrun Libya, if two men had not interfered. One was Winston Churchill. He sent O'Connor's best troops to certain defeat in Greece. The other was a brilliant general, Erwin Rommel. He went to Africa with a small force of Germans in March 1941. After that, the war swayed backwards and forwards until, in November 1942, General Montgomery defeated Rommel at the Battle of El Alamein.

Writing letters

In this section you see what it was like to live, fight and die in the Western Desert.

A British soldier, Rifleman R. L. Crimp, describes the desert itself:

There's gritty sand, good for travelling on, and finer sand where the trucks get stuck. Some of the low-lying areas have perfectly flat pans of hard-baked sand-mud, beautiful for driving over. There are large areas of limestone, scattered with loose slabs which clink like bottles as they burst away from the tyres of the truck. Here and there are midget hills or bumps, with cairns of stones to help navigation by maps and compass. Occasionally you find islands or 'tables' with flat tops supported on shallow sand-cliffs: also the opposite – shallow basins with cliff

walls and flat floors. Everywhere shells lie, as though in a kind of 'land-sea'.

Our life is dominated by the sun. Every day we see it rise from under the eastern desert rim and, waxing rapidly in heat and light, climb into its course over the glaring sky. At noon the desert face is burning hot, the heat is like a solid wall. Mirages cut off the horizon: not palms and oases as people imagine, but stretches of shimmering blue, as though patches of sky have been drawn down onto the earth. Objects lying in the mirage area become strangely distorted. Men are split into several portions, vehicles stretched into tall-masted ships.

Diary of a Desert Rat

1. What surfaces does the desert have in different places?
2. What natural features are there? (In Britain 'natural features' are such things as hills and valleys.)
3. What does Crimp mean by 'Our life is dominated by the sun'?
4. What are mirages like? How do they distort things?

Serving food Do you think these men were near the front, or away from it? (See below).

As well as Germans and Italians, Crimp found other enemies:

Then of course, there are the flies. Lord Almighty, that such pests should ever have been created! Bad enough in any climate, the Egyptian sort are almost a different type with a fierce determination to settle on human flesh. This may be due to the dryness of the country and to the fact that the only moisture available is human sweat. Soon after sunrise they arrive in hordes from nowhere, then plague us all through the day, swarming and buzzing round, trying desperately to land on our faces, in our eyes, ears and nostrils, on our arms, hands, knees and necks. And once settled they bite hard. Desert sores draw them like magnets. In fact, everything unwholesome, filthy and rotten is manna to them. That's why we have to make our latrines completely sealed and burn out our refuse dumps with petrol daily. It's the devil's own job keeping our food from their clutches, and as soon as a meal's on the plate they always get the first nibble. At this moment there are five crawling over my hands and I'm spitting as many again away from my mouth. You can whack them a hundred times and still they come back. It's a blessed relief at sunset when, as at some secret signal, they all disappear.

Diary of a Desert Rat

1. When do the flies arrive? When do they leave?
2. How do they annoy?
3. What precautions do the troops have to take? Why do you suppose this is?

A big problem was to keep the troops supplied with food and water. During the fighting they might have nothing but 'bully beef' (corned beef), dry biscuits and very little water. Away from the front they were luckier. R. L. Crimp wrote:

At 6 o'clock armed with sacks, canisters and empty watercans we accompany the corporal to platoon H.Q. for rations. The sergeant's already built 'basic' piles on the ground – four cans of bully, a tin of milk, a tin of cheese and six oranges for each section, and as soon as their representatives have shown up, starts doling out the rest. This is one of our happier moments. 'Wot, no fresh meat?' is the opening gambit. Fresh meat, in fact, appears once in a blue moon, but you'd think it was the rule, the way bully's groaned against. 'Cpl. Spear's turn for jam,' says the sergeant, slinging over a 7 lb tin. Cpl. Pearl makes a formal protest. 'That's strawberry,' he says, 'ours was goosegog.' 'Luck of the draw, mate!' says the sergeant, 'who fancies fish?' 'You can stick it on the wall' is the feeling here: tinned fish isn't popular, taken only when things are short. Jam and margarine in 7 lb tins, come once a week and go round in rotation. 'Here's two tins of spuds; you'll have to toss!' Those who lose take 'fresh' potatoes, the yellow, sweet Egyptian types, and curse their luck – for once, the fresh is not preferred. 'Anyone now for the Cruft's Specials?' Biscuits (with bully, our staple diet) can be had ad lib in 28 lb tins, which last some time. Then the distribution of tea, a very careful business, almost every leaf counted. 'One-third mug for each section!' is the sergeant's rule and he dips in his sack and measures carefully before parting with the precious herb. Sugar follows, not so jealously checked, three parts of a mug for each section. Last thing is water, two gallons a man, and we dump our empties in exchange. Then heavy laden back 'home'.

Diary of a Desert Rat

1 What rations do the men draw?
2 What food do they like? What do they dislike?
3 Why do you suppose they call the biscuits 'Cruft's Specials'?
4 What is particularly precious?
5 How much water does each man have? (In Britain we use, on average, 26 gallons a day each.)

R. L. Crimp belonged to a motorised battalion so he rode in a truck. Many troops, though, were infantry and had to march. A Scottish officer wrote:

A shabby, gritty landscape. The sweat oozes and trickles all day. This is war, one kind of war, sweat and tiredness and no water till evening and cigarettes made of dirt. The pain of muscles, not wounded, but twisted from the weight of rifles, automatic guns, heavy equipment. The rubbing of the skin by a sand-paste of desert and sweat. The thud of feet on the sand 94 times every minute, 50 minutes an hour. . . . And every night dig. . . . Dig in case the bombs drop. Dig for discipline. Dig to save your skins. Dig through sand. Dig if necessary, through rock. Dig for bloody victory.

Journey with a Pistol, Neil McCallum

1 What is unpleasant about marching in the desert?
2 How often do the men rest, and for how long?
3 What must the men do at the end of each day?

A soldier looked forward to leave far more than any schoolboy ever looked forward to his summer holidays. However, he could not go home from Africa, so he had to make do with Cairo. Here he could see the sights, such as the Pyramids, and eat and drink at the various clubs that had been opened for British soldiers. Anything else was likely to be disappointing. R. L. Crimp tells what happened when he went into the heart of Cairo with a guide:

Our first call is at the bazaars. The guide leads me through a maze of twisting alleys to a small shop, ushers me inside, introduces me to the manager, then retires.

Arab guide lecturing New Zealand troops

Tanks and footsoldiers It was important for tanks and infantry to work together. The Germans were better at this than the British, which explains much of their success.

The manager, a fat, oily man in European clothes, insists on my taking a small cup of black coffee for my refreshment. Then various sorts of trashy trinkets, alabaster pots and vases, gaudy leatherwork, 'ancient' Egyptian statuettes, and shoddy-looking shirts and mats are produced, described as irresistible bargains and offered at extortionate prices. With no further sign of the guide, I begin to feel a bit uneasy. Visions of drugged coffee and finding myself a few hours later minus my wallet in the back alleys grow vivid in my mind – many a squaddy, wandering off the beaten track in Cairo, has been relieved of all his valuables, with, in one or two cases, a knife between his ribs as well. Eventually, however, I manage to explain that I'm supposed to be doing a sightseeing tour and anyway can't afford any of the goods, then beat a retreat.

The guide is waiting outside and seems somewhat upset at my emptyhandedness.

Diary of a Desert Rat

1 Where did Crimp's guide take him?
2 What did the shopkeeper offer Crimp?
3 Why was Crimp worried?
4 How did he get away?
5 Why do you suppose the guide was 'upset at his empty-handedness'?

The rest of the extracts tell you about fighting and dying in the desert.

At the Battle of El Alamein, R. L. Crimp's battalion was surrounded, and German tanks attacked it several times. The British anti-tank guns destroyed many enemy tanks, but then they ran out of ammunition. Afterwards, Crimp wrote:

The day seems to be going on for ever. The sun's still high. About four o'clock, the enemy tanks, sure of our weakness, attack again. This time they make a more determined approach from South, South-West and West, with other arms in support. Quite a hubbub follows: the brittle rasping and spitting of machine-guns; mortar bombs falling over, whispering gently and crashing suddenly; solids blasting by like express trains: and the mewing and squealing chorus of the 25-pounder shells as they arch down over our heads. Our own six-pounders are silent. But the barrage saves us again. The panzers are forced to withdraw. Except one. He gets to within 50 yards on the western side and halts, as though undecided what to do next. None of our guns has a single round, otherwise he'd be a sitting bird. He lumbers forward, clumsily yet warily, hosing a clear path with his machine gun, right up to our trenches, where the chaps lie low (who wouldn't?) and on until he's almost up to Battalion Headquarters.

Then he stops again. His gun veers slightly till its horizontal. And when he fires the air seems to take a terrific blow. My tin-hat hits my head with a hard jolt. But nothing near seems to get whacked. Then after more waggling, another terrific crash and blast. Yet still no damage.

However, just as some of us are thinking 'This Is It', one of the anti-tank chaps crawls from his trench and with bullets ripping into the sand around him, runs stooping to an abandoned six-pounder facing north, takes out a shell already in the breech and creeps back with it to his own gun which faces the panzer. It's amazing how the stream of machine gun bullets misses him, but he calmly puts the shell in, takes steady aim, and fires. Immediately there's an explosion from the panzer. The machine gun cuts out, and the tank stays still. A strand of smoke comes from the turret and minutes later it starts to blaze.

Diary of a Desert Rat

Note: 'Solids' were shot that were metal all the way through, like large bullets. They would not explode like a shell, and in the main, they were used by tanks against each other.
25-pounders were British field guns.
6-pounders were British anti-tank guns.

1 From how many directions did the German tanks attack?
2 What weapons supported them?
3 What drove most of the tanks away?
4 Why did the one remaining tank seem safe?
5 What did it do as it advanced?
6 What did most of the British soldiers do?
7 How was the tank destroyed, in the end?

That night, Crimp's battalion was able to escape and rejoin the main British army.

Here now is what a British officer, Keith Douglas, wrote after his tank had been face to face with a German tank:

As the turret swung I watched the heavy barrel moving and said, 'On. Fire when you like, but hurry up.' There was a long moment of silence. I remembered suddenly, this corporal is a wireless operator, not a gunner. 'It's stuck,' the corporal said in a voice as if he could not get his breath. He looked up at me and I thought, 'I don't know if I'm flapping, but he is.' 'What's the matter?' I said. 'It's stuck, it's stuck. It won't elevate.' The corporal began to heave and wrench blindly, like a man who has lost his temper. His fingers fluttered to the safety catch, flicking it on and off. That made up my mind for me. I said into the microphone, 'Driver advance. Driver right. Speed up, speed up,' and switching to the A set: 'King Five, my gun has let me down. I'm getting out. Over.' 'Bad luck,' said Picadilly Jim's voice. 'I'm very sorry.' I looked up. We were heading directly towards the German, now only fifty yards or so away. I had already heard the report of one shot, and now cried; 'Driver, right. RIGHT,' into the mouthpiece. He continued steadily forward; I realized I was still switched to A set, shouting my instructions to the whole regiment, but I

Ruined tank It is impossible to say what became of the crew, but they were spared one disaster. What was it? (See page 35).

Desert trenches They were called 'slit trenches'. Why was that, do you suppose? Compare them with the trenches of the First World War. (See Chapter 1).

could not be heard by the driver. I switched hastily and repeated, 'Right, Right,' until he obeyed and swung round. 'Speed up or you'll be blown to glory,' for he was grinding along in second gear. I looked at the enemy again but he had slid behind the ridge out of sight. He must have thought we were going to ram him. I was sweating and out of breath.

Alamein to Zem Zem

1 What did Keith Douglas order his corporal to do?
2 Why did the corporal not obey?
3 What did Douglas decide he must do?
4 What mistake did he make?
5 How did the men in the British tank behave differently from the gunner in the last section?

R. L. Crimp describes how one of the men in his battalion died:

Bill Robinson has been killed. His mate, Freddie Flitch, tells how it happened. 'We were all sitting on the edge of our slit trench,' he says, 'making a brew when things were quieter like, when suddenly a mortar bomb plomps down. We all dived, except Bill – he'd caught a hit in the tummy. We couldn't do much for him, and anyway he told us not to bother. He said he knew he'd got his lot, and just stayed quiet.'

Diary of a Desert Rat

Death in a tank could be terrible. The American Shermans, excellent tanks though they were, caught fire every time they were hit. A man who fought in Shermans wrote:

A tank you see, had four petrol tanks and each one was filled with high octane. If any of these four were hit, the whole machine would go up. ... When that petrol got hit, your choices were, to say the least, limited. Oh, we had a fire extinguisher, but that was for overheated motors: it was useless for an exploded tank. Now, there were two ways to get out. One was via the turret; the other was through a trapdoor on the opposite side of the driver from the bow gun. Often the turret would be inaccessible to anyone inside the tank; if the machine was hit badly, particularly if it was knocked on its side, the trapdoor would jam as well. At best you would have ninety seconds to push it open. That would leave forty seconds for three men to squeeze out. Tick, tick, tick, boom! And what would happen if both the turret and the trapdoor were jammed? What would happen is, you'd die! It takes twenty minutes for a medium tank to incinerate; and the flames burn slowly, so figure it takes ten minutes for a hearty man within to perish. You wouldn't even be able to struggle, for chances are both exits would be sheeted with flame and smoke. You would sit, read Good Housekeeping, and die like a dog. Steel coffins indeed!

Patton's Best, Neil Frankel

1 Why were tanks very likely to explode?
2 Why was it difficult for the crew to escape?

Written Work

Imagine you are a soldier in the Western Desert. Write a letter home describing your life.

Research

What were the main events of the war in North Africa? When and how were the Germans and Italians finally defeated?

The most important battle was El Alamein, October–November 1942. Find out how it was fought, and why the British won.

Chapter 3 Two Problem Areas: The Middle East and South-East Asia

The Fall of the Bar-Lev Line, October 1973

You will know from the Bible that the homeland of the Jews is Palestine. However, for reasons which we do not fully understand, the Jewish people became scattered all over the world. Millions of them lived in Russia. In the middle of the nineteenth century there were only about 24,000 in Palestine itself. Almost all the inhabitants were Arabs and the country belonged to Turkey. Then, in the 1880's the Russians began persecuting their Jews, and many of them fled to Palestine. They came from other countries, too, so that by 1939 there were half a million of them in Palestine. The Arabs were angry that so many Jews had arrived and there was trouble between the two races, with bombing and shooting. The Jews were particularly clever at organising terrorist groups.

In 1919 Palestine became part of the British Empire, and the British did their best to keep order. By 1947, though, they decided this was impossible, and left. The United Nations ordered that Palestine should be divided into two states, one Arab and one Jewish.

The Jews decided to call their state Israel. It came into being in May 1948. At once, all the Arab states surrounding Israel attacked her, determined to destroy her. After months of fighting, though, it was the Israelis who won. They made their country much bigger than the United Nations had intended, and drove out all the Arabs living in its borders. These Palestinian refugees, as we call them, have since lived in wretched camps in one Arab country after another.

There was a second war in 1956 which we know as the Suez Crisis. There was yet another in 1967, called the Six Day War. Hearing that Syria, Jordan and Egypt were planning to attack, the Israelis struck first and thoroughly defeated their enemies in just six days. They then took land from all of them.

The Six Day War was a great triumph for Israel, but in a sense it was also a misfortune. The Arabs and especially the Egyptians, had been so humiliated that they could not rest until they had taken their revenge. They plotted and prepared for years and then, in 1973, the Egyptians and Syrians launched their attack. It came on Saturday October 6th which was Yom Kippur, the holiest day in the Jewish year. We call the conflict the Yom Kippur War.

In 1967 the Israelis had advanced to the Suez Canal. It made an excellent anti-tank barrier, so on its east bank they built a string of forts called the Bar-Lev Line. In the Purkan fort, opposite Ismaelia, was a young Israeli called Avi. He had a tape recorder with him, which he ran for much of the time. This is, of course, an unusual thing for a soldier to do in battle, and it gives us a unique account of the fighting on the Bar-Lev Line.

Egyptian troops raise their flag over a captured fort in the Bar Lev Line

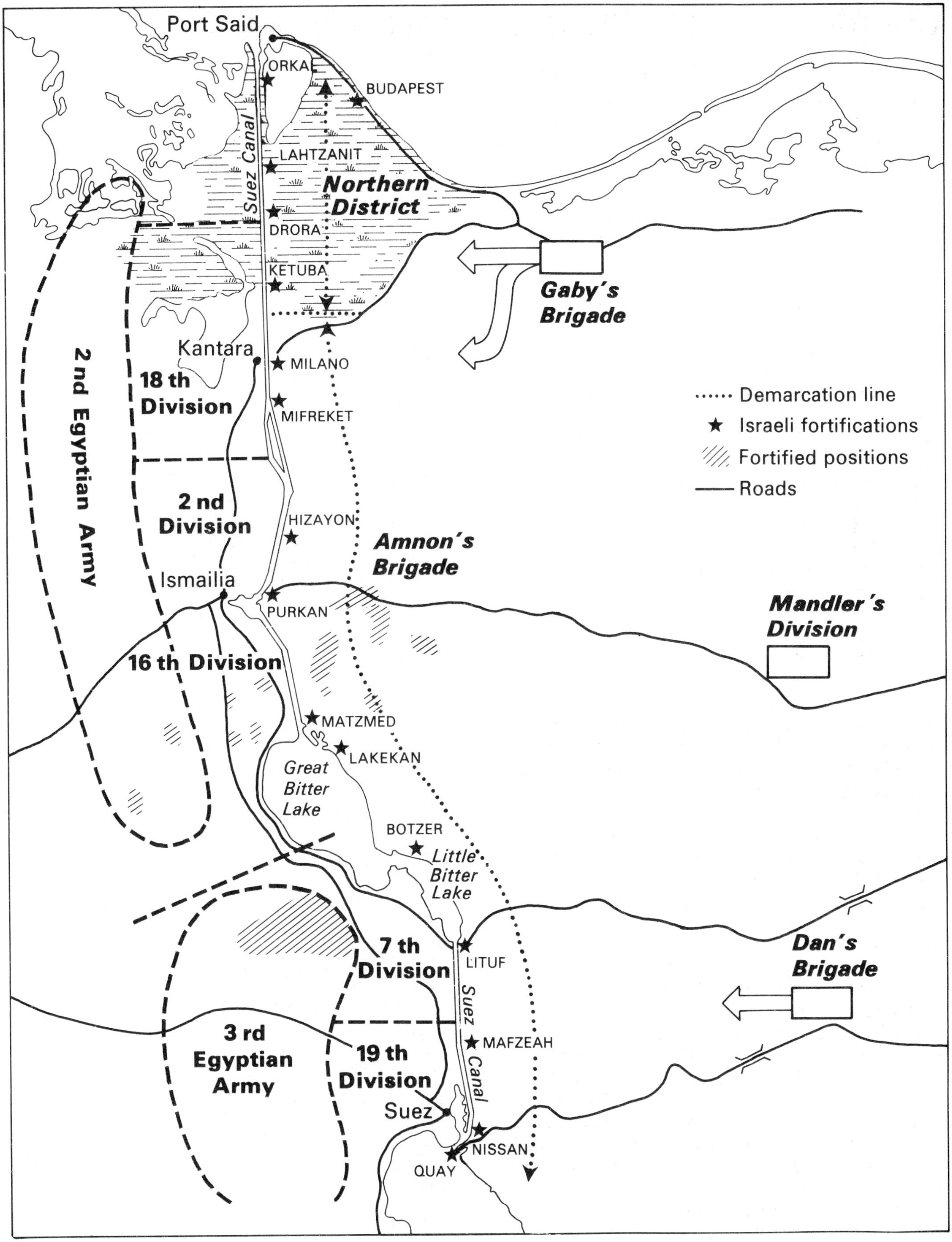
Port Said
ORKAL
BUDAPEST
Suez Canal
LAHTZANIT
Northern District
DRORA
KETUBA
Gaby's Brigade
Kantara
MILANO
18 th Division
MIFREKET
2nd Egyptian Army
Demarcation line
Israeli fortifications
Fortified positions
Roads
2 nd Division
HIZAYON
Amnon's Brigade
Ismailia
PURKAN
Mandler's Division
16 th Division
MATZMED
LAKEKAN
Great Bitter Lake
BOTZER
Little Bitter Lake
7 th Division
LITUF
Dan's Brigade
Suez Canal
3 rd Egyptian Army
19 th Division
MAFZEAH
Suez
NISSAN
QUAY

Here is what Avi recorded when the Egyptians launched their attack:

Egyptians are putting in boats directly below us ... they're crossing now ... full of crowds of infantry ... landing with anti-tank missiles ... a few odd tanks rushing at Egyptians ... artillery fire ... shells falling close, closer, fire getting nearer. Armoured troop carriers crossing ... lots of them jumping on the bank and running forward with missiles ... six helicopters – Egyptian commandos – flying over.

T-54 tank is opposite ... it's shooting at us. More boats crossing, wave after wave ... they're fanning out in our area ... they're putting up a commando flag ... Egyptians are laying a bridge ... automatic trailer is lowering floats ... huge convoys, lots of armour ... tanks, halftracks, trucks with missiles, lines of Jeeps and batteries of artillery.

The forward spotters are complaining – why isn't the Israeli Air Force in action? Planes could make mincemeat of such a traffic jam.

The Yom Kippur War

1. What Egyptian vehicles and weapons are crossing the canal?
2. How are they crossing?
3. What is the only opposition they are meeting?
4. What puzzles the defenders?

Here is a conversation the men in the fort had with their Headquarters. Shuki was second-in-command of the fort and Meyerke was the commander:

HEADQUARTERS (on the radio): What's new with you?
SHUKI (in a voice of unflappable calm): Nothing special here Headquarters. There's fire around us. We've seen one more boat cross the canal. Aside from that there are Egyptians around us.
HEADQUARTERS (puzzled): You asked for artillery?
SHUKI: Yes, we asked.
DOCTOR: Bloody hell! Don't allow Shuki to send situation reports. For him, everything is fine, even now!
AVI (shouting into the radio): We've lots of Egyptians around us.
MEYERKE (taking charge): Hello, Headquarters. I don't know what's happening with you. The guns are firing far from target. I can't see, but it's far from target. It's nowhere near the right direction.

The Yom Kippur War

Egyptians taking supplies over the Suez Canal One problem the Egyptians had was to tear gaps in the great barricade of sand which the Israelis had made. Shelling it would have done little damage. They decided to use powerful hoses, and you can see the result from the picture.

Israeli gun

1 What does Shuki report to Headquarters?
2 Why does the doctor dislike his report?
3 What does Meyerke report to Headquarters?

The following day, the fort was completely surrounded and came under heavy fire:

SHUKI (on the phone): What's happening? They're still shelling. I left the bunker. It's blocked between all the trenches to 3 and 3A. I'm in 4 at the moment, trying to get out. Maybe something will work.
 (By now it is dark. Another powerful explosion is heard.)
MEYERKE: What's that?
SHUKI: It's still falling on me. ... I can't see. I think the shell fell in the middle of the fort. What shells, honey! The trench in Position 4 has also had it. Everything on top's collapsed on me.
MEYERKE: Give me headquarters. Headquarters, listen. We can see lights on the canal road.
HEADQUARTERS: Instead of talking give me targets.
MEYERKE (amid more explosions): I gave you targets. First of all the canal road. All of it. Halftracks are moving on it. The question is whether ours or theirs. I don't know, can't see in the dark. If you can, hit right away, do you hear, because they are wiping us out here. So I want as follows: Shells on Concentration Point G (a coded map reference). After that I want fire by the church in Ismaelia. There's a tank position there. You'll see it on the map between the church and the mosque. Also to the north, 200 northeast. (Another gigantic explosion) ... Oh – Oh. All the bunkers are collapsing. ... I want rapid fire now.
SOLDIER: Can't they send some sort of vehicle to take us away?
MEYERKE: Here? During the shelling? We'd get killed outside. Tanks would just get knocked up in the shelling.
SHUKI (phoning from the ruins of Bunker 4): We've just caught a whopper. We're completely covered in sand.
MEYERKE (voice choking with dust): We can't see a thing. We're choking here. The ventilator has bust.
 (This is however, the last Egyptian salvo. The barrage subsides almost as quickly as it began.)
The Yom Kippur War

1 What damage does the Egyptian bombardment do to the fort?
2 What information does Meyerke send to Headquarters?
3 What does the soldier want to happen? Why is this impossible?

On Tuesday, Meyerke decided they would have to evacuate the fort, but with many Egyptians behind them it was going to be difficult to escape:

> They wait for the early hours for the setting of the moon and set out in pitch darkness. Barbed wire is in their way and the dunes are pockmarked with craters. They are worried mainly about the two wounded, Marciano and Baruch, but both make their way without help. Flares flicker in the sky. The men freeze until the lights go out.
>
> At five-thirty dawn breaks. At six o'clock a large tank battle starts up and the men find themselves trapped between the opposing armoured forces. They take cover in a dip in the dunes.
>
> MARCIANO: When we passed through them in the night, we actually heard them shouting. Enough to make you feel faint.
>
> MEYERKE: When I set out I wasn't scared. And when we passed by them I wasn't scared. You know when I began to worry? You didn't even notice it. There was this embankment of sand, all sorts of guys lying in foxholes. I thought we were coming on the Egyptians so I got hold of that one who speaks Arabic – where is he – that's you Roni. I told him to mutter something aloud in Arabic about wanting to get there quickly to smash those Jews.
>
> Burning tanks are now scattered in all directions, but Meyerke encourages his men to press on. They come under machine gun fire. Avi calls base on the radio. 'We're sending a tank to rescue you' he is told.
>
> As the tank arrives the thirty-three men clamber all over it holding onto anything available, even the gun barrel. Exposed to fire, the tank zigzags at full speed to where a halftrack is waiting. The military road that they reach, just a little way farther, is still under full Israeli control.
>
> *The Yom Kippur War*

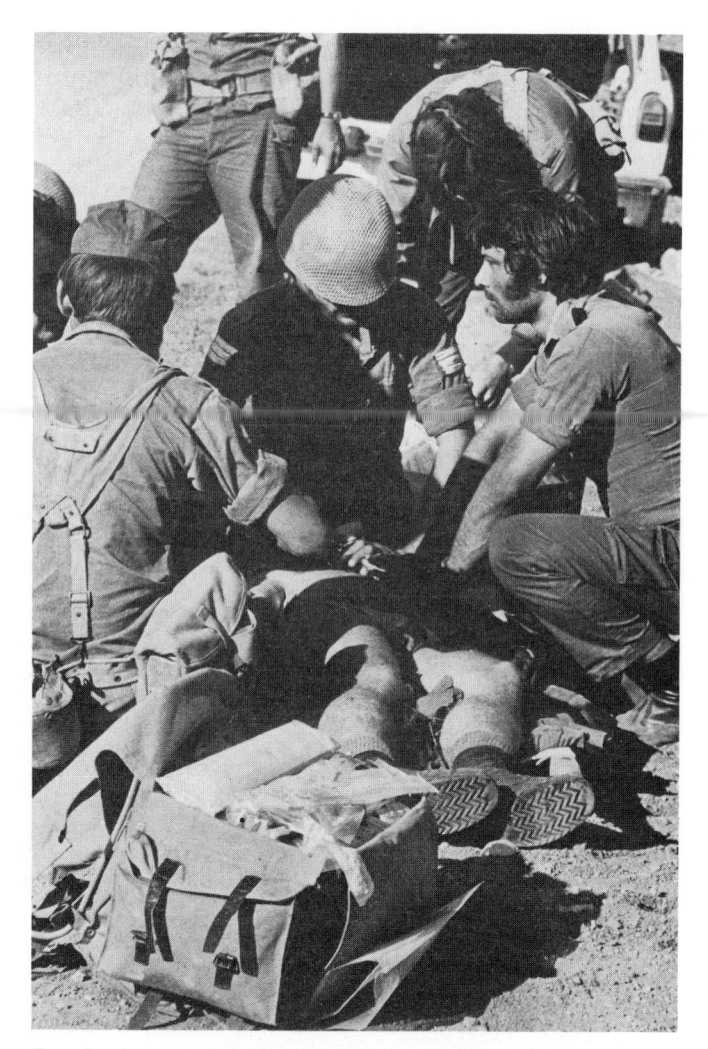

First Aid for a wounded Israeli tank commander Why were many Israeli tanks hit during this war? (See page 42).

1. What problems did the men have, in the night?
2. What frightened Meyerke most?
3. What trick did he play?
4. What dangers did the men face in the day?
5. How were they rescued?

By now, the Egyptians had taken all the forts in the Bar-Lev Line, except one called 'Budapest' in the far north. It was a major victory for them and we must see why they won it.

An important reason was that the Israelis were taken completely by surprise. All their young men are trained soldiers, but in time of peace most of them are doing civilian work. Very few are under arms, for Israel just cannot afford to keep a large army in being for long periods. After the Yom Kippur war an Israeli officer, Major-General Chaim Herzog, described the two forces which faced each other across the Suez Canal:

> Deployed along the Canal the Egyptians had five infantry divisions backed by three mechanised divisions and two armoured divisions. Each infantry division had a total of 120 tanks. The three mechanised divisions had a total of 160 tanks per division. The two armoured divisions had a total of 250 tanks per division. In addition there were two parachute brigades, some twenty-eight battalions of commandos and a marine brigade.
>
> Facing this force in Sinai along the 100 miles of the Suez Canal was a total of 436 Israeli soldiers in a series of fortifications 7–8 miles apart and three tanks actually on the water front. Seven artillery batteries were in the line and the remainder, a total of some seventy guns followed on later. Of the tanks planned to be holding the line, 277 were forward in Sinai.
>
> *The War of Atonement*

1. How many infantry did the Egyptians have on the canal? (An infantry division is about 16,000 men, a brigade is about 3,000 and a battalion is 800).
2. How many tanks did the Egyptians have?
3. How many men did the Israelis have on the canal?
4. How many tanks did the Israelis have on the canal and close by in Sinai?
5. How many times did the Egyptians outnumber the Israelis in men and tanks?

Major-General Herzog also had this to say about the Israeli soldiers holding the Bar-Lev line:

> The troops from the Jerusalem Reserve Brigade holding the northern half of the Suez Canal were a mixture. There were shopkeepers, tradesmen, new immigrants with little knowledge of Hebrew, university professors, senior government officials, farmers and Kibbutzniks from the hill villages in the Jerusalem corridor. Some of the troops were old-timers who had served in the brigade in the Six Day War, but most were newcomers to Jerusalem who had never been in a war. Large numbers of them had not served a period of conscription in the regular army, and had merely had enough basic training to enable them to do reserve duty.
>
> *The War of Atonement*

1. What impression does this description give of the Israeli soldiers?
2. Having read some of the transcripts of Avi's tapes do you think they fought well or badly? Give reasons for your answer.

As you saw in the first extract, Avi and his friends hoped the Israeli Air Force would help them. But it was having problems. Major-General Herzog said:

> Four Israeli planes were lost in the first strike. Thereafter the situation can be described only as bedlam, with the Air Force spread to its utmost and with demands for air support pouring in from all along the front – from the hard-pressed fortifications along the Bar-Lev Line, from units along the Gulf of Suez as far south as Sharm-el-Sheik, and from units fighting a desperate holding battle in the Golan Heights. All this, while the Air Force also had to ensure that the skies over Israel were kept 'clean'.
>
> The Israeli Air Force fought a desperate battle, flying into the teeth of one of the most concentrated missile systems in the world. There were 150 batteries of SAM missiles in Egypt.
>
> The mobile SAM 6, with a range of 22,000 metres, fits into a pattern with the SAM 2 (with a range of 50,000 metres) and the SAM 3 (30,000 metres). The main advantage of the SAM 6 lies in its mobility. It is mounted on a tank chassis and can be moved into action rapidly. It needs only minutes to be folded up before being moved to another site and then another short period to be ready for action again. To seek out a SAM 6 missile, a plane must enter the range of the SAM 2.
>
> As well as this formidable system there were hundreds of SAM 7 portable missile launchers held by the infantry together with conventional anti-aircraft weapons, in particular the multi-barrelled ZSU 23.
>
> *The War of Atonement*

Note: 1 A ZSU 23 fired 4,000 shells a minute.
2 All these weapons had been sent to Egypt by the Russians.

SAM 6 Missiles What does the document above tell you about these missiles?

1. What did the Israeli Air Force have to do?
2. How many batteries of SAM missiles did the Egyptians have?
3. Draw a scale diagram to show the ranges of the SAM 2, 3 and 6 missiles.
4. What was the great advantage of the SAM 6?
5. What would probably happen to an Israeli plane that went after a SAM 6 launcher?
6. What other dangers did the Israeli planes face, in addition to the SAM 2, 3 and 6 missiles?

Avi and his friends also hoped the Israeli tanks and artillery might help them. This is what happened on the first day. The story is reconstructed from Avi's tapes:

> Underground in the command bunker, Avi and Meyerke listen by radio as the small Israeli armoured forces in the area try to check the Egyptian attack. One mile behind the fort is an Israeli tank unit and a mobile artillery unit. The artillery commander wants to join forces with the tanks for a joint attack on the Egyptian bridgehead, but before that can happen the enemy attacks. The Egyptians are armed with deadly Sagger anti-tank missiles, and the artillery commander sends out an urgent warning to the tanks: 'Take care not to get hit. Take cover! I want you to save all your strength for a counterattack.'
>
> The artillery opens fire on the Egyptian tanks, but it, too, is attacked with missiles. From his firing position, Shuki can see the battle raging and reports that the tanks will not now be able to come to the aid of the fort. 'They're pretty messed up,' he says.
>
> *The Yom Kippur War*

1. What plan did the Israeli commander have?
2. How did the Egyptians attack the Israeli tanks and guns?
3. How successful were the Egyptians?

An Israeli tank commander describes what happened to him:

> We were advancing, and in the distance I saw specks dotted on the sand dunes. I couldn't make out what they were. As we got closer, I thought they looked like tree stumps. They were motionless and scattered across the ground ahead of us. I got on the intercom and asked the tanks ahead what they made of it. One of my tank commanders radioed back: 'My God, they're not tree stumps! They're men!' For a moment I couldn't understand. What were men doing out there – quite still – when we were advancing in our tanks towards them? Suddenly all hell broke lose. Many of our tanks were hit. We had never come up against anything like this before.
>
> *The Yom Kippur War*

Damaged Israeli tank

1. What did the Israeli tank commander think he saw in the desert?
2. What unpleasant surprise did he have?

Here is a description of the missiles the Egyptians were using. It was written by English journalists of the *Sunday Times*.

> Ground missiles demanded courage of their operators. The RPG 7 (rocket propelled grenade) is best fired at little more than 100 yards – and it takes considerable nerve to let an enemy tank get that close. Even if the tank is then disabled, its crew will probably survive, to machine-gun the infantryman. The Sagger wire-guided missile is most effective at about one mile. At that range the missile can easily be seen in flight, like a high speed model aircraft, for up to thirty seconds, a long time when you are exposed and at risk of being machine-gunned. Yet, throughout, the operator must cooly pilot the missile, keeping his sight fixed on the target by means of a small joystick. The Israelis were certainly not expecting the new confidence of the average Egyptian soldier.
>
> *The Yom Kippur War*

Note: These missiles were given to the Egyptians by the Russians.

1. What is an RPG 7?
2. What is its range?
3. How is the Sagger missile guided?
4. What is its range?
5. What qualities are needed in the men who use these missiles?

The *Sunday Times* journalists also wrote:

> The only hope of serious damage to the bridgeheads was from the Israeli 155 mm and 175 mm guns ranging in from the road fifteen miles back from the canal. But that artillery had been seriously damaged by missiles. There is also evidence of another, very strange reason for the failure of the Israeli artillery. The gunners depended entirely on forward spotters – tank crews and the last surviving Bar-Lev strongholds such as Meyerke's. An enquiry after the war found such confusion in the use of coded map references by the spotters – 'Concentration Point G' and so on – that it seems the artillery may in some cases have been using different maps or codes from the spotters. There were even incidents when the Israeli artillery hit their own side in Sinai, including the shelling of an Israeli tank unit that resulted in the deaths of the crew of the command tank and possibly of two other tanks.
>
> *The Yom Kippur War*

1. What was the Israeli artillery expected to do?
2. How had the artillery suffered from the Egyptians?
3. Who told the Israeli gunners where to fire? Find evidence of this happening in the transcripts of Avi's tapes.
4. Why, possibly, did the gunners fire in the wrong places?
5. Having read the transcripts of Avi's tapes, do you agree that this is likely?

After the war, the Egyptian Minister of Information, Mohamed Heikal wrote:

> The plan had gone like clockwork. Credit for this success, which went beyond the wildest dreams of the planners, must without doubt go to the junior commanders, and to the N.C.O's and men of the infantry, artillery, engineers and tanks. Many of them were later to speak of the delight they felt, when they found themselves with the chance to wipe out the disgrace of defeat and humiliation under which the Egyptian army had suffered for six years.
>
> *The Road to Ramadan*

1. According to Mohamed Heikal:
   a. Who was mainly responsible for the Egyptian victory?
   b. How did they feel about their victory?
2. Do you think they were right to feel as they did? Give reasons for your answer.

It was not only the Israelis who were taken by surprise in the early days of the war. The Egyptians were as well, by their very success. They advanced only a short way into Sinai and then paused, wondering what to do next. This gave the Israelis time to call up their army and, on Tuesday, October 9th they launched a big counter-attack. It was through this battle that Avi and his friends made their way, when they were escaping. On October 16th, an Israeli force commanded by Ariel Sharon crossed to the west bank of the canal, and swung round behind the Egyptian Third Army, cutting it off. Sharon was about to inflict a resounding defeat on the Egyptians when the Russians and Americans ordered both sides to stop fighting. They had no choice but to obey, and there was a cease fire on October 22nd.

Egypt was saved before she lost the war. Moreover, at the start of the fighting she had won the victory she so badly needed to satisfy her honour. That meant she was ready to make a lasting peace with Israel, something which, until then, she had stubbornly refused to do. Probably, Israel gained as much from her defeat on the Bar-Lev Line as she did from any of her victories.

Written Work

1. You are a high ranking officer in the Israeli army. Write a report on the fall of the Bar-Lev Line for your government.
2. You are an ordinary soldier in the Egyptian army and were among the first men who crossed the Suez Canal. Write a letter home describing your experiences in the first few days of the war.

Research

1. Find out more about Israel's earlier wars with her Arab neighbours. (There is an account of the Suez Crisis in **Oxford Junior History**, Book 6, *The Twentieth Century World*, Chapter Eight, section 2.)
2. Read more about the Yom Kippur War, for example, the fighting on the Syrian front and Israel's victories after her earlier defeats.
3. Find out why the United States and the U.S.S.R. stopped the war, and how they were able to do so.
4. Find out how Israel and Egypt came to an agreement after the Yom Kippur War.

The War in Vietnam

In the nineteenth century the French conquered Vietnam, making it part of their empire. Many Vietnamese did not like the French and after the Second World War there was a rebellion led by a man called Ho Chi Minh. He was a communist, and so were most of his followers. Finally, in 1954, a communist army under General Giap defeated the French at Dien Bien Phu.

Vietnam was then divided into two, at the 17th parallel. The north had a communist government under Ho Chi Minh, while the south had an anti-communist government led by Ngo Dinh Diem. However, there were plenty of communists in the south. They were known as the Vietcong. They rebelled against Diem, hoping to overthrow him and unite the whole of Vietnam under communist rule.

The Americans were alarmed. They were afraid that if South Vietnam become communist, so would the other countries of South-East Asia. Accordingly, the Americans sent weapons and supplies to Diem. But his army still failed to crush the Vietcong, so American soldiers came as well. In the end, there were 500,000 United States troops in Vietnam. Most of them were sent by Lyndon Johnson, who became President in 1963.

American troops on patrol in Vietnam Why is their work unpleasant and dangerous?

Much of Vietnam is mountainous, and covered with jungle, so the Vietcong were able to use guerilla tactics. The first extract describes an American attack on some Vietcong guerillas. It was written by an Austrian reporter, Hugo Portisch:

'Tiger 5, Tiger 5 calling Puma 2, Puma 2' crackled the steady voice from one of the walkie-talkie sets in the command post of the American 1st Cavalry Division.

Fifteen minutes later, thirty of the latest jet bombers were flying over a particular map reference in the Highlands of Vietnam. Hundreds of rocket bombs, containers of napalm, and thousands of shells from the aircraft cannons were beating down on this target. An American patrol was hiding in the area. Fifteen minutes before, it had fallen into a Vietcong ambush. One of the soldiers had turned the knob of his radio set to 'Transmit': 'Tiger 5, Tiger 5....'

The use of aircraft was just to pin down the Vietcong and give some help to the American patrol. Soon, a black cloud appeared on the horizon; some dozens of helicopters of the 1st Cavalry Division.

The first wave of the helicopters reached the map reference. There was another hail of steel and fire as each of them fired its air-to-ground rockets to check the Vietcong anti-aircraft fire. While the black clouds from the rocket explosions were still smoking up through the jungle tree tops, heavily weighted nylon rope ladders were thrown from the helicopters. The weights smashed through the branches of the trees and reached the ground. While they were still falling the first American soldiers were beginning to slide to the ground on these ladders, like trapeze artists in a circus. In twenty minutes thousands of men from the Cavalry Division had landed to the rear of the enemy.

At An Keh, in the middle of the Vietnamese Highlands, where the Vietcong have not met an enemy in twenty years, the Americans have moved in. Some hundreds of helicopters, many of which carry ninety-six men, flew in to attack An Keh. Not only did they bring a whole division into the jungle in one day, but they also delivered heavy artillery. Here in the Highlands, where the Vietcong's heaviest weapon is a little portable trench mortar, the Americans brought heavy howitzers into position.

While the troops pressed back the Vietcong in heavy hand-to-hand fighting, giant bulldozers, likewise brought in by the airborne cavalry, were clearing the jungle and laying down an emergency airstrip. On the evening of the same day, the first supply planes could already land in the jungle.

Up at the front the most lethal modern weapons were in action and squadrons of fighter bombers in more than 600 raids a day were unloading hundreds of tons of bombs and rockets. Out in the bush dozens of walkie-talkies were in use. Every little squad was linked with the

American troops leaving helicopter Why were helicopters particularly useful in Vietnam? What stopped the ladders being caught in the trees? (See opposite).

neighbouring one by radio. If it fell into an ambush, it could immediately call for help.

Over the battle area one aeroplane was circling at a great height. In this plane there was a unit which the Americans call the ABCCC – Airborne Battle Control and Command Center. The equipment of this aeroplane is worth two and a half million dollars. Inside it sit officers in front of several television screens. A series of detailed maps appears on these screens showing the movements one might almost say of each individual American soldier. Up there orders are worked out. Computers help the officers to reach the right decisions which are then sent by radio to the fighting troops.

The ABCCC is not only in touch with the ground: it is permanently linked with the helicopter bases, with the airfields from which the combat planes operate, with the aircraft carriers in the China Sea, with General Headquarters in Saigon, with the reconnaissance planes and even with meteorological aircraft.

At night the American reconnaissance planes switch on an apparatus called 'Tipsy 53'. It works with infra-red rays – rays which sweep the ground, rays which pierce the thickest clouds, the densest fog and the darkest night. They distinguish trees from men, rifles from rice sacks, rucksacks from trench mortars. When these rays have once caught the supply convoys of the Vietcong, they do not let them go. In the middle of the night, in the middle of a tropical storm, under conditions in which the Vietcong used to feel themselves completely safe, the American airforce attacks them.

The Vietcong are not only afraid of rockets and napalm bombs and aircraft cannon shells. It is above all the American rifles which have inflicted heavy losses on them. This newest American rifle fires bullets with the effect of shells. Without even hitting the enemy it is enough if one of these shells strikes the ground two yards away from him, and the result at this distance is terrible. I have seen Vietcong snipers open fire on American troops who answered with 25 rounds per rifle in a few seconds; the trees were stripped of their foliage, the snipers swept away.

Eyewitness in Vietnam

1. Why did the American patrol send a radio message?
2. What help did the aircraft give the patrol?
3. What troops did the helicopters bring? How would this unit have travelled in the days of the Wild West?
4. What did the helicopters do as soon as they arrived? Why?
5. How did the troops leave the helicopters?
6. How long did it take all the troops to land?
7. How long had the Vietcong been undisturbed in this area?
8. What heavy weapons did the helicopters bring in? What was the heaviest weapon the Vietcong had?
9. How was the airstrip made? Why was it needed?
10. What aircraft attacked the Vietcong? What weapons did they use?
11. How did the American units on the ground keep in touch with each other?
12. Who was in the aeroplane high above the battlefields?
13. What were they doing?
14. What equipment did they have to help them?
15. With whom did they keep in contact?
16. What are the American reconnaissance planes able to do at night?
17. Why, according to the writer, are the Vietcong afraid of the American rifles?

South Vietnamese troops question a prisoner The soldiers suspect that the man belongs to the Vietcong, but how can they prove it?

18. Make a list of the American weapons and equipment mentioned in this extract.

As time went on, the communists in North Vietnam sent more and more help to the Vietcong, even units from their regular army. President Johnson called North Vietnam a 'fourth-rate, raggedy ass little country', and was sure she could be defeated. He ordered his aircraft to bomb North Vietnam, but he dared not invade because he was scared that China might come to the rescue. All the land fighting took place in the south. Here, the Americans found they could not win. The war cost the United States millions of dollars, and their men were being killed or wounded the whole time. At last, Johnson's successor, President Nixon, decided to bring the American forces home. A

West German news reporter, Peter Scholl-Latour, watched some of them go:

In the giant US base in Bien Hoa, the evacuation of the last remaining GIs continued (the election promises of the American president had to be kept). When the soldiers from the New World first arrived here they had garlands of flowers hung round their necks by young South Vietnamese girls. Now they were leaving in an atmosphere of almost shame. Surly military policemen had Alsatian dogs sniff over the luggage of the returning soldiers in search of drugs. The use of heroin among Americans in Indochina had reached alarming proportions, and now it was feared the epidemic would spread to the United States. The army, demoralized, was pulling out of Vietnam. A few soldiers tried to impress the crowd of press photographers by popping one last champagne cork and giving the V-for-Victory sign before they boarded the transport plane for Guam. It was grotesque.

Death in the Rice Fields

1. How had the South Vietnamese greeted the Americans when they arrived?
2. How did Scholl-Latour think the Americans felt as they left?
3. What were the military police using dogs for?
4. How did some of the soldiers try to put on a brave face?

Three years later, in 1976, Scholl-Latour visited Hanoi, the capital of North Vietnam. He wrote:

How on earth could a victory like this ever have happened? How could this divided country, robbed of its richest provinces, survive thirty years of war – and not only survive but win? How did North Vietnam, this poor, under-fed dwarf, manage to take on the spectacular might of the American army and beat it? Every time you walked through the streets of Saigon these questions would come to you again and again. There was no easy answer. When you looked around you in Hanoi everything was dilapidated, worn out and run down. The buildings were neglected and crumbling in the monsoon rains. The French shops, Indian bazaars and Chinese markets had been replaced by drab state-run stores. The choice of goods was poor, and the articles themselves were expensive and of low quality. The people in the streets looked thin and long-suffering: their yellow skin was like old parchment. The children were the only ones who had rosy cheeks and laughed.

Death in the Rice Fields

1. What questions did Scholl-Latour ask himself?
2. What did he say about: **a** the buildings **b** the shops **c** the people of Hanoi?
3. How far do you think Scholl-Latour would have agreed with Johnson's description of North Vietnam as a 'fourth-rate, raggedy ass little country'?

North Vietnamese repair a road destroyed by American bombing What equipment are the people using? What does this picture tell you about the spirit they are showing?

In the rest of this section we will look at some of the reasons for America's defeat.

Hugo Portisch said of the jungle in South Vietnam:

A division can disappear in it like a needle in a haystack. The paths which the troops have to hack through the jungle may be only a yard away from a Vietcong convoy without the convoy being noticed. You can be walking over an underground headquarters of the Vietcong without knowing that in the next bamboo thicket there is the main entrance to an enormous tunnel, without noticing that the tree in front of you is hollow and serves as an air shaft.

Eyewitness in Vietnam

1. What does Portisch say the Americans can miss in the jungle?
2. How does Portisch seem to contradict himself? (See his description of American reconnaissance planes on page 46).

In 1967 the Commander-in-Chief of the army of North Vietnam, General Vo Nguyen Giap wrote:

When they sent troops into the south, the United States imperialists wanted to use their great military superiority, concentrate their forces and attack and wipe out the Liberation Armed Forces (Vietcong). Yet, although they have more than one million troops they have not been able to do this. Although they wanted to concentrate their forces they have had to scatter them in many theaters of war, and give them many tasks.

In the First Army Corps area, U.S. Marines have been scattered over an area of roughly 500 to 600 kilometres. In the highlands U.S. forces, which are not large, have

Jungle damaged by American bombing Here we can see the results of bombing and spraying 'defoliants'. What are defoliants and why did the Americans use them, do you suppose?

been scattered over a 200 kilometre area. In eastern Nam Bo, American forces have had to spread out on many fronts and have found it necessary to defend all areas. As a result, large U.S. forces have become small, and are not strong enough.

U.S. and puppet troops have not only been scattered but have also been given many tasks. It had been the U.S. imperialists' intention to concentrate on wiping out the Liberation Armed Forces. Yet faced with growing resistance in the south the imperialists have had to use U.S. and puppet troops to hold the people in check. This will certainly lead the U.S. imperialists to great political and military defeats.

Although the American imperialists wanted to launch an offensive, they have fallen into a defensive position. At present about 70 per cent of the U.S. troops perform defensive tasks in South Vietnam. To defend the Da Nang airbase alone, the U.S. imperialists have one division of American troops, and spread them over a 25 kilometre perimeter.

The U.S. imperialists have had to use their fighting forces for the defence of their bases, cities, lines of communication and even the puppet army which is falling apart. As a result, although the U.S. troops are very numerous, they are thinly spread and lack the strength to attack.

Big Victory, Great Task

Note: When Giap says the Americans have 1 million troops, he includes their ally, the army of the government of South Vietnam. He calls it the 'puppet' army.

1 How, according to Giap, did the Americans hope to use their troops when they entered the war?
2 List the things which Giap says they have had to do instead.
3 Giap was writing to encourage his troops, so we must be careful about believing him. Does what he says sound convincing? It will help you to know the area of South Vietnam which is about 160,000 square kilometres.
4 Why does Giap call the army of South Vietnam a 'puppet' army, do you suppose?

In 1967 an American university lecturer, David Schoenbrun, visited North Vietnam. He wrote:

On the night of August 24th, after one of the heaviest raids of the year, I rode south out of Hanoi along National Route 1. It is no longer anything like a national highway. A few miles out of Hanoi it becomes a crater-filled obstacle course. One does not drive down it, one bounces along over ruts and rocks. Within ten miles it runs out completely, and the Route detours across a river and on to a dike. The bridge at the river crossing is out,

The Vietnam War The Ho Chi Minh trail was the route along which the North Vietnamese sent weapons and supplies to the Vietcong. Note that it ran through two neutral countries.

too. There are almost no roads or bridges left intact in North Vietnam.

Yet the supplies keep moving, day and night, without let up, along no roads and across rivers without bridges.

How do you move supplies without roads and bridges? By the 'Legion of Porters', the brilliant creation of Vo Nguyen Giap.

The back of the coolie has been the backbone of Vietnam's struggle in past history. Today the backs of the people and the modern bicycle make up the supply train in the North and in the South. I saw the bicycles, with planks fixed over back wheels, weighted down at each end with straw baskets carrying up to fifty pounds each: 100 pounds per bicycle, or one ton for every twenty bicycles. And they have tens of thousands of bicycles in the 'Legion of Porters'. It is impossible to stop the movement of bicycles. Bicycles do not need paved roads.

Bicycle used to carry supplies How would the stake help the porter? (Remember the saddle and carrier would be covered with a bag of rice). How has the front been adapted to carry loads?

1. What kind of war does Giap say the Americans are having to fight?
2. Why does he give it this name?

This is what David Schoenbrun saw:

> One night, just before dawn, my car was caught in a convoy on a dike, waiting in line to cross a floating bridge. A huge truck and trailer slowly lumbered across and then lurched forward up a steep embankment on the far side. The left rear wheel sunk suddenly in a mudhole, more than hub-cap deep.
>
> I walked across the bridge to watch the attempt to get the ten-ton truck out of the mudhole, an almost impossible task without a power crane. From a nearby village came a stream of peasants, each armed with a shovel and a pail or basket of sand and gravel. They covered the truck like ants on a sugar cube. Dozens of shovels dug deeply into the mud around the wheel. More dozens of sand pails and gravel scoops filled in the sucking hole, while up ahead of the truck, their backs straining against cable lines tied to the bumpers, the legion of porters pulled and hauled until inch by inch the truck moved forward and then, in one burst, shot out of the mudhole. The entire operation took less than an hour. A crane on wheels, with a power winch, could not have done it better or more quickly. At that moment I think I fully understood for the first time what Giap and Ho Chi Minh mean when they talk about a 'People's war'.

Introduction to *Big Victory, Great Task*, Giap

1. What happened to the truck?
2. How was it rescued?
3. What did this incident help Schoenbrun to understand?

People need roads even less than bicycles do. In uncountable numbers the people of Vietnam like columns of ants, lope along the rivers, across the paddies, and through the forests and jungles, with long, thin, flexible bamboo poles balanced on their shoulders, each with its straw baskets on the ends, forming the human freight trains that supply the armies, and the markets of the war-ravaged land.

As for bridges, Giap has come up with a typically Vietnamese invention: the portable floating bridge. It is astonishing to see the floating bridge put together. Flat-bottomed sampans, hidden in reeds while bombers are overhead, are floated down to the river ford, lashed together with pontoons. Then a covering of wooden planks is laid over them and traffic begins to move. I have seen ten-ton trucks with trailers cross a floating bridge.

Introduction to *Big Victory, Great Task*, Giap

1. What has happened to the roads and bridges in North Vietnam?
2. How do the North Vietnamese carry supplies to the south?
3. How do they cross rivers?
4. Why did the North Vietnamese allow Schoenbrun, an American, to visit their country during the war, do you suppose?

General Giap wrote:

> In sending U.S. troops to South Vietnam, the U.S. imperialists have met a people's war. This people's war has successfully developed the people's strength, has succeeded in gathering all the people to fight their attackers in all ways and with all kinds of weapons – from primitive to modern, and has created a very great strength.

Big Victory, Great Task

Written Work

You are a United States soldier who has fought through the war in Vietnam. Why, when you arrived, did you think your side was going to win? Why do you think you lost?

Further Work

1. Read about the siege and capture of Dien Bien Phu in 1954.
2. Find out what you can about Ho Chi Minh, Vo Nguyen Giap and Ngo Dinh Diem.
3. What were the main events of the war in Vietnam?
4. Who were the 'Vietnamese boat people'?

Chapter 4 *Hitler's Germany*

The Nazis

Hitler came to power in 1933. He was Germany's Führer, or Leader, and it was a position he meant to keep. To do that he had to persuade the people to believe in the ideas of his Nazi party. Most of these ideas were quite crude. Here are some of the most important:

1. Hitler was the greatest leader Germany had ever had.
2. The Germans were a master race, and far better than any other nation.
3. Germany's chief enemies were Jews and communists, and they must be destroyed.
4. Germany must become once again the most powerful country in Europe, even if it meant fighting another war.

Children greeting their teachers

Hitler was very interested in education. If his new empire was to last, he would have to make the children and young people into good Nazis. Here is a rule that was made for the schools:

Teachers and pupils are to give one another the German salute within and outside the school.

At the beginning of each lesson the teacher goes in front of the class, which is standing, and greets it by raising his right arm and with the words 'Heil Hitler!'; the class returns the salute by raising their right arms and with the words 'Heil Hitler'. The teacher closes the lesson after the pupils have risen by raising his right arm and with the words 'Heil Hitler'; the pupils reply in the same way.

Apart from this the pupils greet the members of staff by raising their right arms in the proper way within the boundaries of the school.

Where hitherto Catholic religious instruction began and ended with the verse and response: 'Praised be Jesus Christ.' 'For ever and ever Amen', the German salute is to be given *before* this at the beginning of the lesson and *after* it at the end of the lesson.

Decree of December 18th, 1934

1 What is the 'German salute'? (Look at the picture on page 51.)
2 Who has to give the German salute? When?
3 What words are given with the German salute? What do they mean do you suppose?

Here is a school dictation:

Just as Jesus saved people from sin and from Hell, Hitler saved the German nation from ruin. Jesus and Hitler were persecuted, but while Jesus was crucified, Hitler became Chancellor. While the disciples of Jesus denied their master and deserted him, the sixteen comrades of Hitler died for their leader. The apostles completed the work of their Lord. We hope that Hitler will be able to complete his work himself. Jesus built for heaven: Hitler for the German earth.

Dictation given in a Munich school, 1934

Note: The 'sixteen comrades' were the men who died in the 'beer hall putsch' of 1923. It was Hitler's first attempt to seize power, and it failed.

According to this dictation:
1 How were Jesus and Hitler alike?
2 How were Jesus and Hitler different?
3 Which seems to be the greater of the two men?
4 How were Jesus's disciples different from Hitler's 'sixteen comrades'?

Here is an account of a court case:

An eleven year old girl has been noticed at school continually refusing to give the German salute. She gives her religion as the reason and quotes several passages from the Bible. At school she shows a complete lack of interest in matters concerning the Führer.

The parents, who have another daughter of six, approve of this attitude and stubbornly refuse to make the child change her ways. They also refuse to give the German salute, quoting the passage from the Bible, 'Do nothing with a raised hand for this displeases the Lord.' They stick to this in spite of instructions from the court and the headmaster of the school. The mother utterly refuses to speak to the child about it. The father is willing to do so, but says the child must decide for herself. The parents show themselves to be enemies of the Nationalist Socialist State in other ways. They do not possess a swastika flag. They have not put down their child for the

Hitler Youth They are going to work in the forest, but they march, like soldiers. Compare them with the children in the last photograph. What does this tell you about the Nazi movement?

Hitler Youth. They are not members of the Nazi Party, because they have not paid their contributions, even though the father could afford it. Nevertheless they deny being opponents of the movement.

Because of their attitude the Youth Office has proposed the removal of both children from the care of their parents.

The Minister of Justice agreed with this, saying:

> Parents who openly profess the ideas of Jehovah's Witnesses are not suited for the education of their children in the National Socialist spirit.
>
> *Judge's Letter No. 14, 1942*

1. What is the religion of the family described here?
2. How has the older daughter annoyed her teachers?
3. What excuse does she give?
4. Why do the parents object to the Nazi salute?
5. In what other ways have they annoyed the Nazis?
6. What happened to the two children?

In the last extract there was mention of the Hitler Youth. This was a movement for young Germans between the ages of ten and eighteen.

Here Hitler describes its aims:

> There were times which now seem to us very far off and almost impossible to understand, when the ideal young man was the chap who could hold his beer and was good for a drink. But now his day is past and we like to see, not the man who can hold his drink, but the young man who can stand all weathers, the hardened young man. Because what matters is not how many glasses of beer he can drink, but how many blows he can stand: not how many nights he can spend on the spree, but how many kilometres he can march.
>
> What we want from our German youth is different from what people wanted in the past. The German youth of the future must be slim and slender, swift as the greyhound, tough as leather and as hard as Krupp steel.
>
> *Speech to the Hitler Youth*, September 1935

1. What, according to Hitler, was the ideal young German before the Nazis came to power?
2. How does Hitler want young Germans to be?
3. Is there anything wrong in these aims? (What do you suppose were Hitler's real reasons? Look back to the ideas of the Nazi movement on page 51.)

To carry out Hitler's aims, the members of the Hitler Youth did physical exercises, played a lot of sport and went camping regularly. They also learnt to be good

Hitler Youth

Nazis. As we have seen parents were expected to encourage their children to join the Hitler Youth. They were not alone. Here is a letter written by a Catholic priest in Trier:

> In the 5th Class there are ten members of the Catholic Youth Club. These boys have been youth club members for years and remained when the Hitler Youth was founded. Because of this, they have had to put up with a good deal of bullying from their teacher. He puts such pressure on them, that it is almost unbearable for them. For example: last Saturday he set them the essay, 'Why am I not in the Hitler Youth?', while all the other children in the class had no homework. On setting the essay he added: 'If you don't write the essay, I shall beat you until you can't sit down.' Another case: a member of the Hitler Youth had come back to the Catholic Youth Club. When the teacher heard of this he threatened he would set him forty sums every time he stayed away from the Hitler Youth parade. He also threatened to beat him as well. After this, the boy stayed in the Hitler Youth. The teacher even went so far as to threaten the boys in the Catholic Youth Club that he would 'muck up' their reports at Easter and would not move them up, and so on. When he was asked why as a rule he only punished members of the Catholic Youth Club he said, 'It goes against the grain to beat a boy wearing the brown shirt of honour.'
>
> It would be better for the whole class if the Catholic Youth Club members were given the same freedom and just treatment as the other members of the class.
>
> *Letter*, February 14th, 1934

Nazi rally at Nuremburg How did such rallies affect the people who attended them? What are your impressions of the Nazi movement, from this photograph?

1. What rival organisation was there to the Hitler Youth?
2. How did the teacher try to persuade the boys to join, and remain in, the Hitler Youth?
3. What does the priest want to happen?

In 1936, the Nazis made a law saying that all young Germans must join the Hitler Youth.

Of course, Hitler had to win over adult Germans as well as the young. One of the ways he did this was by organising great rallies at different times of the year. The most important was at Nuremberg. It lasted a week and was to celebrate the anniversary of the 'beer hall putsch'. William Shirer, an American news reporter went to the 1934 Nuremberg rally. He wrote:

> I'm beginning to understand, I think, some of the reasons for Hitler's astounding success. Borrowing ideas from the Roman Catholic Church he is restoring pageantry and colour and faith to the drab lives of twentieth century Germans. This morning's opening meeting in the Luitpold Hall was more than a gorgeous show: it also had something of the mystery and religious fervour of an Easter or Christmas Mass in a great Gothic cathedral. The hall was a sea of brightly coloured flags. Even Hitler's arrival was made dramatic. The band stopped playing. There was a hush over the thirty thousand people packed in the hall. Then the band struck up the 'Badenweiler March', a very catchy tune and used only, I'm told, when Hitler makes big entries. Hitler appeared at the back of the auditorium, and followed by his aides, Goering, Goebbels, Hess, Himmler and others he strode slowly down the long centre aisle while thirty thousand hands were raised in salute. Then an immense symphony orchestra played Beethoven's 'Egmont' Overture. Powerful lights played on the stage, where Hitler sat surrounded by a hundred party officials and officers of the army and navy. Behind them the 'blood flag', the one carried down the streets of Munich in the ill-fated putsch. Behind this, four or five hundred S.A. standards. When the music was over, Rudolph Hess, Hitler's closest adviser, rose and slowly read the names of the Nazi 'martyrs' – brown shirts who had been killed in the struggle for power – a roll call of the dead. The thirty thousand seemed very moved.
>
> In such an atmosphere no wonder, then, that every word dropped by Hitler seemed like an inspired Word from on high. Man's – or at least German's – ability to think for himself is swept away at such moments and every lie is accepted as high truth itself.

Berlin Diary, September 5th, 1934

Note: The S.A., or Brown Shirts, were Storm Troopers. They were Hitler's private army, and their violence had done much to bring him to power.

How does this German girl think of Hitler?

1. What does Shirer say Hitler is copying?
2. To what does Shirer compare the meeting?
3. Which other extract in this section shows the Nazis themselves were thinking along the same lines as Shirer?
4. What was done to make the rally impressive?
5. According to Shirer, how did the rally affect the minds of the people there?

There was another display at the rally:

> Hitler sprung his Labour Service Corps on the public for the first time today, and it turned out to be a highly trained semi-military group of fanatical Nazi youths. Standing there in the early morning sunlight, which sparked on their shiny spades, fifty thousand of them, with the first thousand bared to the waist, suddenly made the German spectators go mad with joy when, without warning, they broke into a perfect goose-step. Now, the goose-step has always seemed to me to be a crude exhibition of the human being in his most undignified and stupid state, but I felt for the first time this morning how it touches the strange soul of the German people. They jumped up and shouted their applause. The Labour Service boys formed a huge chanting chorus and with one voice intoned such words as these: 'We want one Leader! Nothing for us! Everything for Germany! Heil Hitler!'

Berlin Diary, September 6th, 1934

1. What men took part in this parade? What were they carrying? What did they shout?
2. What is the goose-step?
3. What did the crowds think of the goose-stepping? What does Shirer think of it?

Here is what happened to Shirer one evening during the rally:

> At ten o'clock tonight I got caught in a mob of ten thousand hysterical people who jammed the moat in front of Hitler's hotel shouting: 'We want our Führer!' I was a little shocked at the faces, especially those of the women, when Hitler finally appeared on the balcony for a moment. They reminded me of the crazed expressions I once saw in the back country of Louisiana on the faces of some Holy Rollers who were about to hit the trail. They looked up at him as if he were a Messiah, their faces transformed into something positively inhuman. If he had remained in sight for more than a few moments, I think that many of the women would have swooned from excitement.

Berlin Diary, September 4th, 1934

Note: Holy Rollers were certain Americans with very strong religious beliefs, who travelled round the country, preaching.

Nazi slogan 'One People, One Empire, One Leader'.

1 Where was the crowd? How big was it? What was it shouting?
2 What was it about the people that shocked Shirer?
3 How did the people seem to view Hitler?
4 What did Shirer think some of the women were likely to do?

Here now is another view of Hitler. William Shirer wrote it in 1938:

> This morning I noticed something very interesting. I was having breakfast in the garden of the Dreesen Hotel, where Hitler is stopping, when he suddenly appeared, strode past me and went down to the edge of the Rhine to inspect his river yacht. One of Germany's leading editors, who secretly despises the Nazis, nudged me: 'Look at his walk!' It was a very curious walk indeed. In the first place it was very ladylike. Dainty little steps. In the second place, every few steps he cocked his right shoulder nervously, his left leg snapping up as he did so. He had ugly black patches under his eyes. I think the man is on the edge of a nervous breakdown. And now I understand the meaning of an expression the party hacks were using when we sat around drinking in the Dreesen last night. They kept talking about the 'Teppichfresser', the 'carpet-eater'. At first I didn't get it, and then someone explained it in a whisper. They said Hitler had been having some of his nervous crises lately and that in recent days they've taken a strange form. Whenever he goes on a rampage about Beneš or the Czechs he flings himself to the floor and chews the edges of the carpet, hence the Teppichfresser. After seeing him this morning I can believe it.
> *Berlin Diary, September 22nd, 1938*

1 What did Shirer notice was strange about Hitler?
2 What does Shirer think is the matter with Hitler?
3 What nickname has Hitler been given? Why?
4 What does the extract show about the feelings of the 'party hacks' towards Hitler? Why do you suppose they felt differently from the crowds at the Nuremberg Rally?

Study this table:

Number of Germans Unemployed (Millions)

January 1933	6.0
„ 1934	3.7
„ 1935	3.0
„ 1936	2.5
„ 1937	1.9
„ 1938	1.1
„ 1939	0.3
August 1939	0.03

1 Plot these figures on a graph.
2 How do you suppose the fall in unemployment helped Hitler?
3 Hitler was preparing for war. How would this have helped end unemployment?

Written Work
It is early in 1939. You are a German, and you are giving Hitler your full support. Explain why.

Research
Find out what you can about:
1 The 'beer hall putsch' of 1923.
2 The S.S. and the concentration camps.
3 Hitler's successes in foreign policy before 1939. (The Rhineland, Austria, Czechoslovakia.)
4 Find out about other Nazi leaders, especially Goering, Goebbels, Himmler and Hess.
5 What work did: **a** Hjalmar Schacht and **b** Albert Speer, do for Hitler?

Anti-Semitism

According to legend, the Jews are descended from Shem, one of Noah's sons. For that reason they are known as Semites. Anti-Semitism is hatred of the Jews.

The worst enemy the Jews ever had was probably Hitler, but he was not alone. When he was still a small boy many Germans disliked the Jews and there was even a society which wanted all the Jews in the world to be killed. Anti-Semitism was also strong in Austria, and it was here that Hitler was born in 1889. This is his description of his first meeting with a Jew. It was in 1909:

> I do not remember ever having heard the word 'Jew' at home during my father's lifetime. Then, one day, when passing through the Inner City of Vienna, I suddenly saw a creature in a long caftan and wearing black sidelocks. My first thought was: is this a Jew? I watched the man secretly, but the longer I gazed at this strange face and examined it section by section, the more the question shaped itself in my brain: is this a German? I turned to books for help in removing my doubts. For the first time in my life I bought myself some anti-Semitic pamphlets for a few pence.
> *Mein Kampf*

1 What, apparently, was the attitude of Hitler's parents towards the Jews?
2 Where did Hitler meet his first Jew?
3 What did he find strange about the man's appearance?
4 What was Hitler unable to decide?
5 What did he do to make up his mind?
6 What kind of thing do you suppose he read in the anti-Semitic pamphlets?

Hitler fought in the German army throughout the First World War. When it was over he stayed in Germany and formed the Nazi party. Nazis were very much against the Jews. This was one of the reasons why they were popular and why, eventually, they came to power. When they did, they began to attack the Jews in earnest.

German girl forced to wear a placard This is her punishment for being friendly with Jews.

Here is an extract from a Nazi school book:

'It is almost noon,' says the teacher. 'Now we must summarize what we have learned in this lesson. What did we discuss?'

All the children raise their hands. The teacher calls on Karl Scholz, a little boy on the front bench. 'We talked about how to recognise a Jew.'

'Good! Now tell us about it!'

Little Karl takes the pointer, goes to the blackboard and points to the sketches. 'A Jew is usually recognised by his nose. The Jewish nose is crooked at the end. It looks like the figure 6. So it is called the "Jewish Six". Many non-Jews have crooked noses too. But their noses are bent, not at the end, but further up. Such a nose is called a hook nose or eagle's beak. It has nothing to do with a Jewish nose. . . .'

'Right!' says the teacher. 'But the Jew is recognised not only by his nose . . .', the boy continues. 'The Jew is also recognised by his lips. His lips are usually thick. Often the lower lip hangs down. That is called "sloppy". And the Jew is also recognised by his eyes. His eyelids are usually thicker and more fleshy than ours. The look of the Jew is sly and sharp. . . .'

Then the teacher goes to the desk and turns over the blackboard, on its back is a verse. The children recite it in chorus:

From a Jew's countenance / the evil devil talks to us,
The devil, who in every land / is known as evil plague,
If we are to be free from the Jew / and to be happy and glad again,
Then youth must join our struggle / to overcome the Jew devil . . .

Der Giftpilz: The Poisonous Mushroom, 1938

According to this extract:
1 How is it possible to recognize a Jew?
2 What kind of people are the Jews?
3 What is the duty of the young people of Germany?

School's over Jewish children and also a Jewish teacher are expelled so that 'discipline and order' can now be taught properly.

Nazi leaders The four men facing the camera are, from left to right, Hess, Goering, Streicher and Goebbels.

Here is a discussion between two Nazi leaders, Goebbels and Goering. Goebbels was Minister of Propaganda while Goering was Air Minister and Commander-in-Chief of the Air Force.

GOEBBELS: It is still possible for a Jew to share a compartment in a sleeping car with a German. Therefore we need a law stating that Jews shall have separate compartments: when compartments are full up, Jews cannot claim a seat. They will be given a separate compartment only after all Germans have secured seats. They are not to mix with Germans, and if there is no more room, they will have to stand in the corridor.

GOERING: I'd give the Jews one coach or compartment. And if the train is overcrowded, believe me, we won't need a law. We'll kick him out and he'll have to sit alone in the lavatory all the way!

GOEBBELS: I don't agree. There ought to be a law. Furthermore, there ought to be a law barring Jews from German beaches and resorts. Jews should not be allowed to sit around in German parks. I am thinking of the whispering campaign on the part of Jewish women in the public gardens on the Fehrbelliner Platz. They go and sit with German mothers and their children and begin to gossip and work upon their feelings. I see here a particularly grave danger. I think it is imperative to give the Jews certain public parks, not the best ones, and tell them: 'You may sit on these benches.' These benches shall be marked 'For Jews only'. Besides, they have no business in German parks. Furthermore, Jewish children are still allowed in German schools. That's impossible. It is out of the question that any boy should sit beside a Jewish boy in a German grammar school and take lessons in German history. Jews ought to be put out of German schools. They ought to take care of their own education.

Conference on the Jewish Question, November 12th, 1938

1. List the things which Goebbels thinks Jews should be forbidden to do.
2. Where does he disagree with Goering?

Laws were made against the Jews from time to time. The most important were the Nuremberg Laws of 1935. We give them that name because they were announced at a rally of the Nazi party in Nuremberg. Here are extracts from two of them:

Marriages between Jews and citizens of German blood are forbidden. Marriages concluded in defiance of this law are void, even if, for the purpose of evading this law, they were concluded abroad.

Jews will not be permitted to employ female citizens of German blood as domestic servants.

Jews are forbidden to display the national flag or the national colours.

Law for the Protection of German Blood and German Honour, 15th September, 1935

A Jew cannot be a citizen of the Reich. He has no right to vote in political affairs and he cannot occupy public office.

Regulation under Reich Citizenship Law, November 14th, 1935

1 What are Jews forbidden to do?
2 What rights are taken from them?

Here are some other laws:

1. From January 1st, 1939 the running of retail shops, mail order houses and the practice of independent trades are forbidden to Jews.
2. Moreover, Jews are forbidden from the same date to offer goods or services in markets of all kinds, fairs or exhibitions or to advertise them or accept orders for them.
3. Jewish shops which operate in violation of this order will be closed by the police.

Decree of October 18th, 1936

In 1938 an Order of the Police President of Berlin placed these restrictions on the Jews in that city:

1. All theatres, cinemas, cabarets, public concert and lecture halls, museums, amusement places, the exhibition halls at the Messedamm including the exhibition area and radio tower, the Sportplatz, the Reich Sports Field, and all sport places including the ice skating rinks.
2. All public and private bathing establishments and indoor baths as well as open-air baths.

Note: Jews were also fobidden to go into certain of the more important streets.

1 What are Jews forbidden to do by the Decree of 1936?
2 What kinds of places must they keep out of in Berlin?

Jews throughout the world were very angry with the Nazis and, on November 7th 1938, a Polish Jew living in Paris murdered a German official there. The American consul at Leipzig describes what happened in his town. It was much the same all over Germany:

At 3.00 a.m. on 10th November 1938 was unleashed a barrage of Nazi ferocity, the like of which had never been seen before in Germany, or, probably, anywhere else in the world since savagery began. Jewish buildings were smashed into and contents destroyed or looted. In one of the Jewish sections an eighteen-year-old boy was hurled from a three-storey window to land with both legs

Anti-Jewish sign in shop Why is the notice in English as well as German, do you suppose?

broken on a street littered with burning beds and other furniture from his family's and other flats. In another part of the town a small dog was flung down four flights of steps and broke his spine. One flat belonging to some rich people was violently ransacked for valuables and one of the looters thrust a cane through a priceless medieval painting.

Jewish shop windows by the hundreds were smashed throughout the entire city at a cost of several millions of marks. There were heavy losses as many of the windows were full of expensive furs which were seized. The main streets of the city were a positive litter of shattered plate glass. It seems the damage was done by S.S. men and Stormtroopers not in uniform, each group using hammers, axes and incendiary bombs.

Three synagogues in Leipzig were fired and all sacred objects destroyed, in most cases hurled through the windows and burned in the streets. The fire brigade made no attempt to quench the flames, but played their water on adjoining buildings. All of the synagogues were gutted by fire. The blackened frames have been the centre of attraction during the past week of terror for silent and bewildered crowds.

Fierce as was the destruction of property, even more hideous was the arrest and transportation to concentration camps of male German Jews between the ages of sixteen and sixty. This has been taking place daily since the night of horror.

Report of David Buffum, November 21st, 1938

1 What damage was done to Jewish property?
2 Who was responsible?
3 What did the fire brigade do? Why do you suppose it acted in this way?
4 What happened to many Jewish men?

So many shop windows were smashed on the night of November 10th that it was known as Kristallnacht, or Crystal Night.

The next day a woman member of the Nazi party, Melita Maschmann went to her work in Berlin. Later she wrote:

Next morning – I had slept well and heard no disturbance – I went into Berlin very early. On my way I had to go down a rather gloomy alley containing many small shops and inns. To my surprise almost all the shop windows here were smashed. The pavement was covered with pieces of glass and fragments of broken furniture.

I asked a policeman what on earth had been going on. He replied: 'In this street they're almost all Jews.'

'Well?'

'You don't read the papers. Last night the National Soul boiled over.'

I went on my way shaking my head. For the space of a second I was clearly aware that something terrible had happened there. Something frighteningly brutal. But almost at once I switched over to accepting what had happened as over and done with. I said to myself: The Jews are the enemies of the New Germany. Last night they had a taste of what this means. Let us hope that World Jewry will take the events of last night as a warning. If Jews sow hatred against us all over the world, they must learn that we have hostages for them in our hands.

Account Rendered, 1963

1 What was Melita Maschmann surprised to see?
2 What did the policeman say had happened? What did he mean? Do you suppose he had done anything to stop the rioters?
3 What were Melita Maschmann's first thoughts?
4 What were her second thoughts?

Hitler had left Vienna in 1913, a penniless tramp. He returned in 1938, a conqueror. He had sent his soldiers into Austria but instead of fighting them, the people cheered them. They wanted their country to be part of Germany. When Hitler himself arrived, they gave him a hero's welcome.

At the same time, an American news correspondent, William Shirer, was in Vienna. Here are some of the things he saw:

I fought my way out of the crowd towards the Karntnerstrasse. Crowds moving about all the way. Singing now. Singing Nazi songs. A few policemen standing around good naturedly. What's that on their arms? A red-black-white Swastika arm band! So they've gone over too! Young toughs were heaving paving blocks into the windows of the Jewish shops. The crowd roared with delight.

Berlin Diary, March 11th–12th, 1938

1 What shows the crowds welcomed the Nazis?
2 What proved that the police did as well?
3 What were some of the young men doing? What did the Austrian crowd feel about it?

A few days later Shirer wrote:

On the streets today gangs of Jews with jeering storm troopers standing over them and taunting crowds around them, on their hands and knees scrubbing the Schuschnigg signs off the sidewalks. Many Jews killing themselves. All sorts of reports of Nazi cruelty, and from the Austrians it surprises me. Jewish men *and* women made to clean lavatories. Hundreds of them just picked at random off the streets to clean the toilets of the Nazi boys. The lucky ones get off with merely cleaning cars – the

Jews killed in countries occupied by Germans

Country	Previous number of Jews	Losses Lowest estimate	Losses Highest estimate
1 Poland	3,300,000	2,350,000	2,900,000 = 88%
2 U.S.S.R.	2,100,000	700,000	1,000,000 = 48%
3 Romania	850,000	200,000	420,000 = 49%
4 Czechoslovakia	360,000	233,000	300,000 = 83%
5 Germany	240,000	160,000	200,000 = 83%
6 Hungary	403,000	180,000	200,000 = 50%
7 Lithuania	155,000	—	135,000 = 87%
8 France	300,000	60,000	130,000 = 43%
9 Holland	150,000	104,000	120,000 = 80%
10 Latvia	95,000	—	85,000 = 89%
11 Yugoslavia	75,000	55,000	65,000 = 87%
12 Greece	75,000	57,000	60,000 = 80%
13 Austria	60,000	—	40,000 = 67%
14 Belgium	100,000	25,000	40,000 = 40%
15 Italy	75,000	8,500	15,000 = 26%
16 Bulgaria	50,000	—	7,000 = 14%
17 Denmark	—	(less than 100)	—
18 Luxemburg	—	3,000	3,000 —
19 Norway	—	700	1,000 —
Total		4,194,200	app. 5,721,000 = 68%

thousands of cars which have been stolen from the Jews and 'enemies' of the government. The wife of a diplomat, a Jewess, told me today she dared not leave her home for fear of being picked up and put to 'scrubbing things'.

Berlin Diary, March 22nd, 1938

Note: Schuschnigg was one of the Austrian leaders who opposed Hitler.

1 What are Jews having to do?
2 Who is making them?
3 How can you tell that many Austrians were pleased?

Look back to page 57 and you will remember that it was in Vienna that Hitler himself first learnt to hate the Jews.
After the war began the Nazis decided to destroy the Jews completely. They set up death camps where Jews were killed in gas chambers, hundreds at a time.
Study the above table:

1 What is the lowest estimate of Jews killed in Europe? What is the highest?
2 In which country were most Jews killed?
3 Which country lost the highest percentage of its Jews?

The Nazis who ran the death camps all belonged to the S.S. The man in charge of the S.S. was Heinrich Himmler. Here is part of a speech he made to some of his men in 1943:

We have exterminated a disease, because we did not want to be infected by the disease and die of it. All in all we can say we have carried out this most difficult duty for the love of our people. And our spirit, our soul, our character has not suffered injury from it.

Speech at Posen, October 6th, 1943

1 What does Himmler think of the Jews?
2 What reason does he give for killing them?
3 How does he say the members of the S.S. have been affected by all the killing?

William Shirer, who met Himmler, said of him:

Heinrich Himmler is such a mild little fellow when you talk to him, reminding you of a country school teacher, which he once was – pince-nez and all.

Berlin Diary, December 21st, 1939

Written Work
It is 1939 and you are a Jew living in Germany. Describe how the Nazis have been persecuting your people, and what you fear may happen in the future.

Research
1 As well as the Nuremberg Laws there were some Nuremberg Trials. What were they?
2 Find out about the persecution of the Jews in countries other than Germany, especially Russia before the First World War.

Chapter 5 *Russia*

The Communist Revolution in Petrograd, November 1917

Until 1917 Russia was ruled by an Emperor, or Tsar. The last of the Tsars was Nicholas II. He governed with the help of the nobles, the Church and his secret police. He was very unpopular and his government was inefficient. When the war came in 1914, the Germans defeated the Russian armies quite easily. This made the Tsar even more unpopular, so in March 1917 there was a revolution which overthrew him. The men who led the revolution were, for the most part, members of the middle classes, such as doctors, lawyers and factory owners. They set up what they called the Provisional Government. Its leader was Kerensky.

The Provisional Government made some serious mistakes and the worst of these was to go on with the war. Russian soldiers died in their thousands while, in the cities, people starved. Soon, Kerensky and his ministers were as unpopular as the Tsar had been. This was the opportunity for a small group of determined men, the Bolsheviks, or Communists. Their leader was Lenin.

The Communists had little difficulty in winning over most of the ordinary soldiers and sailors. All they had to do was promise that if they came to power they would at once make peace. Many discontented factory workers also joined the Communists. Early in November 1917, Lenin and his friends decided the time had come to overthrow the Provisional Government. In the capital, Petrograd,* they had their own private army of Red Guards. Also, the soldiers in the fortress of St. Peter and St. Paul were on

*Today this city is called Leningrad.

Storming the Winter Palace This is a photograph, not of the event itself, but of a diorama. Compare it with the descriptions of the attack on page 66.

their side, as were the sailors in the naval base at Kronstadt.

This section tells you what happened at Petrograd from the night of November 6th to the night of November 7th. We shall see the events mainly through the eyes of two men. They were John Reed, an American newspaper reporter and Louis de Robien, an official in the French Embassy. Reed was strongly in favour of the Communists: de Robien had nothing against them at first, but he changed his mind later.

The only troops in Petrograd who were loyal to the Provisional Government were the Women's Battalion, and the boy soldiers in the officer training schools. John Reed describes the Women's Battalion:

> The Women's Battalion is known to the world as the Death Battalion, but there were many Death Battalions composed of men. They were formed in the summer of 1917 by Kerensky, to strengthen the discipline and fighting spirit of the army by heroic example. The Death Battalions were composed mostly of intense young patriots. They were, for the most part, the sons and daughters of landowners.
>
> *Ten Days that Shook the World*

Louis de Robien wrote:

> I watched the women's regiment going along the Embassy quay, with bands and machine guns, beautifully in line, with their rifles held straight on their shoulders, with fixed bayonets. One could have mistaken them for a splendid Guards regiment of the old days.
>
> *The Diary of a Diplomat in Russia*, November 6th, 1917

1. What was the Women's Battalion known as?
2. Who formed it, and others like it? Why?
3. Who were the parents of the soldiers in these battalions?
4. What are 'intense young patriots'?
5. How was the Women's Battalion marching when de Robien saw it? To what did he compare it?

The Provisional Government met in the Winter Palace, which had belonged to the Tsar before he was deposed. On the night of November 6th the Communists seized most of the important buildings in Petrograd, but the Women's Battalion and the cadets still held the Palace. John Reed went there on November 7th:

> Three cadets stood beside us and we fell into convers-

Soldiers of the Women's Battalion Does this photograph agree with de Robien's description above? What happened to these girls on the night of November 7th? (See page 66).

ation. They said they had entered the officer training schools from the ranks, but now they didn't want to be officers any more, because officers were very unpopular. They didn't seem to know what to do as a matter of fact, and it was plain that they were not happy.

But soon they began to boast, 'If the Bolsheviks (Communists) come we shall show them how to fight. They do not dare to fight, they are cowards. But if we should be overpowered, well, every man keeps one bullet for himself.'

Ten Days that Shook the World

1. What did the three cadets feel about becoming officers?
2. What did they say they would do if the Communists attacked?
3. What did they think of the Communists?
4. What did they say they would do, if they were defeated?

The next extract is from the memoirs of Kerensky, the head of the Provisional Government:

The night of November 6–7 was tense. We were waiting for troops to arrive from the front. They had been summoned by me in good time and were due in Petrograd on the morning of November 7th. But instead of the troops, all we got were telegrams and telephone messages saying that the railways were being sabotaged.

By morning (November 7th) the troops had not yet arrived. The telephone exchange, post office and most of the government offices were occupied by Red Guards. After a brief discussion it was decided that I should drive out at once to meet the troops.

Red Guards had been posted in all the streets around the Winter Palace. Check-points at the approaches to Petrograd were also occupied by armed Bolsheviks. I decided to take a big risk and drive all the way across the city. The driver was told to drive at his usual speed through all the main streets of the capital, which led to the check-points. This plan worked very well. My appearance in the streets of the city among the rebels was so unexpected that they failed to react as they should have done. Many of the 'revolutionary' sentries stood to attention! At the Moscow check-point our car was fired at, but we arrived safely at Gatchina.

The Kerensky Memoirs

Note: Kerensky could not find enough soldiers to help him recapture Petrograd so he fled abroad.

1. What excuse did the troops give for not coming to Kerensky's aid? Do you suppose this excuse was genuine?
2. Why did Kerensky decide to leave Petrograd?
3. Why was this dangerous?

Kerensky addressing troops Kerensky was an excellent speaker, but he failed to keep the support of the army.

4. How did Kerensky escape from the city?
5. What did some of the rebel sentries do as Kerensky drove past? What should they have done?

Later, it was said that Kerensky fled from Petrograd disguised as a nurse. This, he denied.

Here is Louis de Robien's account of what happened on the night of November 7th–8th:

According to this morning's information the battle was fairly heated. The Bolsheviks had decided to seize the Winter Palace, the government's last stronghold. It was being defended by a few cadets and by the women's battalion, who had entrenched themselves inside the Palace and in the square behind mountains of firewood. The Palace was surrounded by Bolshevik troops who set up a battery of about twenty machine guns in front of the Ministry of Foreign Affairs, and installed two cannon under the Red Archway of Morskaya Street. In addition, the cruisers who had brought the sailors from Kronstadt were moving broadside on to the Palace firing their guns. Firing was also coming from the Peter and Paul Fortress. Under those conditions the defenders could not hold out for long. It is impossible to know the casualty figures. Three hundred women soldiers are said to have been killed, but this figure seems to me exaggerated.

Diary of a Diplomat in Russia

1. Who defended the Winter Palace?
2. How had the Communists attacked the Palace?
3. How many of the defenders were reported dead? What did de Robien think of this figure?

A few days later, de Robien wrote:

According to the information I have been able to collect, the fighting at the Winter Palace was less murderous than was at first believed. It appears that the Kronstadt sailors shot a number of cadets, and some women soldiers were killed during the fighting. However, the hospital which occupies the centre of the building has not suffered, and the wounded remained there throughout the battle. During this time, the windows of the rooms used by the hospital remained brilliantly lit, to prevent them being shot at. But all these dear Russians are so clumsy that those windows got just as badly riddled by bullets as the ones which they were aiming at.

The gunners in the Fortress did not do much better, and at a range of about four hundred yards they missed the target with almost every shot, sending their shrapnel either into the water at their feet or else to the devil. And yet the Palace made a lovely target. Seeing them at work like this, one realised why they did so little damage to the Germans who consider a spell at the Russian front to be a rest-cure after France.

Diary of a Diplomat in Russia, November 10th, 1917

1. How fierce does de Robien now think the battle was?
2. How could the Communists tell which part of the Winter Palace was a hospital?
3. What happened to the hospital windows? Why?
4. What does de Robien think of the artillery fire?
5. What, according to de Robien, did the attack on the Winter Palace help explain?

John Reed arrived at the Winter Palace just as it surrendered. He and some other journalists were with the first Communist troops to go inside it:

Just as we came up, someone was shouting 'The cadets have sent word that they want to surrender!' Voices began to give commands, and in the thick gloom we made out a dark mass moving forward, silent but for the shuffle of feet and the chinking of arms. We fell in with the first ranks.

Like a black river, filling all the street, without song or cheer we poured through the Red Arch. The man just ahead of me said in a low voice, 'Look out comrades! Don't trust them. They will fire surely!!' In the open we began to run, stooping low and bunching together, and jammed up suddenly behind the Alexander Column.

After a few minutes huddling there, some hundreds of men, the Army seemed reassured, and without any orders suddenly began again to flow forward. Over the barricade of fire-wood we clambered, and leaping down inside gave a triumphant shout as we stumbled on a heap of rifles thrown down by the cadets who had stood there. On both sides of the main gateway the door stood wide open, light streamed out, and from the huge building came not a single sound.

Carried along by the eager wave of men we were swept through the entrance. A number of huge packing cases stood about and upon these the Red Guards and soldiers fell furiously, battering them open with the butts of their rifles, and pulling out carpets, curtains, linen, porcelain, plates, glass-ware. One man went strutting around with a bronze clock perched on his shoulder; another found a plume of ostrich feathers which he stuck in his hat. The looting was just beginning when somebody cried, 'Comrades! Don't take anything! This is the property of the People!' Immediately twenty voices were crying, 'Stop! Put everything back! Don't take anything! Property of the People!' Many hands dragged the looters down. Roughly and hastily the things were crammed back in their cases, and self-appointed sentinels stood guard.

Ten Days that Shook the World

1. What shows the Communists were nervous?
2. What, finally convinced them that the cadets had surrendered?
3. What did some of the Communists do as soon as they entered the Palace?
4. How were they stopped?

Inside the Palace were some cadets, the Women's Battalion and those members of the Provisional Government who had not managed to escape. John Reed describes what happened to each group:

1. Cadets came out in bunches of three or four. The Committee seized upon them with remarks like, 'Ah, the Provocators! Counter-revolutionists! Murderers of the People!!' But there was no violence done, although the cadets were terrified. Their pockets were full of plunder. It was carefully noted down by the scribe and piled in the little room. The cadets were disarmed. 'Now, will you take up arms against the People any more?' demanded the clamouring voices.

'No,' answered the cadets, one by one. Whereupon they were allowed to go free.

2. 'What happened to the Women's Battalion?' we asked an officer. 'Oh – the women!' He laughed. 'They were all huddled up in a back room. We had a terrible time deciding what to do with them – many were in hysterics and so on. So finally we marched them to the Finland Station and put them on a train to Levashovo, where they have a camp.'

3. A soldier and a Red Guard appeared in the door, and other guards with fixed bayonets. After them followed single file half a dozen men in civilian dress – the members of the Provisional Government. First came Kishkin, his face drawn and pale, then Rutenberg,

Lenin addressing a meeting Lenin was an even better speaker than Kerensky. Also, he told the people what they wanted to hear.

looking sullenly at the floor: Tereshchenko was next, glancing sharply around. They passed in silence: the victorious rebels crowded to see, but there were only a few angry mutterings. It was only later that we learned how the people in the street wanted to lynch them, and shots were fired – but the sailors brought them safely to Peter-Paul.
Ten Days that Shook the World

1. What did the Bolsheviks call the cadets?
2. What did they do to them?
3. What did they make them promise?
4. Where did the Communists find the members of the Women's Battalion? What sort of state were they in?
5. What happened to the Women's Battalion?
6. What did the crowd want to do with the members of the Provisional Government?
7. What, in fact, happened to them?

A few days after the capture of the Winter Palace, de Robien wrote:

> Trams and cars are circulating as usual, and it does not seem to occur to all these armed thugs, who are themselves in rags, to remove the fur-lined coats of the wealthy people driving past in cars. They are not really bad at heart, and in any other country, days like these would have been much more terrible.
>
> I was able to get about undisturbed all day. I lunched with Ermolovs and I dined with Madame Lindes and came back along the Liteiny Prospekt. The fog made great haloes round the few street lamps, in which the silhouettes of the Red Guards with their guns and bayonets appeared immense and fantastic.

The Diary of a Diplomat in Russia, November 11th, 1917

1. What is life like in Petrograd after the revolution?
2. What was de Robien able to do?
3. How are the Communists behaving?
4. What does de Robien think of them?

A month later, however, de Robien wrote in his diary:

> Yesterday, on the corner of the Liteiny Prospekt, two soldiers were bargaining for apples with an old woman street vendor. Deciding that the price was too high, one of them shot her in the head while the other ran her through with his bayonet. Naturally, nobody dared to do anything to the two soldier murderers who went quietly on their way munching the apples they had acquired so cheaply, without giving a thought to the poor old woman whose body lay in the snow for part of the day, near her little stall of green apples.

The Diary of a Diplomat in Russia, December 12th, 1917

1. Why did the two soldiers kill the old woman?
2. What did de Robien think of the Communists after this incident?

The old woman was one of the first of millions who died in Russia as a result of the Communist revolution.

Written Work
Write your own account of what happened in Petrograd from the night of November 6th–7th, to the following night. Say what you think of the troops on both sides.

Research
1. Find out what you can about Tsar Nicholas II, his family and the monk Rasputin. What happened to them in the end?
2. Read about the Revolution of March 1917 which brought Kerensky and the Provisional Government to power.
3. Read about the Civil War in Russia that followed the Revolution of November 1917. What part did Britain and other countries play in it?

Communists and Peasants

The Russian revolution which you read about in the previous section was the work of a handful of Communists. They were helped by some of the town workers who were close to starvation and, more important, by soldiers and sailors who were tired of the war. Between them, they seized power in the capital, Petrograd. However, eight Russians in every ten were peasants, so the Communists could not gain control of the whole country unless they made friends with them. Accordingly, one of the first things which the Communists did was to pass a Land Decree. This took away the land belonging to the nobles and gave it to the peasants. Next, the peasants were invited to send representatives to a special Congress at Petrograd. Here, the Communists persuaded the peasants to work with them.

The Communists met in a former girls' school, the Smolny Institute. The Peasants' Congress met in the Duma, or parliament building. When the two sides had made their agreement, the peasants went to the Smolny Institute in a body. John Reed saw them go:

> The peasants poured out of the building. It was already dark, and on the ice-covered snow glittered the pale light of moon and star. Along the bank of the canal were drawn up in full marching order the soldiers of the Pavlovsky Regiment, with their band, which broke into the Marseillaise. Amid the crashing full-throated shouts of the soldiers, the peasants formed in line, unfurling the great red banner of the All-Russian Peasants' Soviets, embroidered newly in gold, 'Long live the union of the revolutionary and toiling masses!' Following were other banners: of the District Soviets, of Putilov Factory.
>
> So the great procession wound through the city, growing and unfurling ever new red banners lettered in gold. Two old peasants, bowed with toil, were walking hand in hand, their faces lit up with child-like joy.
>
> 'Well,' said one, 'I'd like to see them take away our land again *now!*'
>
> On the steps of Smolny about a hundred Workers' and Soldiers' Deputies were massed. Like a wave they rushed down, clasping the peasants in their arms and kissing them: and the procession poured in through the great door, and up the stairs with a noise like thunder.

Trotsky This picture is obviously posed. What impression is Trotsky trying to give of himself?

> Zinoviev announced the agreement with the Peasants' Congress, to a shaking roar which rose and burst into a storm as the sound of the music blared down the corridor, and the head of the procession came in.
>
> Then, Trotsky, full of fire: 'I wish you welcome comrade peasants! You come here, not as guests, but as masters of this house, which holds the heart of the Russian Revolution. The will of millions of workers is now concentrated in this hall. There is now only one master of the Russian land: the union of the workers, soldiers and peasants.'

Ten Days that Shook the World

1. Who marched with the peasants?
2. Why were the two old peasants pleased?
3. What did Zinoviev announce?
4. Who, according to Trotsky, ruled Russia?

Many peasants had not waited for the Land Decree, or the agreement with the Communists. Louis de Robien describes what happened on one estate even before the revolution in Petrograd:

> We heard some appalling details about the pillaging and burning of the chateau at Lapotkovo. Old Princess Urussov was ill, and the peasants dragged her out of bed and left the unfortunate woman for several hours in the courtyard, shivering with fever and cold, while they ransacked everything and squabbled over the furniture and clothes. Not one of them would agree to lend a cart to drive the poor woman to the station and it was some Austrian prisoners of war who took pity on her and saved her from being murdered by taking her to the station. Those peasants behaved like savages. They dug up the body of the Princess's son, who had been killed at the beginning of the war, to see if they could find any jewellery or medals on it: then they left the corpse, half out of the grave. Not one man could be found in the village to help the Princess and her daughter who had, in fact, been very kind to their peasants and had done them a great deal of good. And these are those very same peasants whose gentleness and kindness are praised by Tolstoy, who wrote a few kilometres from there! There is moreover something very disturbing about these outbreaks. It is a kind of sudden madness. In fact, a few days before, these same peasants, while dividing up the land on the estate between themselves, had decided to protect their former masters and declared that they would not allow them to be insulted, even verbally. Then all at once they burst into the chateau in a fury, pillaging everywhere and burning everything.
>
> *The Diary of a Diplomat in Russia*

Note: Leo Tolstoy, 1829–1910, was a Russian nobleman and a famous author.

1 What did the peasants do to Princess Urussov?
2 Who saved her life?
3 How does de Robien describe the way the peasants behaved?
4 Why does de Robien find the peasants' behaviour strange and disturbing?
5 What had the peasants done a few days before they attacked the chateau?

After the Revolution there was a terrible Civil War in Russia. It was between the Communists, or 'Reds' and their enemies who were called 'Whites'. In the end, the Reds won, and the main reason was that the peasants helped them. They did so because, as we have seen, the Communists allowed them to take land from the nobles.

When the Civil War was over, many peasants made quite a lot of money, especially the more prosperous ones who were called 'kulaks'. But the good times did not last. Lenin, the man who had led the Revolution died in 1924. The new ruler of Russia was Josef Stalin. He was a strict Communist and he did not like the peasants owning land. People who have property cannot be true Communists. It is like eating meat, and calling yourself a vegetarian. Also, Stalin thought the peasants were inefficient. Most of them had tiny farms, they were very old fashioned and they were not growing nearly enough food for the Russian people. Stalin decided the answer to both

Peasants massacred by Communists

problems was to take land from the peasants and make them work in teams on huge collective farms. A Russian writer, Raphael Abramovitch, describes what happened to them:

> The kulaks were deported to the northern provinces to do forced labour, such as making roads, drainage works, lumbering and work in the mines.
>
> They were transported in appalling conditions. So many of them were crammed into freight and cattle cars that often there was no room to sit down: they were sent off, sometimes without water, usually without warm clothing and frequently without enough food. Many died on the journey, disease was rife, and when they arrived the terrible working conditions killed even more. Their families were not much better off: they were driven from their homes to beg for bread in other villages, whose inhabitants were well aware that it was dangerous to help the relatives of a kulak.
>
> *The Soviet Revolution*

1. Where were the kulaks sent?
2. What did they have to do when they arrived?
3. Why did many die on the journey?
4. What happened to their families?

Peasants harvesting

Many peasants did go to work on the collective farms. The next two extracts tell you about them:

> Many peasants, before joining the collective farms began to slaughter their livestock: cows, sheep, pigs, even poultry. Just in February and March 1930 around 14 million head of cattle were destroyed: also one third of all pigs and one fourth of all sheep and goats.
>
> *Let History Judge*, Roy Medvedev

> The peasants worked on the collective farms without any real desire to do well. Sowing and harvesting were carried out lazily, carelessly and late in the season: farm machinery was kept in poor repair. Many cattle died because of poor fodder, polluted water and lack of care: calves perished and the milk yield sank to a very low level. Even greater were the losses in horses, which no longer had the loving care of their former owners. The losses in livestock were so enormous that it took Russia more than a generation to recover.
>
> *The Soviet Revolution*, Raphael Abramovitch

1. What did many peasants do before they joined the collective farms?
2. In what ways did they do their work badly?
3. What happened to many of the animals?
4. Why do you suppose the peasants behaved as they did?

These figures show what happened as a result of making the peasants work on collective farms:

> If we take 1928 food production as 100 per cent, in 1929 it was 98 per cent, in 1930 94.4 per cent, in 1931 92 per cent, in 1932 86 per cent, and in 1933 81.5 per cent. The total number of cattle dropped from 60.1 million head to 33.5 million. The number of goats, sheep and pigs fell to less than half its pre-war level. The number of draft animals, especially horses, fell by more than a half.
>
> *Let History Judge*, Roy Medvedev

1. Draw a bar diagram to show how food production fell from 1928 to 1933.
2. How many cattle were lost?
3. What proportion of other farm animals died?

A Russian writer describes the countryside in the early 1930's:

> It was frightening to walk through the villages. Houses with boarded-up windows, empty barnyards, abandoned equipment in the fields. And a terrifying number of deaths, especially many children.
>
> On the deserted road to Stavropol I met a peasant with a knapsack. I asked him, 'Where are you tramping comrade?'
>
> 'To prison.'
>
> Astonishment kept me from saying anything. I only

looked my amazement at the old man. He told me his story. He was a peasant who had been sentenced to ten years for refusing to join a collective farm. The village policeman lacked the time or the inclination to escort him to Stavropol, so he was going alone.

On the surface the man did not care about anything, but he also had his peasant cunning: in prison he would be saved from starvation. Famine, in early 1933 was striking down hundreds of people in the villages.

Memoirs, A. E. Kosterin

1. What did Kosterin find in the villages?
2. Why had the old man been sent to prison?
3. Why was he going there on his own?
4. What did he feel about going to prison?
5. Why were so many people dying?

Some ten years later, during the Second World War, Winston Churchill went to Russia to meet Stalin. This is a conversation he had with him:

'Tell me,' I asked, 'have the stresses of this war been as bad to you personally as carrying through the policy of the Collective Farms?'

This subject immediately roused Stalin.

'Oh no,' he said, 'the Collective Farm policy was a terrible struggle.'

'I thought you would have found it bad,' said I, 'because you were not dealing with a few score thousand of aristocrats or big landowners, but with millions of small men.'

'Ten millions,' he said, holding up his hands. 'It was fearful. Four years it lasted. It was absolutely necessary for Russia, if we were to avoid periodic famines, to plough the land with tractors. We must mechanise our agriculture. When we gave tractors to the peasants they were all spoiled in a few months. Only the Collective Farms with workshops could handle tractors. We took the greatest trouble to explain it to the peasants. It was no use arguing with them. After you have said all you can to a peasant he says he must go home and consult his wife, and he must consult his herder.'

'After he has talked it over with them he always answers that he does not want the Collective Farms and he would rather do without the tractors.'

'These were what you call Kulaks?'

'Yes,' he said, but he did not repeat the word. After a pause, 'It was all very bad and difficult – but necessary.'

'What happened?' I asked.

'Oh well,' he said, 'many of them agreed to come in with us. Some of them were given land of their own to cultivate in the province of Tomsk or the province of Irkutsk or farther north, but the great bulk were very unpopular and were wiped out by their labourers.'

There was a considerable pause. Then, 'Not only have we vastly increased the food supply, but we have improved the quality of the grain beyond all measure. All kinds of grain used to be grown. Now no one is allowed to sow any but the standard Soviet grain from one end of our country to the other. If they do they are severely dealt with. That means another large increase in the food supply.'

History of the Second World War, Vol. IV: *The Hinge of Fate*, Winston Churchill

1. How, according to Stalin, did the struggle with the peasants compare with the war with Germany?
2. Why did Stalin say he wanted collective farms?
3. What did the peasants feel about them?
4. What did Stalin say happened to the kulaks?
5. What did Stalin say was the result of having collective farms?
6. Where does Stalin's account agree with the other sources? Where is it different? Which do you believe? Why?

By 1936 the worst of the famine was over because Stalin allowed each peasant to have at least some land for himself and grow food for sale. That year the leader of Britain's trade unions, Walter Citrine, visited Russia where he saw a collective farm. These extracts are from his book *I Search for Truth in Russia*.

1. The farm was once the property of some wealthy landowner. There were 183 families and they farmed 3,000 acres. This was divided up among cattle, dairy farm, vegetables, wheat etc. etc. They had 120 cows on the collective farm and the peasants had 80 others on their own property.

Every member of the farm worked on task work which was fixed at so many labour days. These days were entered in the books of the collective farm. When the crop was sold, after the Government had taken its share, the surplus was divided amongst members according to the number of working days they had to their credit.

1. Who had once owned the farm? When had he lost it, do you suppose?
2. How big was the collective farm? How many families were there on it?
3. How many cows belonged to the collective farm? How many belonged to individual peasants?
4. Who took much of the crop?
5. How were the peasants paid?

2. We went to inspect the farm buildings. First we visited the restaurant which was in an old and somewhat dilapidated main building, with places for about forty people at small tables. Most of the peasants were awfully

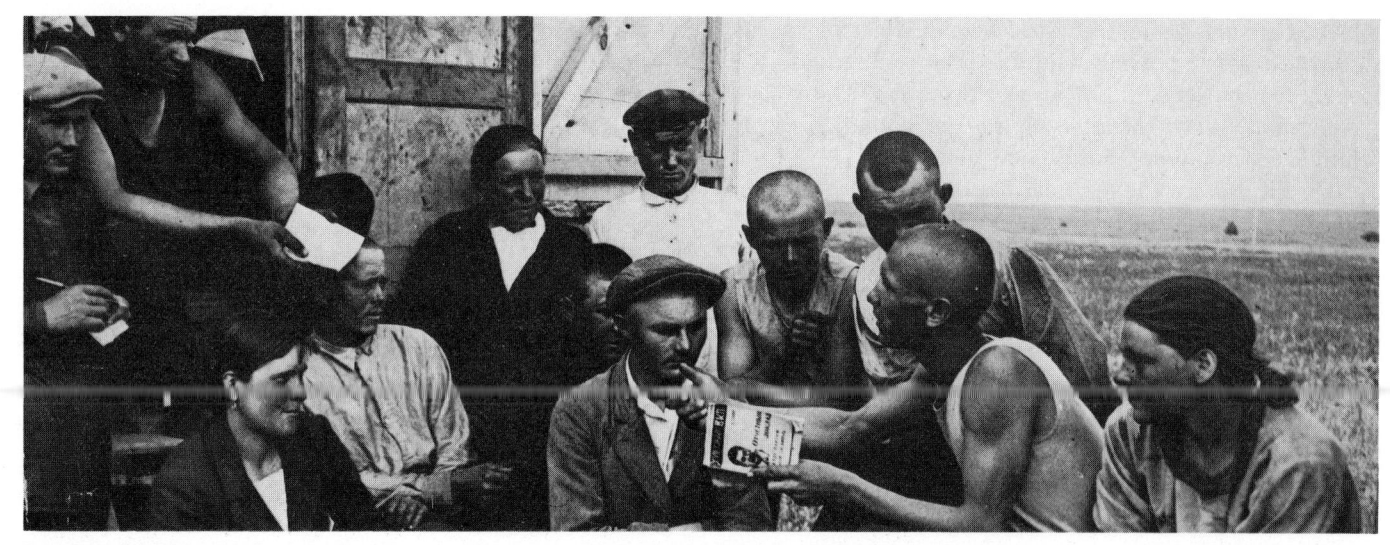

Peasants listening to a Communist Why was it important for the Communists to win the peasants over to their ideas? How are the peasants reacting to the speaker?

poor looking. They were drinking a soup which appeared to be quite nourishing.

We then went to the village club, a wooden building which had a small meeting hall as well as a tiny library. There were pictures of tractors showing the spare parts, and pictures showing how necessary it was for the peasants to work steadily instead of lazing their time away and not attending to their crops. In every room there was a picture of Stalin.

1. What building did the peasants share?
2. What was hanging on the walls?

3. I was struck by the ragged dress of many of the peasants. Some of them wore good boots, but their clothes were for the most part mud-stained and tattered. Scarcely any of the women wore boots and none of the children. As for the clothes of the children, particularly the boys, much of it had been cut down after serving for many years their parents' or someone else's use.

One house which I saw consisted of two rooms about 12 feet square. There was only one bed for the family of five. Mother, daughter aged about twenty-five and a younger girl about fourteen, slept in this one bed. The boy slept on a sort of wooden bench in the other room. The father was on night work as a watchman. There was no covering whatever on the floor, but there were several religious pictures, including ikons, on the walls. All of them were crude but colourful. There were only two chairs, both of them small basket armchairs. The elderly woman had a pair of ancient shoes, but the younger woman no shoes at all.

1. Describe the peasants' clothes in your own words.
2. What was the floor area of the house? How many square feet was that for each person? What is the figure, roughly, for your own home?
3. What furniture was there?
4. How did the family sleep?

Study this table:

Grain Imported into Russia from the United States of America

	Wheat	Coarse Grains
1976–1977	2.9 million tonnes	4.6 million tonnes
1977–1978	3.3	9.2
1978–1979	2.9	8.3
1979–1980	3.9	11.4
1980–1981	3.0	5.0

1. Show this information as a bar diagram.
2. What do the figures tell you about Russian farming in the 1970's? Bear in mind that Russia has far more good farming land than the United States.
3. The wheat is used to make bread. The coarse grains are chiefly maize, which is cattle food. How is the Russian government trying to improve the diet of its people, do you think?

Written Work

1. It is 1936. You are a Russian peasant. Tell the story of your life since 1917. How did you feel about the Communists when they first seized power? How do you feel about them now?
2. Now write the story of farming in Russia from 1917 to 1936, pretending you are a Communist.

Research

Find out more about the way Stalin ruled Russia. Look especially at his Five Year Plans and his great purge of 1934–1938.

Chapter 6 *China*

China Before the Communist Revolution

In the seventeenth century, China was conquered by a race called the Manchus. They governed badly. Then, in the early twentieth century a man named Sun Yat-sen organized the Chinese Nationalist Party. In 1911 it rebelled against the Manchus and overthrew them. However, the Nationalists were not strong enough to rule China themselves. There was no proper government, so there was chaos almost everywhere.

Here, we shall look at China's problems during these troubled times.

The Chinese are a quarter of the world's population, but under the Manchus the country was backward, and, as a result, it was weak. Foreigners took advantage of this to win control of China's main ports. In 1928, an American newspaper reporter, Edgar Snow, went to Shanghai. This is what he saw:

> In this river are grey or white ships, lean and slenderly fashioned of steel, with armored decks on which the guns are turned westward into China. These are the foreign watchdogs: American, British, French, Italian and Japanese cruisers, destroyers, submarines and aircraft carriers that patrol the Whangpoo, the Yangtze and the coasts of China. In the threat of their cannon, poised so gracefully, is the explanation of Shanghai's safety. Stationed ashore are French, American and Italian marines, British Tommies and Japanese bluejackets: their bayonets form a rim of steel around the foreign Settlement. They guard the largest foreign investment in any city in the world.
>
> *Edgar Snow's China*

Note: The Settlement was the part of the town where the foreign merchants, bankers and factory owners were. They had special privileges, for example their own courts of law. No foreigner could be tried by a Chinese court.

1. What different kinds of warship does Snow see?
2. To which countries do they belong?
3. What soldiers are there on shore?
4. Why are the ships and soldiers there?
5. How would the British feel if something like this was happening in, say, Liverpool?

The Settlement, Shanghai Who lived and worked here? How can you tell they were prosperous?

During the 1930's China's worst enemy was Japan. In 1931 she invaded Manchuria. Edgar Snow went there and wrote this letter to his brother:

I had an interesting trip to Manchuria last month. I went up to Tsitsihar, where it was ten below in November. Six of us went up on the Chinese Eastern Railway the same day the Japanese occupied the town. There were still numerous bodies spread over the fields. They were all frozen. Despite the fact that 5,000 Japanese drove back 20,000 Chinese and killed nearly a thousand, the latter put up a better fight than anyone expected. Those northerners are tall and strong limbed, used to the cold and are full of courage. Against them the Japanese had eight giant air bombers, tanks, heavy artillery, armoured cars and all under the operation of a highly efficient, well-disciplined army. The Chinese were mostly bandits and peasants, had no airplanes and only light artillery. But they managed to kill more than 200 Japanese before the latter wiped out their front line trenches.

Edgar Snow's China

1. How many Chinese were there in the battle? What does Snow say about them?
2. How many Japanese were there? How many times were they outnumbered?
3. Why did the Japanese win?

While the fighting was still going on in Manchuria, Edgar Snow returned to Shanghai. He saw this:

It was dark midnight, January 28th, 1932.

Suddenly Japanese rifle and machine-gun fire laced Jukong Road, up which I hurried from the Shanghai North Station. I saw a figure stop and fall. Beyond, a Chinese soldier dropped to his knees, crawled inside a doorway and began firing. The street emptied like a drain: iron shutters closed as if clams lived inside, and the last light disappeared.

In that stinking alley the 'greatest' battle since World War 1 was beginning.

Outrage piled on outrage: cases of banditry, kidnapping, murder and brutality. Obviously, certain Chinese had been marked well in advance; these were leading merchants or businessmen who had refused to trade with Japanese. Some were taken away, not to be heard of again: their families were attacked and often wiped out completely. I saw a helpless old Chinese woman dragged from her home and kicked in the face. The reign of terror was not be checked for days.

Edgar Snow's China

Shanghai 1932 Japanese troops about to attack.

1 Why were there Japanese soldiers in Shanghai? (See page 73.)
2 According to Snow, how serious was the fighting in Shanghai?
3 Which Chinese, in particular, suffered?
4 How long did the trouble last?

Japan overran Manchuria in 1932, but she was far from satisfied. In 1937 she attacked again, meaning, this time, to take the whole of China.

As there was no proper government in China, men called warlords were able to seize power in many provinces. The next extract will give you some idea of the kind of men they were. It is about **Marshal Tang Kiao**, who ruled over Yunnan, with help from the French. The writer is Lucien Bodard, the son of the French Consul in Yunnan. He was then a young boy:

> Like every warlord, there is plotting round him the whole time: treason follows him like his own shadow. He stays on his guard, and will make a refined dinner party even more elegant by unmasking one of his people, and having him executed on the spot, even during the banquet. He is so kind that he shares the pleasure of his revenge with his western guests. One evening, in the middle of an official dinner of some fifty courses, he announced in the nicest possible way, that a punishment had been arranged on the floor below. His favourite general had become a little involved in a plot to assassinate him. The guests are cordially invited to see the show. No-one is surprised. They know China. The gentlemen get up to watch the execution. The ladies stay where they are.
>
> Afterwards my father told me that the condemned man was about forty, very handsome, wearing a dress uniform and a snow leopard cap. All was done with great ceremony. The executioner, with a pointed hat, and holding a long, straight sword with a square end, asked him to kneel on a silk carpet. He obeyed, but suddenly objected because he felt something rough under his knee. It offended his dignity. They lifted the carpet and took out the stone which was annoying the fastidious general. Thereupon he knelt down again, bent his neck below the enormous cutlass which took off his dainty head with ridiculous ease. Afterwards, everybody went back to the banqueting room where the feast went on as if nothing had happened.
>
> *Le Fils du Consul*

1 Why is Tang Kiao always on his guard?
2 When does he like to have people executed?
3 Who is invited to watch?
4 Whose execution is described here? What had he done?

Woman road worker

5 How was the man executed?
6 What did the people do afterwards?

In one way this man was lucky. Others who displeased Tang Kiao were tortured to death in public. The heads of the victims were hung in cages above the gates of the town.

In Shanghai, the foreigners and wealthy Chinese lived in luxury, but this is how **Edgar Snow** found some of the ordinary people:

> I remember the hundreds of factories where little boy and girl slaves sit or stand at their tasks twelve or thirteen hours a day, and then drop, in exhausted sleep, to the dirty cotton quilt, their bed, directly beneath the machine. I remember little girls in silk mills and the pale young women in cotton factories – all of them literally sold into these jobs as virtual slaves for four or five years, unable to leave the heavily guarded, high walled premises, day or night, without special permission. And I remember that during 1935 more than 29,000 bodies were picked up from the streets and rivers and canals of Shanghai. There is a perpetual famine among the hundreds and thousands of poor in the great city just as severe, maybe worse, than famine in the farm country.
>
> *Edgar Snow's China*

1 What hours did the factory children work?
2 Where did they sleep?
3 How had they come to work in the factories?
4 Why did they need permission to leave the factories, do you suppose?
5 What seems to show that the factory workers were luckier than many of the people outside?

Most Chinese were not townsmen, but peasants. Lucien Bodard describes something of the lives of those who lived in Yunnan:

I can remember one winter when the village streets were empty. The people stayed in their huts, eating as little as possible. Every mouthful was precious, for their stocks of beans were vanishing. The father would give each member of the family what he thought fit, and often those who could not work had almost nothing. Pigs were more important than people, especially the elderly. In the Chinese countryside, respect for the old was often a joke. If there was a shortage, they died quickly. Sometimes, newly-born babies were killed. If there was absolutely nothing left to eat, the men chased away the peasant women, those sturdy females who, in normal times, worked tremendously hard. Their husbands would snap 'Get out! Go and look for food somewhere else.' Later, their bodies were found at the bottoms of cliffs, or in the rivers. It wasn't that the last harvest had been bad, but there were too many soldiers at Tcheng Tu. A warlord would send his men with their bayonets who would say: 'We need so much rice, so many pigs, so many dried beans.' And after them, would come another detachment from another warlord, with the same demands.

Le Fils du Consul

1 Why were the village streets empty?
2 Who gave out the food when it was short?
3 Who were the first to suffer during a famine?
4 What did the men do when all the food was gone?
5 Why was there a famine at that particular time?

In 1966 an English traveller, Maslyn Williams, visited a museum in Peking. There he saw a display of life-size clay sculptures called the 'Rent Collection Court'. It was supposed to show what had happened in the old days, when peasants went to pay their rents:

The peasants in tattered rags, bring their grain to be weighed. They bring it in baskets or bundled up in old bits of cloth. All of them are gaunt, some little more than skin and bone. An old woman leans miserably on a stick awaiting her turn to pay. She has brought along a skinny chicken to make up for the short measure of millet she

Peasant woman and child, during a famine

has been able to glean from the tiny patch of land from which she must eke out a living.

A blind man, almost naked, is led in by his grandchild and because he cannot pay his tally she is taken to be a housemaid in the landlord's house, leaving the old man helpless and alone. Next to him an angry young man has raised his shoulder pole to strike at the landlord's agent while his frightened wife puts out her hands to restrain him.

Mr. Wang says that the peasants used to call the rent collection court the 'Gateway to Hell' because when they went there each year they were always afraid about what would happen to them. If they had not enough grain to pay the rent or the money they owed, the landlord would take the children in payment or make the women come and work for him, or conscript the men into the army of the local warlord. If the harvest was poor nobody knew what would happen to them on rent collection day. Any one of the family could be taken.

A group of visitors stood close by us, the guide standing on a box to address them. Her eyes flashed and her voice was loud with contempt as she pointed with a long white stick to the dominating figure in the group. This was the landlord's agent, standing with legs apart, hand on hip, a panama hat on the back of his head, a mastiff squatting beside him. She indicated his fine clothes, the pistol in his waistband, the fan in one hand, a long cigarette holder in the other. How heartless he looks, how arrogant and how well fed!

'And look at his helpers! See how roughly that despicable class traitor empties the poor widow's grain into a wooden bucket to check whether or not it will meet the amount of her debt. See how he lets some of it spill onto the ground while she watches anxiously. And remember that the measuring bucket is a false one made especially big to cheat the peasants.'

Again she swung her stick, and her anger went with it.

'Then see how viciously this other man strikes with his whip at her hungry little son, because he tries to pick up the grain that was spilt.'

The East is Red

1. What are the peasants using to pay their rents, in place of money?
2. What shows that the peasants are very poor?
3. What happened if a peasant could not pay his rent?
4. How is the landlord's agent made to seem?
5. How are the peasants cheated?

Scene from the Rent Collection Court What impression is the sculptor giving of the landlord and his agent? Compare this with the photograph on page 79 which shows peasants paying their taxes after the Revolution!

In 1962 a Swede, Jan Myrdal, went to live for a time in a Chinese village. One of the men, there, Chang Shi-ming, told him about his early life:

We have always been farmers. But we did not have our own land. We rented it. For three generations we rented the same land. There were 120 mu. The landlord's name was Wang Ting-tung. When I was a child I worked at home. When I was fourteen I went out to work as herd-boy for Wang Ting-tung. I was not given any wages, but I got my food. Three meals a day, millet gruel and 'sticky millet' bread. The landlord lived in the town, he had several houses and stone caves. We had an ordinary earth cave.

Landlords did not eat as we others did. They never worked, and they ate meat and vegetables every day. Wang Ting-tung was incredibly mean. He made you give back the tiniest coin due to him. He was hard. If people could not pay, he punished them. He did not hit you, but he threatened and swore and took your possessions away.

When I was eighteen I began working with father in our fields. People hated the landlords, but there was no way of getting round them. 'As long as we have our daily food, we must be satisfied,' people said. 'We must do what our masters say. They own the land and the oxen.' Wang was called 'Wang the Bloodsucker'. Everybody owed him money. As long as you owed him money, you could not get permission to leave the village in order to look for a better landlord.

Every year he put up our rent. In 1928 the rent was 15 jin per mu. In 1930 18 jin per mu. In 1931 21 jin per mu and that year we could not pay it all. We owed him 600 jin. It was a normal year without crop failure, but there were so many mouths to feed in our family and the rent was so high that we could not pay it. Wan Ting-tung said: 'You must pay your debt before you can have permission to move.' We had to give up our land, but we could not move from there because we owed 600 jin.

The landlords ate up people's work. They ate and we worked.

Report from a Chinese Village

Note: A mu is about one sixth of an acre. A jin is 1 lb 1½ oz.

1. How much land did Chang's family farm?
2. What did Chang think of his landlord?
3. How did people think they should behave towards the landlords? Why?
4. What happened to Chang's rent? What happened when the family could not pay?
5. How far do you think Chang would agree with the ideas behind the exhibition at Peking?

Edgar Snow wrote:

In most districts in the interior the only roads are cart tracks, worn deep through centuries of use. Most of the country folk rarely see, never use, a train, airplane, automobile, radio, electric light or newspaper. From 80 to 90 per cent of them are unable to read, and almost all are incredibly poor.

Tax collectors had police powers and could imprison any peasant for failing to pay taxes and rent. The tenant who did not wish to go to jail had to borrow from the moneylender – quite often the selfsame landlord and tax collector. Sometimes the interest was 100 percent a year.

Probably, the average farming family earns a living from less than two acres of soil.

Children in Yunnanfu are used for hauling extraordinary loads. One day I met an old woman leading a dozen juveniles laden with enormous loads of wood. One of them, frailer than the rest, had fallen down weeping and refused to go on. The old lady stood over her and beat her with a hunk of wood.

'Why don't they revolt?' I asked myself. 'Why don't they march in a great army and attack the scoundrels who can tax them, but cannot feed them, who can seize their lands, but cannot repair an irrigation canal? Or why don't they sweep into the great cities and plunder the wealth of the rascals who gorge on thirty-six course banquets while honest men starve?' I was very puzzled. For a while I thought nothing would make a Chinese fight.

I was mistaken. The Chinese peasant was not a coward. He would fight when given a method, an organization, leadership, a workable program, hope – and arms.

Edgar Snow's China

1. In what ways are the peasants backward?
2. What powers did the tax collectors have?
3. Why might a peasant have to borrow money?
4. Who might the moneylender be?
5. What might the peasant have to pay?
6. How much land might a peasant family farm? (Compare this with Chang Shi-ming's farm)
7. In what ways was the old woman ill-treating the children?
8. What other evidence is there in this section that peasants could be cruel?
9. What questions did Snow ask himself about the peasants?
10. What conclusion did he reach? Which of Chang Shi-ming's remarks seem to show he was right?
11. What did Snow discover later?

Written Work

You have visited China in the early 1930's. Write a report on the country saying what her problems are.

Research

1. Find out about:
   The Empress Tz'u-Hsi
   Sun Yat-sen
   Yuan Shi-kai.
2. Read about the Japanese invasion of China from 1937 onwards.

The Peasants in Communist China

You have seen that in the early part of the twentieth century, China had serious problems. One of these was that the warlords and the landlords treated the peasants badly. For a time, things became even worse. The Japanese attacked and overran much of the country and, if that was not enough, there was a civil war. It was between the Nationalists under Chiang Kai-shek and the Communists under Mao Tse-tung. Then at the end of the Second World War, the Americans defeated the Japanese and, soon afterwards, the Communists defeated the Nationalists. Mao Tse-tung proclaimed the People's Republic of China in 1949.

During the Civil War the landlords had supported the Nationalists while the peasants had supported the Communists. Therefore, when the Communists won, the peasants had the landlords at their mercy. You will now read two extracts which will tell you the kind of thing that went on in villages all over China. The first was written by a Chinese woman, Ting Ling.

A group of peasants made their former landlord, Schemer Chien, stand on a stage before them. He glared at them and they had been so frightened of him for so long that no-one dared to do anything. Then this happened:

A man suddenly leapt out from the crowd. He had thick eyebrows and sparkling eyes. Rushing up to Chien he cursed him: 'You murderer! You trampled our village

Peasants paying their taxes in grain, 1973

under your feet! You killed people for money. Today we're going to settle all old scores, and do a thorough job of it. Do you hear that? There's no place for you to stand on this stage! Kneel down! Kneel to all the villagers!' He pushed Chien hard, while the crowd echoed: 'Kneel down! Kneel down!' The soldiers held him so that he knelt down properly.

The man who had cursed Chien now turned to face the crowd. 'Friends!' he said, 'We've poured our blood and sweat to feed him, but today we want him to give back money for money, life for life, isn't that right?'

'Right! Give back money for money, life for life!' People surged up to the stage, shouting wildly, 'Kill him! A life for our lives!'

A group of villagers rushed to beat him. It was not clear who started, but one struck the first blow and the others fought to get at him, while those behind who could not reach him shouted, 'Throw him down! Throw him down! Let's all beat him!'

One feeling moved them all – vengeance! They wanted to give vent to their hatred and loathing. They would have liked to tear him with their teeth.

The Sun Shines over the Sangkan River

1 Why did the villagers hate their former landlord?
2 What did they do to him?

The next extract is a story a peasant told a Swedish visitor, Jan Myrdal:

We were very strict and we destroyed the landowners as a class. When we turned our attention to a certain Chang Pei-yi, 600 of the people on his estates came to the meeting and told us how he had oppressed them. It was a long meeting. We found that he had 300,000 jin of grain, 400 goats, 6 donkeys and 21 oxen. He told us he only owned 10,000 mu, but he really owned more. He had more than 20 villages under him and received 60,000 jin a year in rents. Well, we divided up his land and shared his corn and his animals and his tools and implements. Chang Pei-yi himself had fled, for he knew what his tenants would do with him if they got hold of him.

Report from a Chinese Village

1 How many people came to accuse Chang Pei-yi?
2 What property did he own?
3 Why did he pretend he had less than he really did, do you suppose?
4 What did the peasants do with Chang Pei-yi's property?
5 What did Chang Pei-yi do? Why?

Having taken the land from the landlords, what were the peasants to do with it? As the last extract sug-

Peasants take revenge on their landlord This is another scene from the Rent Collection Court.

gests, they might share it among themselves, each family having its own little farm. However, Mao Tse-tung and the Communists did not like that. True Communists do not own property like factories, shops, houses and land. Moreover, little farms are not usually very efficient. What the Communists wanted the peasants to do was to form 'collective farms', or 'co-operatives'. All the families in a village would put their land together to make a co-operative, that is, one big farm, and work on it as a team. The land would belong to the co-operative and not to any individuals. The peasants would share the crops and any money they might make, according to the amount of work they had done.

The problem was to persuade the peasants to join the co-operatives. Here is what happened to one man, Li Hai-yuan, who had been in a co-operative, but decided to leave it:

For two years I stayed on my own. It was difficult. I had to see to everything myself. I sweated my guts out. I saw that Liu Ling Agricultural Co-operative was flourishing and I began to think that I was stupid to have left it.

Then, in the third year I did not manage to finish my ploughing. I had two mu left. I wasn't going to manage it in time. Then the farmers' co-operative people came along: they stopped and watched me and then, without a word, they began ploughing those two mu for me. There were seventeen of them, and they did the work in less than an hour. I myself would have needed two days. Then I thought: 'It's good to be many.' But I said nothing and they said nothing.

Later, when I was weeding a field of maize that I was behind with, they came once again to help me. I told them that I would pay them for their work. But they replied, 'You are in difficulties and you can't manage this.

We are strong and we are many, and we can help you as a brother.' But I hadn't asked for any help. They had just seen for themselves how things were with me, and come of their own accord.

Liu Ling Farmers' Co-operative had been reorganized as East Shines Red Higher Agricultural Co-operative. They had bigger fields than before. The millet fields were very big and I looked at them and they were so beautiful. Just after that they came to me from the Co-operative and talked with me. They were polite and asked me to do them the service of joining. They said: 'Do you see how rich we've become? We've pooled our land now. It's hard farming on your own. Come to us.' I thought they were right and as they had been polite and had come to me themselves I agreed to become a member of the East Shines Red Higher Agricultural Co-operative.

In 1955, my last harvest on my own, I had got 1,800 jin. In 1956, in the Co-operative, I got 2,000 jin and also sixty yuan in cash. And I had not needed to work so hard.

Report from a Chinese Village

Note: The East Shines Red Higher Agricultural Co-operative would have been a village.

1 How long did Li Hai-yuan farm on his own?
2 What first made him think he had been wrong to leave the co-operative?
3 In what two ways did Li Hai-yuan fall behind with his work?
4 Why did the people from the Co-operative help him, do you suppose?
5 Why did Li Hai-yuan like the look of the Co-operative?
6 How did the people of the Co-operative persuade Li Hai-yuan to join them?
7 How did they make it easy for him to agree? (Find out what a Chinese means by 'losing face'.)
8 In what ways did Li Hai-yuan say he had gained by joining the Co-operative?

In 1958 Mao Tse-tung said China must make a Great Leap Forward. Among other things this meant grouping the Co-operatives into Communes, each one of about 35 villages. A commune is something like an English county in size.

In 1936 Edgar Snow had visited Pao An in northern China. He returned in 1970 and it was then the capital of a commune. He describes the changes the commune had made:

A motor road now leads into Pao An. The roadless badlands I had known were steep, uncultivated hills, divided by ravines, dry except in flood, with only here and there patches of grain and tumbledown caves. The few peasants wore rags, their uneducated urchins ran naked, and salt, needles, thread and matches were luxuries. They could scarcely feed themselves when the weather was kind, and they starved when it was not.

The motor road was built for trucks, jeeps and carts. Our passenger car brought many people to greet us and the quiet hills seemed to sprout smiling children to cry 'Long live Chairman Mao!' as we drove past. Cut from steep yellow clay the road had slipped away here and there under recent rains. In such places, work teams had been brought up by radio to do quick repair jobs.

As the valley widened we began to see the results of land reclamation – hills with their tops cut off, garden-like terraces making giant steps down impossible slopes, new rock walls beside the river, and rank upon rank of poplars and willows planted to bring the stream under control and win precious new valley land. Herds of goats and fat-tailed sheep (three to a household I was told) grazed along the hilltops.

Fortunately the earth here is worth the effort. 'Loess' land is very rich. On such slopes bulldozers would be useless and there are none. To make just one such man-

Terraces

made terrace, covering one-third of an acre of useful farmland, needed 20,000 baskets of earth carried on people's backs.

In 1936 there were scarcely a hundred people living in Pao An. Now there were 3,000. There was a new theatre with a thousand seats. There had been no industry at all: now there were thirteen handicraft workshops, a machine repair shop, and a power plant. In 1936 I saw only one store in the whole country. Now a main street was lined with miniature shops. In a small department store we found much the same goods as are sold everywhere in China.

Li Shih-pin, vice-chairman of the revolutionary committee welcomed us to the new government headquarters of small clean buildings and guest houses, set beside the river. An open-air feast was spread and we ate with farmers who had helped produce it: huge ears of corn on the cob, delicious yams, hot-spiced chicken and pork, and a variety of luscious local fruits.

The Long Revolution

1. What had the countryside been like in 1936?
2. How had the people lived?
3. What had been done since then to the slopes of the hills?
4. What had been done to the river valleys?
5. How were farmers using the hilltops?
6. What changes had there been in the town of Pao An itself?
7. What did Snow and his party have to eat? Where had the food come from?
8. This extract tells you several of the ways in which a commune tries to improve its area. What are they?
9. How can you tell that the commune of Pao An is still backward compared with a country like Britain?

The next extract is from a Chinese novel by Chou Li-po. It is a conversation between a courting couple. Chen Ta-chun and his girl friend, Sheng Shu-chun:

'Shu-chun, I want to tell you something. I have plans in my mind.'

'What kind of plans?'

'After the co-operative is established, I'm going to propose that we do away with all the ridges between the fields, and make small plots into large ones. With large fields, the Iron Buffalo can go into the water.'

'What Iron Buffalo?'

'Tractors. They don't get tired and can work the fields day and night. Then we would be able to grow two crops of rice in all the fields.'

Communist poster What message is the artist trying to give?

'Even in dry fields!' Shu-chun was doubtful.

'We must build a reservoir. Look!' He points to a ravine in the hills opposite. 'Isn't that just the place for a reservoir? When we've built a reservoir, all the dry fields in the village will be irrigated and even after paying taxes we shan't be able to eat all the grain we grow. We'll send the surplus grain to help feed the factory workers in the town. Won't that be wonderful! Then they, all smiles, will come in their jeeps to the countryside, and say to us. "Hello, peasant-brothers, would you like to have electric light here?" "Yes, paraffin lamps are really too inconvenient and wasteful." "Very well, we'll install it. Do you want the telephone?" "Yes, we want that as well." And so, electric light and the telephone will come to the countryside.'

'You talk as if the electric light was just going to come on!'

'It will be soon. Then we'll use some of the funds the co-operative has saved to buy a lorry and when you women go to the theatre in town, you will ride by lorry. With electric light, telephone, lorries and tractors we shall live more comfortably than they do in the city, because we have the beautiful landscape and the fresh air. There will be flowers all the year round, and fruit, more than we can eat.'

Great Changes in a Mountain Village

1. In what two ways does Chen Ta-chun say the co-operative should improve its farming?
2. Where will the people of the co-operative send their surplus grain? What will they have in exchange?
3. Is this the sort of conversation you would expect a courting couple to have?

One of China's main problems is that her population is growing rapidly. By the late 1970's it was already close on 1,000 million, a quarter of the human race. All these people must have food to eat and somewhere to live. Most of them are crowded in the fertile valleys and coastal plains. Meanwhile there are thousands of square miles of less fertile land which are almost empty. In 1978 an American author, Arthur Miller, visited China. Here he met another American called William Hinton, who was an agricultural engineer. Hinton was trying to help the Chinese develop some of their less fertile land. Here is a conversation he had with Miller:

'It's the mechanisation of the land that's the problem. They just took delivery of a million buck's worth of John Deere tractors: the John Deere engineers didn't think they needed those giant machines, but the Chinese insisted. When the Deere people saw fields as big as two thousand acres, they were surprised but relieved.'

'Will they know how to operate them?'

'Oh, they're quick learners. They'll do that okay. But the way to get food out of spaces like that is to let the machines do what they were designed to do. But they're allowing a flood of people to come into the area. They'll defeat the good that might come from the machines. You don't *want* tens of thousands of peasants loose on open land like that, not if you've got the machines to work it. They'll slow it down, they'll bring it to a halt. I produce, all by myself, plus machines, more corn on second-rate Pennsylvania hill sides than a Chinese work brigade of more than four hundred people. They're creeping up to a billion population, they can't afford to waste land. The problem is they keep their bad habits. Too many people were sent into the area. The newly opened lands are being populated at the same rate as the old – about three families to seventeen acres. One hand doesn't seem to know what the other is doing. One farm has American equipment replacing ninety percent of the workers, while a few miles away they are letting people in as fast as they can. The result is that all these farmers eat most of the grain that they grow.'

'I guess they don't know what to do with all those people.'

'Exactly, and I don't either, but this way is not the answer.'

Chinese Encounters

1. What equipment have the Chinese bought from America?
2. How big are some of the fields in which they will be used?
3. What does Miller suggest is the reason the Chinese government is allowing so many people to settle in the area?
4. Why does Hinton say this is a mistake? (Think of buying a tractor to plough a field, then employing a hundred people to dig it with spades.)
5. Why was the author of the previous extract wrong to have so much faith in the 'iron buffalo'?

Written Work
Write a report describing the changes that took place in the Chinese countryside after the Communists seized power. Say what serious problem remains.

Research
1. Read about Chiang Kai-shek, Mao Tse-tung and the Chinese Civil War. Take particular note of the Long March.
2. How did Stalin start collective farms in Russia? How did the Chinese Communists learn from his mistakes?
3. Find out more about the Great Leap Forward.

The Cultural Revolution

In Britain we would be amazed if the Queen went for a long swim in the River Thames. We would be even more amazed if she put up a big notice, urging the ordinary people to start a revolution. Workers were to take over their factories: students and school children were to attack anyone who was important, such as the Prime Minister, the Members of Parliament, the leaders of the political parties, town councillors and so on. It would be amazing, too, if the people of Britain obeyed. Yet things very like this happened in China.

In 1966 Mao Tse-tung swam nine miles down the Yangtze-Kiang. Soon afterwards he put up a poster with the title 'Bombard the Headquarters'. In it he urged the workers, peasants, students and school children to attack the people in authority. This was even more strange than the events we imagined happening in Britain, because the only people who had any real authority in China were Communists. They were members of Mao's own party, most of them people who had fought with him in the Civil War.

Many Chinese needed little encouragement. Workers took control of their factories and ran them themselves. Students and school children called themselves Red Guards, seized what weapons they could find, and attacked anyone they chose. Soon China was in chaos.

Mao called all this the 'Cultural Revolution'. Culture is mainly to do with ideas so, presumably, Mao was trying to change the way the Chinese were thinking. But what new ideas were they to have? Mao had written many books, far too many for ordinary folk to read. What he did, therefore, was to make a short collection of his best sayings. It became known as the *Little Red Book of Mao Tse-tung*.

Here is one of the easier passages from the 'Little Red Book'. Mao first wrote it in 1945:

Section 21 *Self Reliance and Arduous Struggle*
There is an ancient Chinese fable called 'The Foolish Old Man who Removed the Mountains'. It tells of an old man who lived in northern China long, long ago and was known as the Foolish Old Man of North Mountain. His house faced south and beyond his doorway stood the two great peaks, Taihang and Wangwu, obstructing the way. With great determination he led his sons in digging up these mountains hoe in hand. Another greybeard, known as the Wise Old Man, saw them and said

The *Little Red Book of Mao Tse-tung*

scornfully, 'How silly of you to do this! It is quite impossible for you few to dig up these two huge mountains.' The Foolish Old Man replied, 'When I die, my sons will carry on; when they die, there will be my grandsons, and then their sons and grandsons, and so on for ever. High as they are, the mountains cannot grow any higher, and with every bit we dig, they will be that much lower. Why can't we clear them away?' He went on digging every day, unshaken in his belief. God was moved by this, and he sent down two angels, who carried the mountains away on their backs. Today, two big mountains lie like a dead weight on the Chinese people. One is imperialism, the other is feudalism. The Chinese Communist Party has long made up its mind to dig them up. We must persevere and work unceasingly, and we, too, will touch God's heart. Our God is none other than the masses of the Chinese people. If they stand up and dig together with us, why can't these two mountains be cleared away?

Note: By 'imperialism' Mao meant the attempts by foreigners, especially the Japanese, to conquer China. By 'feudalism' he meant the rule of the warlords and landlords.

Mao in silk This is the silk workers' tribute to Mao. What do they seem to think of him?

1. Why did the Foolish Old Man decide to move the two mountains?
2. Why did the Wise Old Man mock him?
3. How did God help?
4. Which two mountains face the Chinese Communist Party?
5. With whom were the Communists fighting when this extract was written in 1945? (See page 79.)
6. According to Mao, who is the God who will help the Communists?

Another statement in the *Little Red Book* is:

> Every Communist must grasp the truth, 'Political power grows out of the barrel of a gun.'

1. What did Mao mean by this? (How did the Chinese Communists come to power?)
2. How does a political party come to power in a country like Britain?

During the Cultural Revolution there was a lot of propaganda about Mao Tse-tung. A Canadian newspaper reporter, Charles Taylor, saw a lavish musical show called 'The East is Red'. This is a translation of the title song:

> The East is red from the rising sun.
> In China appears Mao Tse-tung,
> He works for the people's welfare,
> He is the People's great saviour.
>
> Chairman Mao loves the people,
> He is our guide,
> He leads us onward
> To build a New China.
>
> Beloved Chairman Mao
> Sun in our hearts!
> Your light shines for us
> In whatever we do.

Note: Mao's official position was Chairman of the Chinese Communist Party.

1. What is the song comparing Mao Tse-tung to?
2. According to the song, what kind of man is Mao? What has he done for China?

Charles Taylor describes a singing competition he attended. Almost without exception the competitors had chosen songs of praise to Chairman Mao:

> There was a chorus line of eight lively young girls. Each clutched a volume of the *Works* of Chairman Mao as they sang 'Mao Tse-tung's Thinking Is as Bright as the Sun'. ('If you ask me what I'm busy with, I'm reading Chairman Mao's writings: if you ask me what I've gained, it would be too much to say – so many ideas and so much encouragement.') There was a solo act, a young girl singing 'Chairman Mao is a Member of my Commune', her encore, 'Song of Chairman Mao and the Party'. Another favourite ditty is called 'Last Night I Dreamed of Chairman Mao.'
>
> *Reporter in Red China*

1 What was the subject of all the songs Taylor heard?

This is what a Swedish reporter Hans Grandqvist found in Shanghai:

> In all the buses and trams, groups of young people read newspaper articles and editorials aloud. Once in a while they shouted a number – the number of a quotation in the little red book containing extracts from Mao's writings that everyone carries with him – and urged the passengers to read the quotation aloud, in unison. At certain intervals, they would ask the passengers to shout, 'Long live the Chinese Communist Party!' and 'Long live Chairman Mao!'
>
> *The Red Guard*

Communist poster What impression is the artist trying to give of the Cultural Revolution?

1 What did the young people call themselves, do you suppose? (See page 84.)
2 What were they doing on the buses and trams?
3 What did they make the other passengers do?
4 What would happen if groups of young people tried this on the London buses, do you suppose?

Here is a story which Charles Taylor told:

> At the Shanghai Machine Tool Factory the director, Yu Chang-do, told me about a model worker who had wanted to improve a complicated oil-press controller. He had run into difficulties and felt he was a failure.
>
> 'But he read Chairman Mao's *On Practice* and then he was able to develop a controller of the highest international standards.'
>
> I said that having read the book in question, a rather difficult one on politics, I was somewhat surprised that it had any connection with oil-press controllers.
>
> Mr. Yu shot a glance that had some pity in it.
>
> 'You see,' he said, 'by reading Chairman Mao he gained confidence and realised that failure is the mother of success. He was worried at the start, but after reading Chairman Mao he was full of confidence that he would overcome all his obstacles.'
>
> *Reporter in Red China*

1 Why was the worker in the story disappointed with himself?
2 Which of Mao's books did he read? What did he do as a result?
3 Why was Taylor surprised?
4 What explanation did the factory director give?
5 What book do people in our own country sometimes read for help and comfort?

Charles Taylor reported on some letters he had seen in a Peking newspaper:

Alert readers wrote in to protest against the names given to different varieties of chrysanthemums at a flower show – such as Old Temple in the Setting Sun, the Soft Hand Applies the Rouge, and Dancing Madly when Drunk. The newspaper said: 'The readers maintain that the names of these flowers are a poison left over from feudal times. Today, the names of flowers and flowering plants should also spread the fragrant scent of the Communist era.'

Soon, more readers were getting into the act, jotting down the names of streets, shops, mountains and even railway stations. They came up with such examples as Jade Emperor Mountain, Watching Fairy Bridge, Good Deeds done in Former Lives Lane, Many Blessings Hotel and, worst of all, the U.S.A.-Chinese Hairdressing Salon. These names, they pointed out, 'were obviously not in keeping with the spirit of our times and, therefore, should be changed into meaningful and healthy Communist names.'

Reporter in Red China

1 What do you think of the names given to the chrysanthemums, places and buildings?
2 Why did the people who wrote the letters object to the names?
3 Can you suggest some names they would have liked?

During the Cultural Revolution, a Cambridge professor, Joan Robinson visited a sweet factory in Peking. It was only a small concern, but what was happening there was common in most Chinese factories. The workers had taken over and were deciding what to do with their former bosses:

The Vice-Director had been on the wrong side: he had stirred up quarrels among the workers: but when the rebels took power he came over to them. They looked into his past life. He came from a poor peasant family and he had been a child beggar. At the age of 13 he became a landlord's servant (a kind of domestic slave). At 16 he joined the People's Liberation Army. He became a Communist Party member at 18. His work in the factory had been guided by the Party, and he could not be too much blamed for loyalty to his superiors. He was classed as comparatively good.

The former Director of the factory made serious mistakes. He believed in working with the old capitalist and allowed him to run the supply department of the factory. He was accused also of putting 'feudal' designs of dragons and fairies on the wrapping paper of the sweets.

He did not take the workers into his confidence. He told them to trust the capitalist and built up his authority. He told the workers that without the capitalist they could not produce sweets, though in fact they had improved their sweets since the factory had been taken over. He made the workers obey the technicians, and used a bonus system of wages. He came from a rich family, and lived in a rich style. He was friendly with capitalists – dined with them and exchanged gifts.

He was graded as a man who had made serious mistakes. They proposed to help him recognize his mistakes. He is difficult to help because he is afraid of losing face, but they think he has made some progress. He and the old capitalist are now working on the shop floor.

The Cultural Revolution in China

Note: The 'capitalist' was the man who had owned the factory before the Communists came to power.

1 What wrong had the Vice-Director done?
2 What kind of family had he come from? How had he lived as a child?

Red Guards Read the description of these people on pages 88–89. Compare the photograph with the poster, opposite.

Young Chinese who have just been given their copies of Mao's *Little Red Book* Why is this photograph an effective piece of Communist propaganda? Probably, the books were waved more than they were read.

3 What had he done when he was 16 and when he was 18? What did this seem to prove about him?
4 What excuse did the rebels find for him?
5 How was he classed?
6 What wrongs had the Director done?
7 What kind of family had he come from?
8 Would the Director have been criticized for any of these things in Britain?
9 How was the Director classed?
10 What happened to him?
11 What job had the former owner of the factory been doing?
12 What happened to him?

After Mao Tse-tung had been dead for two years, and the Cultural Revolution had ended, the American author, Arthur Miller visited China. This is part of a conversation he had with Professor Yang who taught Physics at the University of Xian. Miller asked what had happened to him during the Cultural Revolution:

'Did you suffer personally?'
'Well, they had me cleaning the lavatories.'
'Part-time or...?'
He laughed. 'Oh, no, for two years I did not teach at all.'
'I guess you can understand how hard it is for foreigners to understand. What exactly happened?'
'The Red Guards...'
'Who exactly were they?'
'I never knew those people before.'
'Well, what'd they do?'
'I was teaching that day and suddenly there they were.'
'How many?'
'About twenty of them came in.'
'Students?'
'Oh, no. They were not even from Xian.'
'And they burst into the classroom, and then what?'
'Well, they told everyone to leave.'
'And to go where?'
'Wherever they liked.'
'It was just to break up the class?'
'Yes. But later some of them argued with me.'
'What was the argument about?'
'It wasn't quite an argument. It was that they were very angry with me. It was really, I suppose, that they were quite ignorant and did not like or trust anyone like me. I was an expert, you see, and they believed that that

made me unequal. So that I had to do manual work in order to sort of melt into the others.'

'So they had you cleaning the toilets?'

'For two years, but then they said I could teach again. However, they tried to study engineering and they were completely unprepared. Some could barely write and do the simplest mathematics. There were people who'd never been to school at all.'

'So what happened?'

'Well, the department sort of dissolved. The teachers had either been taken off to prison or else simply stopped coming. There was nothing for anyone to do any more. We lost something like twenty years in those ten.'

'It's now two years since Hua Kuo-feng took over..'

'I know, but it takes a long time to find the right teachers. We are beginning, though; there are examinations for entrance once again, and people are willing to study, and there is respect for teachers again.'

Chinese Encounters

Note: Hua Kuo-feng succeeded Mao who died in 1976.

1. What was Professor Yang made to do during the Cultural Revolution?
2. For how long was he forbidden to teach?
3. What people broke up his class?
4. Why did Yang think they disliked him?
5. What did they want to study?
6. Why were they unable to do this?
7. What happened to Professor Yang's Department?
8. Why is it taking a long time to repair the damage?
9. What changes have there been since Hua Kuo-feng took over?
10. How can you tell that Professor Yang was reluctant to talk about his experiences? Why do you suppose this was?

Miller also met another American, William Hinton, who had been working in China for some years. When Miller mentioned the Cultural Revolution he said:

I know for a fact that there were people literally crucified against walls, nails driven through their palms and left to die.

Chinese Encounters

Later the two men had this conversation:

'Do you understand what happened here in the past ten years?'

'I do not, and I doubt anybody else does.'

He stares ahead for a moment, then looks at me.

'It often happened, you know, that they'd suddenly come out of nowhere....'

'Who?'

'People. Thousands of them around a leader. A leader nobody'd heard of before. A new warlord, young, sassy (saucy), who didn't care about anything or anybody – right out of some factory somewhere. They were unknowns in many cases who had only been employed some place for a few months, but they'd appear as powerful leaders with hundreds of thousands of followers. The worst of it was to see how quick they were to tear at each other, to humiliate anyone handy. That was the worst of it, seeing that again, that awful desire to grind somebody into the earth. They had a real civil war going. Heavy artillery battles. Thousands of people were killed....'

'What I find hard to grasp is, what did Mao make of that chaos? I mean, he was still there, right? And still functioning?'

Hinton shakes his head. 'He said both sides were wrong.'

'But he made no move to stop the fighting?'

'Oh, no – he said, "Argue, but don't fight".'

'But they *were* fighting. With artillery even.'

'Yes that's right. But it had gotten completely out of control.'

'So what'd he do?'

Hinton looks down at his hands, then back to me, shaking his head. 'Nobody understands this, Miller. Not yet. Maybe it's too soon.'

Chinese Encounters

1. What type of men became leaders during the Cultural Revolution?
2. What did Hinton dislike most about them?
3. What shows there was serious fighting?
4. What, according to Hinton, did Mao say people should do?
5. Which of Miller's questions did Hinton not answer?
6. What did Hinton make of the Cultural Revolution?

Written Work

Imagine you lived through the Cultural Revolution in China. Describe what happened.

Research

1. Find out why Mao Tse-tung went for his swim in the Yangtze-Kiang.
2. Who were the Gang of Four? What happened to them?
3. Who soon became the most important man in China after Mao Tse-tung's death? (It was not Hua Kuo-feng). What changes did he make?

Chapter 7 *India*
Caste in India

Most of the people of India believe in the Hindu religion. An important Hindu idea is that each person belongs to a caste. He or she is born into it, taking caste from the parents; it cannot be changed. According to the Hindus it was the god Manu who created castes. An old law said:

> In order to protect the universe He (Manu), the most glorious one, gave different duties and occupations to those who sprang from his mouth, arms, thighs and feet.
>
> To the Brahmins he gave teaching and studying the Veda, sacrificing for their own benefit and others, giving and accepting of alms.
>
> The Kshatriya he commanded to protect the people, to make gifts, to offer sacrifices, to study the Veda and to enjoy no worldly pleasures.
>
> The Vaisya to tend cattle, to make gifts, to offer sacrifices, to study the Veda, to trade, to lend money, and to cultivate the land.
>
> Only one duty the lord gave to the Sudra, to serve meekly the other three castes.

The Laws of Manu, A.D. 100

Note: the Veda is the Hindu scriptures so it is a little like the Christian Bible.

1. How many castes are there? From which part of the god did each one spring?
2. Which of the castes may study the Veda?

Poor family The pavement is their home.

3 What may the Brahmins alone do with the Veda? What would we call people who did this kind of work in a Christian country?
4 From which part of the god do you suppose the Brahmins sprang?
5 What is the first duty of the Kshatriya? What would we call such people?
6 From which part of the god do you suppose the Kshatriya sprang?
7 What different jobs may the Vaisya do, to earn a living? What would we call these jobs in our own country?
8 From which part of the god do you suppose the Vaisya sprang?
9 What was the duty of the Sudra?
10 From which part of the god do you suppose the Sudra sprang?
11 Which do you suppose is the highest caste? Which do you suppose is the lowest?
12 Do you think it is a good idea to divide people into castes? Give reasons for your answer.

Here is another Hindu law:

> Whoever kills a Brahmin will be condemned at his death to take the form of one of those insects which feed on filth. Being reborn long afterwards a Pariah, he will remain one of these for many generations, and will be blind for more than four times as many years as there are hairs on the body of a cow. He can, nevertheless, atone for his crime by feeding forty thousand Brahmins.
>
> If a Brahmin kills a Sudra, it will wipe out the sin altogether if he recites the gayatri (a prayer) a hundred times.
>
> Quoted in *Mother India*, Katherine Mayo

Note: Hindus believe in the 'transmigration of souls'. This means that when someone dies his soul goes into another body. If he has led a good life, he will be born into a higher caste. If he has led a bad life he will be born into a lower caste. If he was already in the lowest caste, he might return with no caste at all. Such people are called Pariahs, Harijans, or Untouchables. Anyone who has been particularly wicked will be an animal, or even an insect.

1 List the punishments for killing a Brahmin.
2 How was it possible to make up for this crime?
3 How was a Brahmin punished for killing a Sudra?

An American, Katherine Mayo, visited India in 1926. She wrote this about the Untouchables:

> Looked on as if sub-human, they must do only the worst jobs. Some are allowed to serve only as scavengers, and removers of night soil. They may neither own nor read the Hindu scriptures. No Brahmin priest will minister to them, and they may not enter a Hindu temple to pray.

Indian beggar To which caste does he belong, do you suppose?

> The children may not go to school. They may not draw water from public wells.
>
> They may not enter a court of justice: they may not enter a clinic to get help for their sick, they may stop at no inn. In some provinces they may not even use the public roads, they may not enter the shops, or even pass through the streets where shops are. Some may not work at all. They may only beg. And even for that they dare not use the road, but must stand far off, unseen, and cry for alms from those who pass.
>
> Some, if not all, pollute beyond men's use, any food upon which their shadow falls. Food, after becoming foul in this way, can only be destroyed.
>
> Others again give off 'distant pollution', like a bad smell from their unhappy bodies. If one of them is working less than two hundred yards from a main road, he must place on the road a green leaf, weighted down with a handful of earth. This shows that he, the unclean, is within pollution distance of that point. The passing Brahmin, seeing the signal, halts and shouts. The poor man at once takes to his heels, and only when he has fled far enough calls back, 'I am now two hundred yards away. Be pleased to pass.'
>
> *Mother India*, Katherine Mayo

1. Make a list of the things Untouchables may not do.
2. What work, if any, do they do?
3. How must they do their begging?
4. What happens if an Untouchable's shadow falls on the food of someone belonging to a caste?
5. How far must some Untouchables stay from the Brahmins? Why? How do they make sure they keep their distance?

Probably the greatest Indian leader of the twentieth century was Mahatma Gandhi. Here are two extracts from his writings:

> 1. We Hindus must call no-one unclean, or mean, or inferior to ourselves, and must therefore cease to look on the 'Pariah' class as untouchables. We must think it sinful to regard a fellow-being as untouchable.
>
> 2. We can do nothing without killing the snake of untouchability. Untouchability is a poison that is eating into the heart of Hindu society. No man of God can think another man is inferior to himself. He must think of every man as his blood brother. It is the most important part of every religion.

1. What does Gandhi think of 'untouchability'?
2. How does he say people should feel towards each other?

Throughout his life Mahatma Gandhi tried to persuade his fellow Hindus to give up caste. He was assassinated in 1948, but others went on with his work. One was Mrs. Indira Gandhi*, who was prime minister of India from 1971 to 1977 and again from 1980 until she too was assassinated in 1984. Here is a story she told:

> I went as a girl and sat on a bed in an Untouchable household. They would wash that bed although I came from a higher caste, because the thought was implanted in their mind that any mixing of the castes is bad whether it is a higher caste or a lower one.

Indira. The Speeches and Reminiscences of Indira Gandhi.

* Indira's husband was not related to the Mahatma in any way.

A lesson in the scriptures To which Hindu caste does the man belong? (See page 90).

1. Why did the owners of the bed wash it?
2. From this story, what do you think Indira and her family felt about caste?

Here is an extract from one of Mrs. Gandhi's speeches. She made it in Vienna in 1977:

> Much has been spoken and written about our caste system. Some castes were regarded as low and the people belonging to them gradually became very backward. Our laws now give them equality. And because these backward people (the untouchables) form one sixth of our population, we have said that they should have one sixth of the seats in our parliament, to allow them to catch up with the rest of the community. In these twenty years these classes have found some very outspoken leaders and the old feelings of inferiority are gradually going.
>
> *Indira. The Speeches and Reminiscences of Indira Gandhi*

1. What does Mrs. Gandhi say was wrong with the caste system?
2. What has been done to try and change it?
3. What, according to Mrs. Gandhi, is now happening?

Hindu Festival The figures represent evil spirits. Later, they will be burnt. What do we do which is similar?

The next extract is from a book written in 1973 by Prafulla Mohanti. He comes from the village of Nanpur, near Cuttack. The speaker is Kilas Jana, an Untouchable who lives in the same village:

> 'I knew I was a Hindu, but when I was seven I came to know that there was this difference between Touchables and Untouchables. I felt disgusted. I wished I had not been born.
>
> When I wanted to go to a temple I was forbidden. No, only the Brahmins and the high caste people can go into it. The Harijans (Untouchables) are not allowed to enter. I thought, "If I am a Hindu, why can't I go into a Hindu temple? What is my fault? Why should I be refused?" My parents told me, "It has been like this for a long time. Our forefathers made this caste distinction. If you were not allowed into the temple it's all right."
>
> From that day I haven't been near a temple. If after being born into a Hindu family, I am refused entry into a temple, why should I try to go in? If I love God, if I have respect for life, if I am kind to animals, if I help people who are in need, I am sure God will understand. If I pray, God will listen to me. God is not only in the temple. God is everywhere.
>
> When I went to school there was no caste distinction. Mahatma Gandhi had brought about this revolution. He was asking the people to give the Untouchables equal places in society. So they were obeying him in a way. At school I used to sit with high caste children. We used to worship together and eat together. But when we came out of school it was all different. If I went to see a friend I was only allowed to talk with him outside the house. He would not touch me. The children in school with me didn't understand caste distinction. I was a child like them. I think their parents used to tell them, "When you go to school you shouldn't touch that Untouchable boy, You mustn't eat with him." They said, "Yes, yes" to everything, but when they came to school they forgot and played with me.
>
> We are not allowed to mix or take part in the village activities. Of course a lot is changing. In the old days if somebody had to give food to a Harijan he had to give it on a leaf, but now they are allowed to use plates. The educated young people think that all men are equal and there is only one religion.'
>
> 'Have you suffered from being an Untouchable?'
>
> 'Yes, I wanted to study and get a good job, but I didn't succeed. I became a drop out. I can't do the kind of business which people from the other castes are doing. If I had been born in a high caste I could have a tobacconist's shop or a tea stall, but now if I opened one nobody would come near. So it's a disadvantage to be born into an Untouchable family.'
>
> 'What is your relationship with the high caste villagers?'
>
> 'If we don't have a good relationship with them we can't really manage. We look on them as our guardians and they look on us as their children. We are always in

Shampoo for an Indian girl

need. We farm their land. We work for them. We use their shops. There is no other way of earning a living here.'

'How do they treat you?'

'If we are good to them, then they are very good to us. But if by any chance we have offended them, then they make our lives impossible.'

'Do you think about the future?'

'Yes, I think about it a lot. How our children can stand on their own feet. The future seems dark. I think a lot about the plight of the Untouchables. I was told that because I had done something bad in my last life, I was born into an Untouchable family. I have started believing in it against my will. I'll do some good work in this life so that I'll never be born back into this caste again.'

My Village, My Life

1. When did Kilas Jana first realise he was an Untouchable? How did he feel about it?
2. What happened when he tried to go into a temple? What questions did he ask? What did his parents say?
3. How does Kilas Jana try to behave?
4. How does he hope God will feel about him?
5. Why was there no caste distinction at school?
6. How were things different out of school?
7. What does Kilas Jana think the high caste parents told their children to avoid in school?
8. What custom, connected with food, has changed?
9. Which people in particular, no longer believe in caste?
10. What ambitions did Kilas Jana have? How is he held back by being an Untouchable?
11. Why must the Untouchables be on good terms with high caste Hindus?
12. How do the high caste Hindus treat the Untouchables?
13. Why does Kilas believe he was born an Untouchable?
14. What does Kilas Jana believe is the only way to make things better for himself?
15. In what ways is Kilas Jana better off than the Untouchables Katherine Mayo described in the 1920's? (See page 91.)
16. Do you think that Kilas Jena would agree with what Mrs. Gandhi said in her speech? (See previous page.)

Written Work

1. Write a report on caste in India. What changes have there been since the 1920's? Do you think changes are taking place fast enough?
2. We have no castes in Britain, but people do belong to different classes – upper class, middle class and working class. In what ways are class and caste alike? How are they different?

Research

1. Find out more about Mahatma Gandhi.
2. Who was Jawaharlal Nehru? What was his connection with Mahatma Gandhi?
3. Find out more about Indira Gandhi. What was her connection with Jawaharlal Nehru?

Sacred Cows in India

The British conquered India in the eighteenth and early nineteenth centuries. The country had a very old civilisation, but it had stood still for a long time. The British made important changes, for example by building railways, factories and schools. However, progress was slow. Many Indians blamed the British for this, saying they were robbing their country. Then, in 1947, India won her freedom, and her people had high hopes. Most of these hopes have been disappointed. China, a similar country in many ways, has forged ahead, while India has lagged behind. This is hard to explain, but one reason might be that most Indians belong to the Hindu religion, and some Hindus have certain beliefs which seem strange to Europeans. One of these beliefs is that the cow is sacred.

When Aldous Huxley visited Kashmir in 1926, this is what he found:

Srinagar owns a large population of sacred cows and bulls that wander vaguely through the streets, picking up such vegetable garbage, grass and fallen leaves as they can find. They are small beasts – half as big as good-sized English cattle and marvellously mild.

But though harmless, these animals are a nuisance. They will not attack you as you walk or drive along the streets, but neither will they get out of your way. They stand there, ruminating, in the middle of the road, and no shouting, no ringing of bells or hooting of horns will send them away. Not until you are right on top of them will they move. They have learned by long experience that they can stand in the road as much as they like and

Sacred cows In what ways will these animals be a nuisance? Compare the Indian attitude to cows with the English attitude to dogs.

that, however furiously the horn sounds, nothing will ever happen to them. Nothing: for Kashmir is ruled by a pious Hindu ruler. Up till a few years ago a man who killed a cow was sentenced to death. Under a milder law he now only gets a matter of seven years in prison. A fear of cows is rooted in the breast of every Kashmiri driver. And the cows know it.

Jesting Pilate

1. Where do the sacred cows and bulls wander?
2. What do they eat?
3. How do they compare with English cattle?
4. How are the animals a nuisance?
5. What used to happen to a man who killed a cow? What happens now?
6. In what sense are the drivers afraid of cows, do you suppose?

An American, Katherine Mayo, also visited India at about the same time as Huxley. She wrote:

To kill a cow is one of the worst of sins. His Highness the Maharaja Scindia of Gwalior once had the misfortune to commit this sin. He was driving a locomotive engine on the opening run over a railway that he had just built. The cow leaped upon the track. The engine ran her down before the horrified Prince could do anything. 'I think,' he told a friend, years after, 'that I shall never finish paying for that disaster, in penances and in gifts to the Brahmins.'

Prince or peasant, the cow is his holy mother. She should be present when he dies, that he may hold her tail as he breathes his last. For this reason, she is often kept inside the house, to be in readiness. When the late Maharaja of Kashmir was dying, the chosen cow refused to go up to his bedroom: whereupon it became necessary to carry the Prince to the cow, and with a swiftness that considered the comfort of his soul only.

Also, the five substances of the cow – milk, clarified butter (ghi), curds, dung and urine, set in a row in five little pots, offered in prayer for forgiveness, and then mixed together and swallowed, are the very best means of purifying soul and body.

Mother India

Note: A Brahmin is a Hindu priest.

1. How did the Maharaja kill the cow? Was it his fault?
2. How was the Maharaja punished?
3. What does an Indian want to do, when he is dying?
4. What happened to the Maharaja of Kashmir when he was dying? Why?
5. What are the 'five substances' of the cow? What will a Hindu do with them? Why?

Ploughing What does this photograph tell you about Indian agriculture?

A French visitor to India, the Abbé Dubois, noticed that cow's urine was very important to the Hindus. He wrote:

I have often seen Hindus following the cows to pasture, waiting for the moment when they could collect the precious liquid in vessels of brass, and carrying it away while still warm to their houses. I have also seen them waiting to catch it in the hollow of their hands, drinking some of it and rubbing their faces and heads with the rest. Rubbing it in this way is supposed to wash away all external uncleanness and drinking it, to clean all internal impurity.

Hindu Manners, Customs and Ceremonies

1. What did the Abbé Dubois see Hindus doing with cow's urine?
2. What did the Hindus think the urine did for them?

Some strict Hindus objected to shaking hands with Europeans, because Europeans ate beef and were, therefore, impure. Katherine Mayo wrote:

One Prince, at least, takes care, when he is with Europeans always to wear gloves. But it is told of him that at a London dinner party, when he had removed his gloves, the lady beside him noticed a ring that he wore.

'What a beautiful stone, your Highness,' she said. 'May I look at it?' 'Certainly', said he, and, removing the ring from his finger, laid it by her plate.

The lady turned the jewel this way and that, held it up to the light, admired it as it deserved and, with thanks, laid it beside the plate of the owner. He then, by a sideways glance, indicated the ring to his servant who stood behind his chair.

'Wash it,' ordered the Prince.

Mother India

1. Why does the Prince wear gloves?
2. What did the Prince order his servant to do with the ring?
3. Why was this do you suppose?
4. What would you have said, or done, if you had been the lady in the story?

Bullock cart

To pull their carts, the Indians used bullocks, which are just as sacred as cows or bulls. Katherine Mayo wrote:

I one day said: 'I regret that all over India you torture most bullocks and some cows by the disjointing of their tails. Look at the bullocks in that cart over there. Every bone in their tails is dislocated. As you know it causes dreadful pain. Often the tail is broken short off.'

'Ah yes' replied the young Brahmin, indifferently, 'it is perfectly true that we do it. But that, you see, is necessary. The animals would not travel fast enough, unless their tail nerves were wrenched.'

You may stand for hours on the busy Howrah Bridge in Calcutta, watching the bullock carts pass, without discovering a dozen animals whose tails are not a zig-zag string of breaks. It is easier, you see, for the driver to walk with the animals tail in his hand, twisting its joints from time to time, than it is to beat the creature with his stick.

And only the foreigner in the land will protest.

Mother India

1. In what way did Katherine Mayo find the Indians ill-treating their bullocks?
2. Why did they do this?
3. Who are the only people likely to object?
4. How does this extract strike you as strange, after reading the others in this section?

Here is another description of sacred cattle written by Aldous Huxley when he visited Kashmir in 1926:

It was late in the afternoon when we drove past the Court of Justice. The day's business was over and the sweepers were at work. Outside the building stood a row of brimming waste-paper baskets, and from these, as from mangers, two or three sacred bulls were slowly and majestically feeding. When the baskets were empty, hands from within filled them once more with a fresh supply of torn and scribbled paper. The bulls browsed on.

Watching them at their meal, I understood why it is that Indian bulls are so strangely mild. On a diet of waste paper, it would be difficult for them to be anything else. I also understood why it is that Indian cows yield so little milk and, further, why the cattle of either sex are so often afflicted with hiccoughs. Before I came to India, I had never heard a bull hiccoughing. It is a loud and terrifying sound. Hearing behind me that explosive combination of a bellow and a bark, I have often started in alarm, thinking I was on the point of being attacked. But looking round, I would find it was only one of the mild sacred Hindu animals gorged with waste paper and painfully, uncontrollably belching as it walked.
Jesting Pilate

1. Do you think Huxley is suggesting that all Indian cattle live on nothing but waste paper?
2. What idea is he trying to give about their food?
3. Give three ways that Huxley says the feed affects the cattle.

Katherine Mayo wrote:

The cattle question, by itself, might explain India's poverty. India is being eaten up by its own cattle. And even at that the cattle are starving.

The Live-Stock census taken in 1919 showed a total 146,000,000 cattle. Of these, 50 per cent are unprofitable. Because they have no value, the food they eat is a loss to the country of £117,600,000 every year.
Mother India

1. How many cattle were there in India in 1919?
2. How many of these were useless?
3. How did having so many useless cattle affect the country as a whole?

Five legged cow A five legged cow is particularly sacred. Obviously, the fifth leg has been grafted on to the cow by its owner. What evidence is there in the documents of other forms of cruelty to cows?

In 1973 an Indian, Prafulla Mohanti, wrote a description of his village. This was nearly fifty years after Katherine Mayo and Aldous Huxley visited India. Moreover the country had been freed from British rule since 1947.

Here is what Prafulla Mohanti said about cows:

To a villager, the cow is Gomata, the cow mother. She is respected and looked after and considered a member of the family.

Almost every family has its cow, usually tethered outside the house. Every afternoon, the cows are taken to the common grazing ground and at night they are kept inside. Most villagers have a cowshed, but I have seen some Untouchable families living together with their cows and goats in one hut.

The cows are fed on straw and rice water. People have not enough to eat for themselves, but they will never leave their cows to starve. It is a great sin to do so.

The villagers like their cows to lead a natural life and die a natural death. When a cow dies, it is placed in the cremation ground where the damas, Untouchable dealers in leather, come and take the hide away. The vultures quickly finish what is left.

The cows remain pregnant for ten months. After their calves are born, they are not milked for twenty-one days for the milk is considered poisonous. On average, cows give three pints of milk a day for eight months in the year. Milking is done by hand. The milk is boiled and kept in an earthen pot.

When buying a cow, the villagers have various ways of finding out whether she is a good milker. If she has a raised back, and urinates when her tail is touched, she is capable of giving milk, if fed properly.

Milk from a black cow is thought to be sweeter and creamier than milk from a white, grey or red one. When a black cow is bought the astrologer is consulted. He finds out if the cow is suited to the horoscope of the head of the family.

Milk is looked upon as a life-giver. But it is impossible to get pure milk unless one has a cow. It is sold at 50 paisa ($2\frac{1}{2}$p) a pint, but nearly half of it is water.

At any one time only a few cows in the village give milk. Young children are given preference but there is not really enough to go round. People with money can buy milk, but the poor cannot afford it and if they have milk from their own cow they sell it to get the money.

Cow dung has many uses. Apart from its use as a manure, it even has religious uses. Walls and floors are disinfected by being washed with a paste of cow dung. When dried, it is burnt as fuel by the women, in spite of criticism that to do so is wasteful.

My friends in the West often ask me, 'Why is the cow considered sacred? Why don't the villagers eat beef when there is so much starvation?'

The answer to this is very simple. A cow is more than a pet, it is the most useful animal a villager can have. She is considered sacred to protect her. Various stories were built around this idea. Lord Krishna an Avatar of Vishnu, was a milkman's son: the bull Nandi is the companion of Lord Shiva, the God of Creation. As Hindus worship Vishnu and Shiva, their animals are considered sacred.

The villagers would never think of beef as food. Harming a cow is a great sin, as serious as hurting one's mother. That is why they are worried when Muslims slaughter cows. For this reason a villager will never knowingly sell a cow to a Muslim.

My Village, My Life

Note: An avatar is a god in human form.

1. How do Indians view their cows?
2. Where do they keep them?
3. What do the cows eat? Do you think this is a good diet for them?
4. What happens when a cow dies?
5. How much milk will an average cow give in a year? (For a dairy herd in Britain to be up to standard it must give an average of 1,000 gallons a year for every cow.)
6. How is milking done?
7. How is the milk treated? Why is this, do you suppose?
8. What strange ideas do the villagers have about cows?
9. Why are the villagers short of milk?
10. Which people suffer most from the shortage of milk? Why?
11. In what three ways is cow dung used?
12. What questions do Prafulla Mohanti's western friends ask him?
13. Why are cattle sacred, according to Prafulla Mohanti?
14. Why will villagers refuse to sell a cow to a Muslim?

Prafulla Mohanti had this conversation with a man called Hadibandhu Behera. He kept twenty cows and sold their milk:

'Do you add water to your milk?'

'Yes, we can't manage otherwise.'

'How much water?'

'12 to 25 per cent.'

'How do you know how much to mix?'

'We tell by looking at the milk. If the milk is thick, it needs more water. It it is thin, it can only take a small amount.'

'Can't you really manage without adding water to the milk?'

'No.'

'Why?'

'Because people only pay one rupee for a kilo of milk. How can I manage to give pure milk at that price?'

'Why don't you charge more and give people pure milk?'

'People won't pay more.'

'What sort of water do you mix with the milk?'

'We add drinking water from the well. Its clean, but I strain it first.'

'You are adding water to the milk. Does it every worry you that people may become ill, particularly when your milk is drunk by children?'

'No. We never think that our milk can cause ill-health to anybody.'

'Why don't you go in for dairy farming on a big scale? Why don't you keep good breeds of cows which give more milk?'

'They are very expensive and we don't have the money to buy them. We don't know if they can survive in this part of India and give milk. If we invest money we may lose it.'

My Village, My Life

Note: No Indian village has pure tap water. The people fetch their water from rivers, ponds or wells, and it is full of germs.

1 How much water does Hadibandhu Behera add to his milk?
2 Why does he do this?
3 Why does Prafulla Mohanti think adding water to milk is dangerous?
4 How does Prafulla Mohanti suggest Hadibandhu Behera could improve his business?
5 Why does Hadibandhu Behera say this is impossible?

Indian Dairy Farmer Note the size of the pot. Estimate how much milk the man is expecting. Find out how much an English cow will give at one milking.

Written Work

1 You will remember that Katherine Mayo and Aldous Huxley visited India in 1926, while Prafulla Mohanti wrote his description of his village in 1973. What ideas about cattle remained the same?
2 Compare cattle in India with cattle in Britain. You could use the headings:
   a How the people think of cattle.
   b Uses of cattle.
   c Methods of milking, treating and selling milk.
   d Milk yields.
3 There were about 350 cows and 2,000 people in Prafulla Mohanti's village. How much milk did the cows give for each person in a year? How much was that a day? How much milk would 350 English cows have given each of these 2,000 people every day?

Further Work

1 Find out more about the Hindu religion.
2 Read about India under British rule and how she won her independence.

(See **Oxford Junior History**, Book 6, *The Twentieth Century World*, Chapter Six)

Chapter 8   *The United States of America*

The Great Depression

By the early twentieth century the people of the United States had made themselves very wealthy. After the First World War they prospered even more. They began to think they would go on for ever, becoming richer year by year. Then came a depression which destroyed the dream completely. It began with the 'Wall Street Crash' of 1929. This was a money crisis in New York, which meant that many rich people lost fortunes. Soon, there were money problems all over the United States and ordinary folk began to suffer.

Here is what happened at Akron in Ohio, where the main industry was making tyres:

March 2nd, 1933
The blight which, from Monday, had been gradually falling over the city wormed its way into every eddy and nook of Akron. Life slowed down. The rubber companies alone had money to meet week-end pay rolls. The department stores, the grocery stores, the streetcar company, a hundred other business places had no money to pay their employees.

Grocery stores refused credit to old customers. Even speakeasies* told favoured friends, 'Sales for cash only. Nobody may ever get any money again.'

March 4th, 1933
On Saturday morning all business came to a complete halt. The rubber companies closed. Streetcars ran on half schedules. Coal companies shut. Thousands and thousands of men were sent home from work. Pay rolls were not met. Cheques were not honored.

At nine, the First-Central Trust Company Bank opened for business. The lobby was jammed. Women swung their umbrellas wildly and bank guards rushed here and there removing hysterical clients. Clerks paid out the one per cent allowed, under orders not to argue.

'I haven't got a dime to feed my family or myself', clerks yelled at men who demanded, not asked for, ten dollars anyway, please, from their accounts.

'I didn't get paid this week', men in work clothes shouted. 'You got to give me some of my money!'

*A speakeasy was a bar selling alcoholic drinks which, at that time, was illegal in the United States.

Smile away the Depression!

Smile us into Prosperity!
wear a
SMILETTE!
This wonderful little gadget will solve the problems of the Nation!
APPLY NOW AT YOUR CHAMBER OF COMMERCE OR THE REPUBLICAN NATIONAL COMMITTEE
WARNING—Do not risk Federal arrest by looking glum!

'No!' said the clerks, signalling for the bank guards.

At noon the bank guards hustled the crowd out. 'Closing time,' they shouted.

The old First-Central Trust Company Bank never opened again.

Industrial Valley, Ruth McKenney

1. Why were many workers without wages?
2. What happened if they asked for credit in the shops?
3. What happened in the town as a whole on March 4th?
4. How much of his money could each customer draw from the bank?
5. How were the customers behaving? Why?
6. What happened to the bank, in the end?

Study this table and show the figures on a graph:

Unemployment

Year	Number of unemployed	Percentage of labour force
1929	1,550,000	3.2
1930	4,340,000	8.7
1931	8,020,000	15.9
1932	12,060,000	23.6
1933	12,830,000	24.9

Here is what unemployment meant for one family:

Then began the daily disheartening tramp for a job. Every morning at six and sometimes earlier he was out. His was always a very meagre breakfast, often only a piece of bread, and later there was not enough even of that for him and the kids, so he went without. This was in winter. Once in a while, he picked up a job shovelling snow or cleaning snow from the streets. This helped a little with food but not nearly enough. The children began to lose weight and soon looked pale. His wife was not well and became more and more nervous with the strain. The rent was past due two months and the

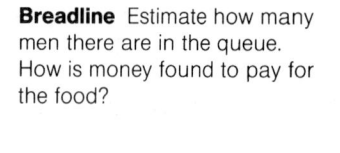

Breadline Estimate how many men there are in the queue. How is money found to pay for the food?

landlady knocked each morning at the door demanding payments: the gas-man knocked: the electric man came; the furniture collector followed. A knock became symbolical of their distress. Then everything fell at once. First came a five-day notice to quit their house; then the gas was shut off; then the electricity; then came a telegram demanding payment on the furniture; then the insurance lapsed. The grocery man, when he found that Pavlowski had no work, refused further credit.

Case Studies of Unemployment, Marion Elderton

1. How did Pavlowski and his family suffer when he was first unemployed?
2. What bills was Pavlowski unable to pay?
3. What happened as a result?

This is how many unemployed families lived:

1. A few weeks ago I visited the public dump at Youngstown, Ohio. Back of the garbage house there are at least three acres of waste land, humpy with ash heaps and junk. From 150 to 200 men live there. The place is a shanty town. It is called by its inhabitants – Hooverville.

I went forward and talked to the men; they showed me their houses. These vary greatly from mere caves covered with a piece of tin, to weatherproof shanties built of packing boxes and equipped with a stolen window-frame or door. Some have beds and one or two a kitchen stove rescued from the junk heap, though most of the men cook together over a fire shielded by bricks in the open.

The inhabitants were not, as one might expect, outcasts or 'untouchables' or even hoboes in the American sense; they were men without jobs. Life is sustained by begging, eating at the city soup kitchens, or earning a quarter by polishing an automobile – enough to bring home bacon and bread. Eating 'at home' is preferred. Men also take part of their food from the garbage house. This I entered: the stench of decaying food is appalling. Here I found that there were more women than men – gathering food for their families. In Hooverville there are no women.

This pitiable village would be of little significance if it

Shanty What has the man used to make his hut? Why is he flying the American flag, do you suppose?

Farmer and his family leaving their home

existed only in Youngstown, but nearly every town in the United States has its shanty town for the unemployed, and the same instinct has named them all 'Hooverville'. The Pittsburgh unit has been taken under the wing of Father Cox who feeds the inhabitants at a soup kitchen in the cellar of his church, and who has supplied each shanty with a printed placard: 'God Bless Our Home.' The largest Hooverville in the United States is in St. Louis with a hovel population of 1,200. Chicago had a flourishing one, but it was felt to be an affront to municipal pride and was ordered burned. The inhabitants were told to get out, and thirty minutes later the 'homes' were in ashes.

Relief and Revolution, Charles R. Walker

Note: the President at the time this was written was Herbert Hoover.

2. Some of the inhabitants of the Hoovervilles forage from the city dumps.... Last summer in the hot weather, when the smell was sickening and the flies were thick, there were a hundred people a day coming to one of the dumps, falling on the heap of refuse as soon as the truck had pulled out and digging in it with sticks and hands. They would devour all the pulp that was left on the old slices of watermelon and cantelupe till the rinds were as thin as paper; and they would take away and wash and cook discarded turnips, onions and potatoes.

The American Earthquake, Edmund Wilson

1. Where are many people living?
2. How do they make their homes?
3. Why do they call their settlements 'Hoovervilles' do you suppose?
4. What people live in Hoovervilles?
5. How common are Hoovervilles?
6. How do their inhabitants find food?
7. What happened to the Hooverville in Chicago?

Some of the unemployed men became 'hoboes'. That meant they stole rides on goods trains and went all over the country looking for work. A young black, called Louis Banks said:

When I was hoboing I would lay on the side of the tracks and wait until I could see the train comin'. I would always carry a bottle of water in my pocket and a piece of tape or rag to keep it from bustin' and put a piece of bread in my pocket, so I wouldn't starve on the way. I would ride all day in the hot sun. I rode atop a boxcar and went to Los Angeles, four days and four nights.

Black and white, it didn't make any difference who you were, 'cause everybody was poor. All friendly, sleep in a jungle. We used to take a big pot and cook food, cabbage, meat and beans all together. We all sat together, we made a tent. Twenty-five or thirty would be on the side of the rail, white and colored. They didn't have no mothers or sisters, they didn't have no home, they were dirty, they had overalls on, they didn't have no food, they didn't have anything.

Sometimes we sent a hobo to walk, to see if there were any jobs open. He'd come back and say: 'Detroit, no jobs.' He'd say: 'They're hirin' in New York City'. So we went to New York City. Sometimes ten or fifteen of us would be on the train. And I'd hear one of 'em holler. He'd fall off, he'd get killed.

I was in chain gangs and been in jail all over the country. I was in a chain gang in Georgia. I had to pick cotton for four months, for just hoboin' on a train. Just took me off the train, the guard. They gave me thirty-five cents and a pair of overalls when I got out. Yes, thirty-five cents, that's what they gave me.

I knocked on people's doors. They'd say, 'What do you want? I'll call the police'. And they'd put you in gaol. They'd make you milk cows, thirty or ninety days. Up in Wisconsin, they'd do the same thing. Alabama, they'd do the same thing. California, anywhere you'd go. Always in gaol and I never did nothin'.

Hard Times, Studs Terkel

1 Find the places where Louis Banks went, on a map of the United States.
2 What food and drink did he carry on a train?
3 How long might he be on a train?
4 How did the hoboes live when they were not travelling?
5 How did they decide which town they should go to?
6 What risks did a hobo run?

We will now see what was happening in the countryside. First of all, study this table:

Prices of Farm Products (1926 = 100 as baseline)

1926	100	1930	88
1927	99	1931	65
1928	106	1932	48
1929	105	1933	51

1 Show these figures on a graph.
2 In what year did farm prices begin to fall?
3 How did the fall in prices affect the farmers, do you suppose?

This is what happened in Iowa:

Grain was being burned. It was cheaper than coal. Corn was being burned. A county just east of here, they burned corn in their courthouse all winter '32, '33. You couldn't hardly buy groceries for corn. It couldn't pay the transportation.

The Blue Eagle from Egg to Earth, Hugh S. Johnson

Here is what the Iowa farmers did after a time:

Suddenly the papers were filled with accounts of highway picketing by farmers around Sioux City. A Farmers' Association had been organised by one Milo Reno, and the farmers were to refuse to bring food to market for thirty days or until they were paid enough for it.

Highway No. 20, leading to Sioux City, has been the scene of some of the sharpest clashes between deputies and farmers. On the night we visited No. 20 a score of men were sitting round a campfire. A boy was sprawled out on an automobile cushion asleep. Everyone was in overalls. Their sunburned faces shone red in the firelight.

'If we farmers go down bankrupt,' says one of the younger men, 'everything in this country goes down. If we got enough to live on, everybody's going to go to work again.'

'When we can't buy,' says another, 'there can't be any prosperity. We ain't been buying nothing, not for four years.'

'My binder's fallen apart, so don't know how I'm going to get through this year.' The conversation moves slowly from one man to another with quiet deliberation. There is a cry:

'Truck!'

They hurry out in the roadway. All of them carry heavy stakes, some made from axe handles. None of them is armed, though a young fellow pointed to a little mound of quarter bricks.

'Plenty of Irish confetti,' he said cheerily. Beside the road, handy to use, are heavy spiked logs and planks bristling with spikes to throw in front of trucks. This truck is empty. There is a short conference. The truck passes on its way.

'Good-night boys,' calls the driver. 'Good luck!' He is one of them, part of the movement that is just beginning to realize its power. We go back to the fire....

Rebellion in the Corn Belt, Mary Heaton Vorse

1 What was happening to much of the grain in Iowa?
2 What were the farmers doing around Sioux City?
3 What did they want?
4 Why do they say good incomes for farmers are important for the whole country?
5 How did they plan to stop the trucks?
6 Why was this particular truck allowed through?

Farm in the dust bowl What has happened to this shed?

To add to the farmers' problems there was a drought on the Prairies during the mid 1930s. Here is a verse from a poem:

> Over the great plains of the buffalo-land,
> The dust-storm blows, the choking, sifting small dust.
> The skin of that land is ploughed by the dry, fierce wind
> And blown away, like a torrent:
> It drifts foot-high above the young sprouts of grain
> And the water fouls, the horses stumble and sicken,
> The wash-board cattle stagger and die of drought.
> We tore the buffalo's pasture with the steel blade.
> We made the waste land blossom and it has blossomed.
> That was our fate; now that land takes its own revenge,
> And the giant dust-flower blooms above five States.
>
> *Is it well with these States?*, Stephen Benet

1 What is happening to the soil?
2 What has man done to help cause this problem?

This is part of a letter written by a farmer's wife from Oklahoma:

> Wearing our shade hats, with handkerchiefs tied over our faces and vaseline in our nostrils, we have been trying to rescue our home from the wind-blown dust which penetrates wherever air can go. It is an almost hopeless task, for there is rarely a day when at some time the dust clouds do not roll over. 'Visibility' approaches zero and everything is covered again with a silt-like deposit which may vary in depth from a film to actual ripples on the kitchen floor. I keep oiled cloths on the window sills and between the upper and lower sashes.
>
> They help just a little to keep back or collect the dust. Some seal the windows with the gummed paper strips used in wrapping parcels, but no method is fully effective. We buy what appears to be red cedar saw dust with oil added to use in sweeping our floors, and do our best not to inhale the irritating dust....
>
> Early in May, with no more grass or even weeds on our 640 acres than on your kitchen floor, and even the scanty remnants of dried grasses from last year cut off and blown away, we decided, like most of our neighbors, to ship our cattle to grass in the central part of the state.
>
> Few residents have left our neighborhood, but on a sixty mile trip yesterday to get tractor repairs we saw many pitiful reminders of broken hopes and apparently wasted effort. Little abandoned homes where people had drilled deep wells for the precious water, had set trees and vines, built reservoirs, and fenced in gardens, – with everything now walled in or half buried by banks of drifted soil, – told a painful story of loss and disappointment.
>
> We have had two most welcome rains in June – three quarters of an inch and one half inch. But the helpful effects of the rains have been for us, and for other people, largely destroyed by the drifting soil from abandoned, unworked lands around us. It fills the air and our eyes and noses and throats, and worst of all, our furrows, where tender shoots are coming to the surface only to be buried by the smothering silt from the fields of those people who persist in their right to do nothing.
>
> *Letters from the Dust Bowl*, Carolyn Henderson

1 Find Oklahoma on a map of the United States.
2 What is happening in the farmer's house? What is his wife doing about it?
3 What has the farmer done with his cattle? Why?
4 What did the farmer and his wife see on their journey?
5 What rain has fallen? Why has it done little good?

Written Work
1 Imagine you are a town worker. Write a letter to a farmer telling him how you are suffering because of the depression.
2 Now imagine you are the farmer. Answer your friend's letter, telling him the problems you are having.

Research
1 Read about America in the 1920's, before the Depression.
2 What was 'Prohibition'? What problems did it cause?
3 Find out more about the Wall Street Crash.
4 Read *Grapes of Wrath* by John Steinbeck.

President Roosevelt and the New Deal

The man who was President of the United States when the great depression began was Herbert Hoover. His answer to the problem was to do little or nothing. There had been other, though less serious depressions in the past and the country had recovered without any help from the government. Hoover thought the same thing would happen again. 'Prosperity', he said, 'is just around the corner.' The American people did not believe him, and at the next election, in 1932, they gave his rival, Franklin Delano Roosevelt, an enormous majority.

When he agreed to stand for President, Roosevelt said, 'I pledge you, I pledge myself, to a new deal for the American people.' The words 'New Deal' became famous, for they summed up all the things which Roosevelt did to save his country.

In fact, when he took office in 1933, Roosevelt was not at all sure what to do for the best. Unlike Hoover, however, he was determined to do something. 'It is common-sense', he said, 'to take a method and try it. If it fails, admit it frankly and try another.'

Members of the C.C.C. being measured for new shoes

Some things, though, were clear. One of Roosevelt's supporters wrote:

> He understood that the suffering of the depression had fallen with terrific impact upon the people least able to bear it. He knew that the rich had been hit hard too, but at least they had something left. But the little merchant, the small householder and home owner, the farmer who worked the soil by himself, the man who worked for wages – these people were desperate. And Roosevelt saw them as the principal citizens of the United States.
>
> When he got to Washington he had no fixed programme. The general situation, however, was clear in Roosevelt's mind and in the minds of his supporters and party. The idea was that all the forces of the community should and could be directed at making life better for ordinary people.

The Roosevelt I Knew, Frances Perkins

1 What people had been hurt most by the depression?
2 What was Roosevelt determined to do?

Before Roosevelt took office the poor had help from charity or from their local authorities, the counties. It was not nearly enough, so Roosevelt decided the Federal Government in Washington must help. His son, Elliott, wrote:

> For the hungry the greatest measure of the New Deal was the Federal Emergency Relief Act, with an immediate grant of $500,000,000 later raised to $5 billion. It was made available through a brand new agency, the Federal Emergency Relief Administration. Harry Hopkins was put in charge of the new agency. During his first morning in office he gave away $5,000,000. 'I'm not going to last six months here, so I'll do as I please', he said.
>
> He received a simple instruction from Roosevelt: 'Get relief to those who need it.' Harry took this to mean cash payments for impoverished families, along with clothing, medical care and shelter in rented rooms.
>
> *A Rendezvous with Destiny*

1. What new agency was created?
2. How much money did it have?
3. Who was in charge of the agency?
4. How much did he give away on his first morning in office?
5. What help was given?
6. How would that have affected the people in Hoovervilles? (See previous section).

As you saw in the previous section, the depression began with money problems. People lost faith in their banks, and drew out all the cash they could. To solve the problem, Roosevelt first declared a 'bank holiday'. That meant the banks closed, and people could not drain them of money. Banks that were badly run, remained closed. The others re-opened, with government loans to help them. This is what happened:

> The measures taken by Roosevelt to check the collapse of the banking system, to coax or force hoarded currency, certificates, silver and gold back into the banks were all successful. Within a single month, money outside the banks declined by about one and a quarter billion dollars. Evidence that the greater part of these funds had been hoarded was found in the fact that most of the paper currency turned back into the banks after March was in the largest notes, rarely used in day-to-day transactions. Moreover, during the first three days after the banking holiday, about seventy-six per cent of all member banks of the Federal Reserve System were opened, and an added seventy-two per cent of all non-member banks were opened by the early part of April.
>
> *Beckoning Frontiers*; Marriner S. Eccles

1. How much money was paid back into the banks?
2. What proved that much of the money had been drawn for hoarding, rather than spending?
3. Roughly what percentage of banks reopened?

Works Progress Administration project, repairing a road

One of the most important things Roosevelt had to do was to find people jobs. For young men there was the Civilian Conservation Corps (C.C.C.). Unemployed youths went to live in camps, where they were given work. A man called Sherwood Anderson wrote:

> Into this camp have come boys, the greater number of them from American cities. They are young boys, most of them about high school age. But for this depression they would have come out of school and would have become clerks or factory hands.
>
> Or – and this would go for a lot of them – they would have become tough city guys – the kind that make bright young gangsters – the kind you see leaning against walls near gang hangouts in cities.
>
> But you see, even the rackets have become a bit thin now, clerkships have fallen away, the factories are not exactly howling for men.
>
> So these C.C.C. camps have gathered them in, all kinds of men. The forester has under him some two or three hundred boys, mostly from the East Side of New York – tough birds, most of them, he says. 'Boy, what we had to do to them – what they did to us.' They had been jerked up from that environment, hauled in fast trains across two thirds of the United States and thrown into a forest camp some seven thousand feet up in the magnificent hills. They had to build the camps, keep themselves clean. Keep their bedding and their quarters clean, learn to swing an axe – 'We had to watch them like babes that they did not kill each other with the axes.' The boys learned to make beds, learned the necessary sanitary laws, the give and take so essential where men live, sleep, talk in one great room – row of beds all in the open – the door at the end of the room open – sight of the wooded hills when you go to sleep at night, when you wake in the morning.
>
> *Puzzled America*

1   What would have happened to the boys, if it had not been for the depression?
2   How many were in the camp?
3   Where had most of them come from?
4   Where was the camp?
5   What did the boys have to learn about camp life?

A boy who was in the C.C.C. said:

> If the fella wouldn't take a bath, we'd give him what we call a 'brushing'. We'd take this fella, and we'd take a big scrub brush and we'd give him a bath, and we'd open up every pore. That's all he needed was one bath. A guy would come in, he'd stink, ten guys would get him in the shower.
>
> *Hard Times*, Studs Terkel

1   What happened to any boy in the camp who was dirty?

The main task of the C.C.C. was to plant trees. Sherwood Anderson explains why:

> The leaves of the forest trees, even the new young trees, now growing, fall and lie on the ground. Next year more leaves fall. There is a soft porous bottom made. Moss begins to grow. It is a great blotter. Pinchot of Pennsylvania, when he was making his first fight against forest destruction, used to go before control committees with a wide board in his hand. He set the board on a table at an angle of forty-five degrees and poured a glass of water down it.
>
> Then he took the same board and tacked blotting paper on it. Again he poured water down the board, but this time it did not rush off. That told the story. It is a thing the government can do and that the individual cannot do. There are these millions of acres of water-shed land, none of it any good for farming. It should go back into forests, making future wealth.
>
> Rains come and wash the plowed lands away and every rain takes its toll of richness. You go through these hill lands in the spring and summer, seeing the hill men at the plow, often on lands so steep you wonder that the man and bony horse do not both roll into the bottom – men slowly and painfully plowing, planting, and hoeing – then the rains – there the fields go.
>
> It would not have mattered so much if it were only one field, a few fields plowed and lost, but there were great gashes in the hillsides, water rushing down pellmell, floods in the low lands, towns destroyed. There are still millions of such fields being plowed. The whole country pays.
>
> *Puzzled America*

1   What damage does rain do, if hillsides are cleared of forests and ploughed?
2   What experiment shows that planting trees would help prevent this damage?

To help adults there was the Works Progress Administration (W.P.A.). At the New York World Fair there was a list of people for whom the W.P.A. had found jobs. It read:

> accountants, architects, bricklayers, biologists, carpenters, chemists, dentists, draftsmen, dietitians, electricians and engravers, foresters and firemen, geologists and gardeners, hoisting engineers and housekeepers, instrument men and iron workers, inspectors, jackhammer operators and janitors, kettlemen and kitchen maids, librarians and linotypers, locksmiths and lumbermen, millwrights and machinists, musicians, nurses and nutritionists, oilers and opticians, painters and plasterers,

Boys of the C.C.C. working in the forest What did these young city dwellers have to learn? (See page 109).

plumbers and pattern makers, photographers and printers, physicians, quarry men and quilters, riveters and roofers, roadmakers and riggers, sculptors and seamstresses, stone-masons and stenographers, statisticians, teamsters and truck drivers, teachers and tabulators, upholsterers and ushers, veterinarians, welders and woodchoppers, waiters and watchmen, X-ray technicians.

1. How many occupations are listed here?
2. How many had you never heard of?
3. What do you suppose the person who wrote this list is trying to tell us about the W.P.A.?

Frances Perkins told this story:

An almost deaf, elderly lawyer, a Harvard graduate, unable to find clients, got a W.P.A. job as assistant caretaker at a small seaside park. He did double the work anyone could have expected of him. He made little extra plantings, arranged charming paths and walks, supervised children's play, and made himself useful and agreeable to the whole community. I saw him from time to time and he always asked me to take a message to the President – a message of gratitude for a job which paid him fifteen dollars a week and kept him from starving to death. It was an honourable occupation that made him feel useful and not like a tramp and a derelict, he would say with tears in his eyes.

The Roosevelt I Knew

1. What was the old man's profession?
2. Why do you suppose he could not find clients?
3. What job did the W.P.A. find for him?
4. How well did he do his job?
5. How did he feel about Roosevelt?

In 1934 a man called Rudd Rennie wrote:

Wandering around the country with one or the other of New York's baseball teams, I find that the National Road to Ruin now is a thriving thoroughfare. It has been redecorated. People have come out of the shell-holes into which they were blown by the explosions of finance and industry. They are working and playing and seem perfectly content to let a busy tribe of professional worriers do their worrying for them. By this happy arrangement, a lot of people seem to be themselves and there is much singing of a song called 'Sweet Ad-o-line.'

A year ago few sang 'Sweet Ad-o-line'. When they did

it sounded sad. It lacked warmth and sincerity. It is no good unless it is warm and sincere. In fact, it is sour.

A year ago, however, everyone was a worrier. I was in Florida with the Yankees when the banks closed and left me with $8.75. For a while I thought about taking a long walk on a short pier, but I couldn't find a short pier.

We came home that year through Southern cities which looked as tho' they had been ravaged by an invisible enemy. People seemed to be hiding. They even would not come out to see Babe Ruth and Lou Gehrig. They simply did not have the money to waste on baseball games or amusements.

Birmingham, a once-thriving, bright city, looked as if it had been swept by a plague and was expecting an air-raid. The factories and many stores were shut. Few people were abroad on the street, and they looked as though they had just been invited to have tea with the Borgias. The streets at night were almost dark, because only a few of the street lamps were lighted.

All over the major-league baseball circuits, one saw stores for rent, silent shops, idle factories, half-empty hotels, and slim crowds in the ball-parks, night clubs and places of amusement.

I went again to Florida this year to the Yankee camp in Saint Petersburgh and to the Giants' camp on Miami Beach. If the ball-club had not arranged transportation for me in advance, I would have had difficulty buying space on a train. People were going to Florida in car-loads.

It costs money to go to Florida, and no one lingers under those palm trees for any length of time free of charge. Yet, hotels were jammed, dog-tracks and race-tracks flourished, night clubs thrived.

I came home this year with the Giants, through Southern cities which a year ago had been gasping and about to die. The change was bewildering. Brass bands met the team at the railroad station. The players were paraded through the streets in automobiles. People elbowed and shoved to get into the ball-parks. There had not been anything like this since the Yankees made their triumphal tour of Texas, Oklahoma and Arkansas in 1929.

The landscape as we moved along was dotted with C.W.A. signs and men were hammering and digging. Smoke issued from chimneys long unused. Stores which had been closed were open and making sales.

When the Giants came home they played to 73,087 more customers in their first nine games than they had in the same number of games the year before.

The Boston Red Sox drew 145,000 more customers in the first six days.

Betting on horse-races was made legal in New York. People flocked to the tracks.

Cocktail bars blossomed in fantastic forms. Restaurants perked up. Hotels dusted entire floors of rooms long unoccupied. Head waiters stopped scowling. Musicians attacked their instruments with renewed vigor. Everywhere I go crowds of people seem to be enjoying themselves. They may not be rolling in wealth, but evidently they have a few 'bucks' to spend on amusements. That's something they did not have last year.

Changing the Tune from Gloom to Cheer

1 Describe in your own words, the changes Rudd Rennie had seen in the first year that Roosevelt was President. Use the headings:
   a Baseball Games
   a Hotels and Restaurants
   b Places of Entertainment
   c Factories and Shops
   d The Way People Felt

2 Study these tables:

Year	Number of Unemployed	Farm Prices (1926=100)
1933	12,830,000	51.4
1934	11,340,000	65.3
1935	10,610,000	78.8
1936	9,030,000	80.9
1937	7,700,000	86.4
1938	10,390,000	68.5
1939	9,480,000	65.3
1940	8,120,000	67.7

   a Show these figures on graphs.
   b Compare the 1940 figures with those for 1929 (See page 102).

3 Do you think Rudd Rennie was right to have been so cheerful in 1934?

Written Work

It is 1936. You are an American citizen. Roosevelt's term of office is over and he has to stand for election again. Explain why you are going to vote for him.

Research

1 Find out about other ways in which Roosevelt helped the United States recover from the depression. What, for example, did he do for farmers? What was the Tennessee Valley Authority, and what did it achieve?

2 Read about the life of Franklin D. Roosevelt both before and after the New Deal.

3 The great depression began in America and then spread to other countries. What happened when it came to Britain? (See Chapter 9.) What happened when it came to Germany? (See **Oxford Junior History**, Book 6, page 46).

The Black Americans

Twelve per cent of the population of the United States is black. Most of those are descendants of slaves who were brought from Africa to work on the cotton and tobacco plantations in the south. Slavery ended in 1865, after the Civil War, but the whites still treated the blacks badly. The southern states had 'Jim Crow' laws which 'segregated' the blacks. That meant they had to use separate hotels, restaurants, parks, schools and public lavatories. Blacks had the right to vote, but few dared to use it for fear of being attacked or even murdered. The southern law courts were unfair, nearly always finding whites innocent, and blacks guilty. As for jobs, the blacks had the lowest wages, and were 'the last to be hired and the first to be fired'.

Homes of black Americans Note the T.V. aerials.

In 1968 an Englishman, Colin Henfrey was visiting the United States. This is what happened when he stopped for a Coca-Cola at a little store in Missouri:

It's just a shack with a yapping dog and crude shelves piled with shotguns, liquor and biscuits; the keeper, a heavy swart character, resting a large paunch on the counter, has a curt, suspicious manner. An older man sits drinking in a corner. He asks where I'm from as the keeper opens the Cokes. Then the keeper joins in. 'Like it here?'

'Pretty country.'

'That's right. And she'd be prettier even, 'cept for all them goddam niggers. You got any niggers over there? Cause we got too goddam many here. Not right in this little county, we put 'em out a long while back and they ain't comin' back again, no sir' – he nods at the shot guns – 'they ain't so stupid they'd come troublin' decent folks. It's up North they're doing that 'cause folks up there's too goddam stupid to keep a goddam nigger down. I heard one of 'em on the radio sayin' how they're gonna take over, drive us white folks right out and take every white woman, yes sir, that's what they're aimin' at. That's all them son-of-a-bitches want, robbin' and plunderin' – right Jeff?'

Jeff nods non-committally, but there's more support from a younger, pinched man who's come in from the back. He adds his piece. 'Tell the truth, Uncle Dean, I wouldn't mind if they did come back here. Have us a little nigger-huntin' – fill 'em with lead and send em back North where they like the sons-of-bitches.'

Manscapes

1 What does the store sell?
2 What does the owner call the blacks?
3 Why does he say there are no blacks in his county?
4 What does he feel about people in the north?
5 What does he say the blacks are planning to do?
6 Why would the younger man like the blacks to return?

Because they were so badly treated in the south, many blacks moved to other parts of the United States. They settled in the city centres where the cheapest and poorest houses were. Soon, all the white families had moved out so the blacks had the city centres to themselves. Such places are called 'ghettos'. Colin Henfrey drove through the Chicago ghetto with a black preacher:

We go screeching down the Gold Coast past the blocks of luxury flats where men in dinner jackets and their bitter-lemon blondes are piling into fancy cars, like ads for expensive cigarettes. 'Brother, it's glory-land up here, another couple of hundred a month and I'd be living right here. Praise the Lord, halleluyah.' He swings south and suddenly the skyscrapers and dainty parks and blondes are gone. The big sweeping avenues give way to narrow streets and small shops and battered cars. Everyone seems to be outside, strolling, murmuring, kids racing, groups on the steps of the little brick houses with broken windows and broken porches. And for mile after mile there isn't a white face to be seen. When the kids see us, they stop in surprise, though it's nothing more. But Brother Eldon suddenly seems nervous, crouches lower over the wheel. 'Brother, see how they live down here, oh glory, ain't it somethin'! I'm a full-blooded negro myself, but I really hate how these folks live. Glory, brother, I wouldn't live here. It's real wild, they'll cut you, rob you, burn your car. I don't agree with no civil rights. These folks has got to blame themselves. Glory. They're so dirty and wild, they don't know how to care for themselves. See down there. That's Blackstone Avenue. Brother, I wouldn't walk down there if you paid me, not if the Lord himself was there. That's where the Blackstone Rangers is, teenage hoodlums. They burn the cars, kill each other. Oh brother, these people. Glory. Maybe the Lord'll help 'em, here we go, halleluyah', and he swings round another corner scattering a group of kids. 'See those kids, oh brother. Ain't safe to drive in these streets.'

Manscapes

1 What does Henfrey see in the richer part of Chicago?
2 What is the black ghetto like?
3 What are the people doing?
4 Why is the black preacher nervous?
5 According to the preacher how do the blacks in the ghettos behave?
6 Whom does he blame for this?
7 Where would he like to live himself?
8 What do you think of this preacher?

In the rest of this section we are going to look at just one of the problems the blacks had. This is the way they were treated on buses.

In 1959 a white American, John Griffin, disguised himself as a black so that he could find out what it was like to be one. Here is what happened to him in New Orleans:

Night was near when I finally caught the bus going towards town. Two blocks before Canal, the bus makes a left turn off Claiborne. I rang the bell to get off at this stop. The driver pulled to a halt and opened the door. He left it open until I reached it. I was ready to step off when the door banged shut in my face. Since he had to remain there waiting for a clear passage through traffic, I asked him to let me off.

'I can't leave the door open all night,' he said impatiently. He waited another full minute, but refused to open the door.

'Will you please let me off at the next corner, then?' I asked, controlling my temper. He did not answer. I returned to my seat.

At each stop I sounded the buzzer, but the driver continued through the next two stops. He drove me eight full blocks past my original stop and pulled up then only because some white passengers wanted to get off. I followed them to the front. He watched me, his hand on the lever that would spring the doors shut.

'May I get off now?' I asked quietly when the others had stepped down.

'Yeah, go ahead,' he said finally, as though he had

Martin Luther King speaks to some of his followers

tired of the cat and mouse game. I got off, sick, wondering how I could ever walk those eight blocks back to my original stop.

Black Like Me

1. What did the driver do when John Griffin tried to leave the bus?
2. Why did the driver stop the bus, in the end?
3. How far did John Griffin have to walk? (A 'block' is a group of buildings between streets.)

In order to win a better life for themselves many blacks joined the Civil Rights Movement. One of its leaders was a Baptist minister, Martin Luther King. In 1954, he went to work in Montgomery, Alabama. His wife, Coretta, describes what happened on the buses there:

Although seventy per cent of the bus company's passengers were black, it treated them like cattle – worse than that, for nobody insults a cow. The first seats on all buses were reserved for whites. Even if they were empty and the rear seats crowded, Negroes would have to stand at the back in case some whites might get aboard; and if the front seats happened to be full and more white people boarded the bus, black people seated in the rear were forced to get up and give them their seats. Furthermore, Negroes had to pay their fares at the front of the bus, get off, and walk to the rear door to board again. Sometimes the bus would drive off without them after they had paid their fare. This would happen to elderly people or pregnant women, in bad weather or good, and was considered a great joke by the drivers. Frequently the white bus drivers abused their passengers, called them niggers, black cows, or black apes. Imagine what it was like, for example, for a black man to get on a bus with his son and be subjected to such treatment.

There had been one incident in March, 1955, when fifteen-year-old Claudette Colvin refused to give up her seat to a white passenger. The high school girl was handcuffed and carted off to the police station.

My Life with Martin Luther King

1. What rules did blacks have to obey on the Montgomery buses?
2. What do we call the separation of blacks and whites in this way? (See page 112.)
3. What trick did drivers sometimes play on black passengers?
4. What happened to Claudette Colvin?

On December 1st, 1955 a black woman, Rosa Parks, was arrested for refusing to give up her seat to a white man. The blacks of Montgomery were furious. They elected Martin Luther King as their leader, and said they would not travel on the buses again until they were 'desegregated'. Since most passengers were black, that meant the bus company would go bankrupt unless it gave way.

At first, Martin Luther King was not hopeful. Boycotting the buses had been tried in other towns and had always failed because not enough blacks had given their support. However, this is what he says happened on the first day of the boycott, December 5th, 1955:

> The first bus was to pass around six o'clock. I was in the kitchen drinking my coffee when I heard Coretta cry, 'Martin, Martin come quickly!' I put down my cup and ran towards the living room. As I approached the front window Coretta pointed joyfully to a slowly moving bus: 'Darling, it's empty!' I could hardly believe what I saw. I knew that the South Jackson line which ran past our house carried more Negro passengers than any other line in Montgomery, and that this first bus was usually filled with domestic workers going to their jobs. Would all of the other buses follow the pattern that had been set by the first? Eagerly we waited for the next bus. In fifteen minutes it rolled down the street and like the first, it was empty. A third bus appeared, and it too was empty of all but two white passengers.
>
> I jumped in my car and for almost an hour I cruised down every major street and examined every passing bus. During this hour, at the peak of the morning traffic, I saw no more than eight Negro passengers riding the buses. By this time I was jubilant. Instead of the 60 per cent co-operation we had hoped for, it was becoming apparent that we had reached almost 100 per cent. A miracle had taken place. The once sleepy and indifferent Negro community was now fully awake.
>
> *Stride Towards Freedom*

1 How many blacks had King expected to join the boycott?
2 How many in fact did?
3 What does King say this proved had happened to the blacks of Montgomery?

This was only the beginning of a long struggle. In the first place, the black leaders had to organise fleets of motor cars to take people to work. Second, they had to keep their own people in order. One man suggested that they should kill eight or ten whites to show they were not afraid. But Martin Luther King was determined that the blacks should not use violence. He felt they must behave like good Christians. Third, the blacks had to stand firm against the whites, who were determined to break the boycott. The police harassed the drivers of cars that were carrying workers: they arrested ninety blacks, including Martin Luther King, on the charge of organising an illegal boycott: other whites sent threatening letters and made abusive telephone calls. Coretta King describes what happened one night. Martin was at a meeting and a friend, Mary Lucy Williams, was keeping her company:

> At about nine-thirty in the evening I had put on a dressing gown and Mary Lucy and I were chatting in the sitting room. I heard a heavy thump on the concrete porch outside. Had I not been expecting an attack, I might have looked out to see what it was. Instead I said, 'It sounds as if someone has hit the house. We'd better move to the back.'
>
> We moved fast – not through the hall, which would have taken us nearer the sound, but straight back through the guest bedroom. We were in the middle of it when there was a thunderous blast. Then smoke and the sound of breaking glass.
>
> Mary Lucy grabbed me and started screaming. Her screaming frightened me, and I was shaken by the impact and the noise. I hurried to my bedroom, two rooms back, where Yolanda was in her cradle. Then I thought, 'Who am I going to call? I'm not going to call the police in this instance.'
>
> Then the doorbell started ringing. My first thought was that it was the person who had thrown the bomb. I was trying to think of what I should do about the baby, and for a split second I got panicky. Then I shouted, 'Who is it?' and a voice said, 'Is anybody hurt?'
>
> I went to the door and let in my neighbours. They were frightened and worried. All over our part of town people had heard the blast and came rushing. The windows had been blown into the living room. The floor was covered with broken glass. The porch had been split, and there was a small hole in the concrete floor.'
>
> *My Life with Martin Luther King*

1 How was the house attacked?
2 Why was no-one hurt?
3 What damage was done?
4 Why do you suppose Coretta was unwilling to call the police?

When he heard the news, Martin rushed home. By the time he arrived there was a large crowd of blacks, some police, the Commissioner of Police, Clyde Sellers, and the Mayor, W. A. Gayle. Coretta King describes what happened:

> The situation outside the house was tense and danger-

ous. Though the crowd was singing, the people were angry and aroused. I remember hearing 'My Country, 'Tis of Thee,' but you could sense the heat of their anger. Many were armed; even the little boys had broken bottles. A policeman held back one black man who said, 'You got your thirty-eight, I got mine. Let's shoot it out.'

Later someone said tension was so high that if a white man had accidentally tripped over a Negro, it could have triggered the most awful riot in our history. The faces of Mayor Gayle and Commissioner Sellers were deathly pale. They went up to Martin and expressed their regret that 'this unfortunate incident has taken place in our city.'

More people were joining the crowd every minute. They stood swaying and muttering and shouting insults at the nervous police. At that point Martin walked out on the porch. In some ways it was the most important hour of his life. His own home had just been bombed, his wife and baby could have been killed; this was the first deep test of his Christian principles and his theories of non-violence. Standing there, very grave and calm, he dominated those furious people. He held up his hand, and they were suddenly silent – the crowd of angry men and women, of excited children and sullen, frightened policemen in a clump by the steps – all were absolutely still. In a calm voice Martin said, 'My wife and my baby are all right. I want you to go home and put down your weapons. We cannot solve this problem through retaliatory violence. We must meet violence with nonviolence. Remember the words of Jesus: "He who lives by the sword will perish by the sword." We must love our white brothers, no matter what they do to us. We must make them know that we love them. Jesus still cries out across the centuries, "Love your enemies." This is what we must live by. We must meet hate with love.'

Then my husband's voice took on the depth and grandeur of its full emotional power as he said, 'Remember, if I am stopped, this Movement will not stop, because God is with this Movement. Go home with this glowing faith and this radiant assurance.'

Many people out there were crying. I could see the shine of tears on their faces, in the strong lights. They were moved, as by a holy exaltation. They shouted, 'Amen.' They shouted, 'God bless you. We are with you all the way, Reverend.'

Mayor Gayle and the commissioner came forward. The crowd turned, began booing and threatening. The police made it worse by shouting, 'Listen to the commissioner!' The crowd yelled furiously. Martin stepped to the edge of the porch, holding up his hand, and the noise suddenly stopped, as when the conductor of an orchestra holds his baton high. Martin spoke, 'Remember what I just said. Let us hear the commissioner.'

Commissioner Sellers said, 'We are going to do everything in our power to find out who did this dreadful thing and bring him to justice.' Mayor Gayle added, 'We are offering five thousand dollars reward for information leading to his arrest.'

After that the crowd began to thin out, and the people went back to their homes. A white policeman's voice was heard in the crowd saying, 'If it hadn't been for that nigger preacher, we'd all be dead.'

My Life with Martin Luther King

Martin Luther King arrested

1 What was the crowd likely to do?
2 How did Martin Luther King say they must behave?
3 How did the crowd reply?
4 What did the police commissioner and the mayor promise?
5 How did the white policeman feel?

All the while, there were legal arguments, and they could only be settled by the United States Supreme Court in Washington. This took a long time, but at last, in November 1956, the Court said that the rules the Montgomery bus company had made for its black passengers were illegal. The first 'desegregated' bus ran on December 21st, 1956, and Martin Luther King decided he would be the first man to ride on it. Coretta King describes what happened:

The next morning, at five-forty-five, a little group gathered in our living room. Mrs. Rosa Parks, Ralph Abernathy, E. D. Nixon, and Glen Smiley (who was white) came to ride the first desegregated bus with Martin. No one knew what would happen, in view of the threats and fury of the white extremists. Reporters and television people waited outside.

Black boys sitting in the section of the bus reserved for whites

Like an anniversary of that memorable morning over a year before, the headlights of the six-o'clock bus flashed down the empty street as it pulled up at the bus stop. The men walked down the steps of our house and through the front door of the bus. The bus driver, smiling broadly said, 'I believe you are Dr. King?'

Martin said, 'Yes I am.'

'We are glad to have you with us this morning,' the driver said.

Smiling too, his tenseness gone, Martin thanked him and sat down in a front seat beside Glenn Smiley. With a clash of gears and a puff of exhaust, the first bus pulled away as though nothing had happened.

My Life with Martin Luther King

1 What was Martin Luther King afraid might happen?
2 How did the bus driver greet him?

Martin describes what happened during the journey:

As the white people boarded, many took seats as if nothing was going on. Others looked amazed to see Negroes sitting in front, and some appeared peeved to know that they either had to sit behind Negroes or stand. One elderly man stood up by the conductor, despite the fact that there were several vacant seats in the rear. When someone suggested to him that he sit in the back, he replied, 'I would rather die and go to hell than sit behind a nigger.' A white woman unknowingly took a seat by a Negro. When she noticed her neighbor, she jumped up and said in a tone of obvious anger: 'What are these niggers gonna do next?'

But despite such signs of hostility there were no major incidents on the first day. Many of the whites responded to the new system calmly. Several deliberately and with friendly smiles took seats next to negroes.

Stride Towards Freedom

1 What were the different ways in which white people behaved on the bus?

Later there was violence. Buses were fired on, blacks were beaten up, houses and churches were bombed. Finally, the police arrested two of the bombers. They signed confessions, but even so, the white jury found them not guilty. However, that was the end of the troubles. Martin Luther King wrote:

The diehards had made their last stand. The disturbances ceased abruptly. Desegregation went ahead smoothly. In a few weeks transportation was back to normal and people of both races rode together wherever they pleased. The skies did not fall when integrated buses finally travelled the streets of Montgomery.

Stride Towards Freedom

Written Work
1 You are an ordinary black living in Montgomery. Say why you wanted the buses desegregated. Tell the story of how this came about.
2 Tell the same story pretending to be a white who is hostile to blacks.

Research
1 What was the Ku-Klux-Klan?
2 Read more about the Civil Rights Movement, and other successes it had.
3 What was the Black Power movement? Why did Martin Luther King dislike it?

Chapter 9 *Britain*

Lloyd George and the Beginnings of the Welfare State

At the start of this century a lady called Mrs. Pember Reeves visited some of the poorest parts of London. She found that numbers of families were living in single rooms. Here is her description of one of them:

> There are four children all living. The man is a dusky, friendly soul. I was so much struck by the brilliance of his teeth shining from his grimy face that I expressed my admiration. 'Yes, mate, an' I tell yer why: 'cause I cleans 'em' and, after a short pause added, 'once a week.'
>
> The room is large – fifteen feet by thirteen feet – and has two windows. Under the window facing the door is the large bed, in which sleep mother, father and two children. A perambulator by the bedside holds the baby, and in the further corner is a small cot for the fourth child. At the foot of the bed is a small square table. Three wooden chairs and a chest of drawers complete the furniture, save for a treadle sewing machine bought by the mother before her marriage. The small fireplace has no oven, and open shelves go up on each side of it. There are two saucepans, both burnt. There is no larder. On the floor lies a loose piece of linoleum, and over the fireplace is an overmantel with brackets and a cracked looking-glass. On the brackets are shells and ornaments. Tiny

Family living in a single room What shows they are trying to keep their pride?

home-made window-boxes with plants in them decorate each window. The whole appearance of the room is cheerful. The overmantel was saved for penny by penny, before marriage, and is much valued. It gives the room an air, as the wife says proudly.

Round About a Pound a Week in London

1. How many children are there?
2. What does the writer hint has happened to other children?
3. Where does everyone sleep?
4. What furniture is there, apart from the beds?
5. How does the woman cook?
6. What have the man and woman done to make their room look pleasant?
7. When did they buy the more expensive things which they own?

Mrs. Reeves also said this about the homes of the poor:

In none of the bedrooms are there any washing arrangements. As a rule, each person just washes his face and hands as he or she comes downstairs. The exception is the little baby who generally has some sort of wash all over every day. Once a week, however, most of the children get a bath.

In one family of eight, the baby has a daily bath in the washing-up basin. On Friday evenings two boys and a girl under five are bathed, all in the same water, in a washing tub before the kitchen fire. On Saturday nights two boys under eleven bathe in one water, which is then changed and two girls of nine and twelve take their turn, the mother also washing her hair. The mother manages to bathe herself once a fortnight in the daytime when the five children are at school, and the father goes to the public baths when he can find time and afford twopence.

In another family the father, who can never afford a twopenny bath, gets a 'wash down' sometimes after the children have gone to sleep at night. 'A bath it ain't' explained his wife: 'it's just a bit at a time like'.

Two pennyworth of soap may have to wash the clothes, scrub the floors, and wash the people of a family for a week. It is difficult to realise the soap famine in such a household. Soda, being cheap, is made to do a great deal. It sometimes appears in the children's weekly bath: it often washes their hair.

Round About a Pound a Week in London

1. What washing do most members of the family do every day?
2. Draw up a time-table to show when the different members of the family have their baths. Bracket together those who share the same water.

Collecting water from the street pump Why will these families find it difficult to keep clean? What problems will they have in cold weather?

3. What are the different reasons why these families find it hard to keep clean? You will find more help on page 121.

In a poor family the man usually did best for food and clothes, because he worked to earn what little money they had. The mother then fed and clothed her children as well as she could, and only took what was left for herself. Mrs. Reeves gave one such woman some new clothes. Afterwards she wrote:

The astonishing difference made by a new pink blouse, nicely done hair and a well-made skirt, on one drab looking woman who seemed to be about forty was too startling to forget. She suddenly looked thirty (her age was twenty-six), and she had a complexion and quite pretty hair – things never noticed before. These women who look to be in the dull middle of middle-age are young: it comes as a shock when you realise it.

Round About a Pound a Week in London

1. What new clothes did the woman have?
2. How old had she seemed before she put them on?
3. How old did she seem when she was wearing them and had tidied her hair?
4. What was her real age?

Fashionable restaurant Why would a working class man feel uncomfortable here?

While many people were very poor, others were comfortable and others rich. There were big differences between them. Here is what a man called Henry Ryecroft saw one day:

I was taking a meal once in a London restaurant when there sat down at the next table a young man of the working class, whose dress showed he was on holiday. A glance told me that he felt uncomfortable, and when the waiter gave him the menu, he stared blankly in confusion. Some stroke of good luck, no doubt, had made him bold enough to enter for the first time such a place as this, and now that he was here, he heartily wished himself out in the street again. However, helped by the waiter, he gave an order for a beef-steak and vegetables. When the dish was served, the poor fellow simply could not make a start upon it: he was embarrassed by all the knives and forks, by the arrangement of the dishes, by the sauce bottles and the cruet stand, above all, no doubt by the other people not of his class, and the unusual experience of being waited upon by a man with a long stiff shirt-front. He grew red: he made the clumsiest and most futile efforts to transport the meat to his plate: food was there before him, but like a very Tantalus, he was unable to enjoy it. At last I saw him pull out his handkerchief, spread it on the table, and, with a sudden effort, fork the meat off the dish and into the handkerchief. The waiter came up and spoke a word to him. Upset and angry, the young man roughly asked what he had to pay. It ended in the waiter bringing a newspaper, wherein he helped to wrap up meat and vegetables. Money was flung down and the victim of a mistaken ambition hurriedly left to satisfy his hunger in more familiar surroundings.

It was a striking and unpleasant example of social differences. Could such a thing happen in any country but England? I doubt it.

The Private Papers of Henry Ryecroft

1. How did the young man feel when he entered the restaurant?
2. What does the writer think is the probable reason he came?
3. What food did the young man order?
4. Why was he unable to eat it?
5. What did he do with his meat? Why was this do you suppose?
6. What happened to the food, in the end?
7. What does the writer say this story shows?

In 1912 the liner *Titanic* struck an iceberg in the North Atlantic and sank. Later, the *Daily Herald* published these figures:

	per cent
Proportion of First Class passengers saved	61
Proportion of Second Class passengers saved	36
Proportion of Third Class passengers saved	23

1. Illustrate these figures with a bar diagram.
2. What conclusions do you draw from them?

Here are descriptions of two very different families. The writer first of all quotes a man called Seebohm Rowntree who wrote a book on the poor of York:

> For instance, we read a brief description of the household of a man of 'no occupation'.
>
> 'Married. Two rooms: parish relief: ill, incapable. Two little girls, one with tuberculosis. The rooms are miserable, badly ventilated and damp. This house shares one lavatory with six other houses, and one water tap with three others.'
>
> Surely we ought to know the description, though it cannot be so brief, of the household of another man of 'no occupation'.
>
> Married. Two children. Four houses. London house in West End. Sixty-two rooms – one of the country houses considerably larger. Thirty-six indoor servants:
>
> | | |
> |---|---|
> | 1 house steward | 1 house carpenter |
> | 2 grooms of the chamber | 1 chef |
> | 1 valet | 1 kitchen porter |
> | 2 under butlers | 4 kitchen maids |
> | 5 footmen | 2 still-room maids |
> | 1 gate porter | 6 housemaids |
> | 1 hall porter | 1 linen maid |
> | 1 usher of the servants' hall | 1 lady's maid |
> | | 1 housekeeper |
> | 2 odd job men | 2 nurses. |
>
> Owns about 20,000 acres of land. (A larger staff of servants than this could be quoted. In one country house as many as ten housemaids are kept.)

The Camel and the Needle's Eye, A. Ponsonby

1. How does the poor man's family suffer?
2. What property does the rich man own?
3. How many rooms are there in his London house?
4. How many servants does he employ in his London house?
5. Why did the writer put these two descriptions side by side, do you think?

Servants

Here is a diagram, drawn in 1904, to show how the wealth of Britain was shared:

British incomes in 1904

Rich	Comfortable
1,250,000 persons	3,750,000 persons
£585,000,000	£245,000,000

Poor
38,000,000 persons
£880,000,000

1. How much money does each rich person have every year?
2. How much does each 'comfortable' person have every year?
3. How much does each poor person have?
4. Draw a bar diagram to illustrate your figures.
5. How many times do the poor outnumber the rich?

Here are the food bills for two families:

Man, wife and child for five weeks:

	s.	d
Meat and liver	8	5
Potatoes and vegetables	2	3½
Fish	0	9
Bacon, eggs, and cheese	3	6¼
Suet	1	0
Butter and dripping	2	9
Bread	8	9½
Flour	4	1½
Rice	0	6
Fruit, jam and sugar	8	4¼
Milk	3	2
Tea and coffee	3	6
Pepper and salt	0	2½
£2	7	4¼
Average for one week	9	5½ (47p)

Household books for one week – seven in family, nineteen servants:

	£
Butcher	16
Baker	5
Poulterer	12
Dairy	9
Fruit, flowers, vegetables	16
Fishmonger	9
Grocer	5
	£72

1. How much does each family spend on food per head, per week?

By now you will have realised that in the early years of this century there were enormous differences between rich and poor. Those differences had always been there, but no government had bothered much about them. Then, towards the end of the nineteenth century, working men were given the vote. At first, they had no political party of their own, so they had to vote either for the Conservatives, or the Liberals. Both stood for different groups of wealthy people. In 1906, the Liberals won a general election with the help of the workers, and they were anxious to keep their support. Accordingly, they decided they must do all they could to help the poor. Even before 1906, the great Liberal leader David Lloyd George said in a speech at Bangor:

> The most startling fact about our country is this – that you have men who have untold wealth living in gorgeous splendour in one street and a horde of miserable, poverty-stricken human beings huddled together in the most abject want and filth in the adjoining alleyways. Great wealth and dreadful poverty dwell side by side. Why, in this very Bangor union, where you have noblemen and squires enjoying riches which they do not know how to squander, I was startled to find that one out of every twenty of the population had parish relief. And it is not that the country around Bangor is barren and desolate. On the contrary, it is rich in agricultural and mineral wealth. But these riches, intended by Providence for the people, are stopped before they reach them. It is well known to all of you that there is not one of the horses of these high-born gentlemen that is not better fed, better housed, and less worked than thousands of working men in this very union. Things must be equalised. This deplorable state of things cannot go on for ever.

According to Lloyd George:

1 What is the most startling fact about Britain?
2 For whom was the wealth of the country meant?
3 How do rich people's horses compare with working men?
4 What must happen now?

David Lloyd George What impression does this photograph give of Lloyd George? What would he have said about the other pictures in this section, do you suppose?

In 1908 Lloyd George became Chancellor of the Exchequer, so he was in a position to give a lot of help to the poor. His schemes were expensive, so he asked Parliament to raise some new taxes which rich people would have to pay. He did this in his budget of 1909. Here is part of a speech he made to Parliament:

> This is a War Budget. It is for raising money to wage implacable warfare against poverty and squalidness. I cannot help hoping and believing that before this generation has passed away we shall have advanced a great step towards that good time when poverty and the misery which always follows in its camp will be as remote to the people of this country as the wolves which once infested its forests.

Hansard, April 29th, 1909

1 Why does Lloyd George call his budget a War Budget?
2 What does he hope it will do?

Soon afterwards Lloyd George made a speech at Limehouse in the East End of London. He said:

It is rather a shame that a rich country like ours – probably the richest in the world – should allow those who have toiled all their days to end in want and possibly starvation. It is rather hard that an old workman should have to find his way to the gates of the tomb, bleeding and footsore, through the brambles and thorns of poverty. We will cut a new path for him – an easier one, a pleasanter one, through fields of waving corn. We are raising money to pay for the new road – aye, and to widen it so that 200,000 paupers shall be able to join in the march. There are many in the country blessed with great wealth. If there are among them men who grudge a fair contribution towards the less fortunate of their fellow countrymen, they are very mean rich men.

We propose to do more by means of the Budget. We are raising money to provide against the evils and sufferings that follow from unemployment. We are raising money to help the sick and the widows and orphans. I do not believe any fair-minded man would challenge the justice and the fairness of the aims which we have in view in raising the money.

1. How wealthy does Lloyd George say Britain is?
2. What does he say the working man's journey through life is like?
3. To what does he compare the new path the government is making?
4. Which poor people in particular does he want to help?
5. Who is going to pay?

The House of Lords did not like Lloyd George's budget, and he had a long hard struggle. In the end, though, his budget was passed and rich people had to pay taxes to help the poor. Lloyd George was able to introduce a number of things which mark the beginning of the Welfare State in Britain. Here are some of them:

1. Old Age Pensions for people over 70.
2. School dinners and medical inspection of school children.
3. Labour Exchanges.
4. National Insurance. The National Insurance Act of 1911 gave the dole to unemployed people in a number of important industries like building and engineering. In addition, it gave sick pay and free medical attention to all workers when they were ill.

National Insurance was particularly expensive, and there had to be a large sum of money set aside. The government found this money in three different ways:

1. For every worker in the country the government itself gave twopence a week. This came from the taxes which Lloyd George made the rich pay to help the poor.
2. Employers paid threepence a week for each one of their employees.
3. Each worker had fourpence a week stopped from his wages.*

The rich were angry because they had to pay extra taxes. The employers were angry because they had to pay contributions for their workers. As for the workers themselves, Lloyd George said they were getting 'ninepence for fourpence' so perhaps they should have been happy. Certainly they were glad to have the dole when they were unemployed, and to have sick pay when they were ill. However, they hated losing fourpence each week from their wages. A mob of servant girls gathered outside Lloyd George's house and shouted, 'Taffy was a Welshman. Taffy was a Thief.'

Written Work

Imagine you are a worker living in 1900. Say why you think life is treating you unfairly. What do you think the government should do to help the poor?

Research

1. Find out about Lloyd George's struggle with the House of Lords and the passing of the Parliament Act of 1911.
2. Lloyd George's work in starting the Welfare State was completed by the Labour Government which was in power from 1945–1950. Find out what it did.

*These figures are in old money, and one old penny was worth less than half of a new one.

Votes for Women

During the nineteenth century women did not have anything like as many rights as men. They could not go to either of the Universities of Oxford or Cambridge: they could not become lawyers or doctors: if they were allowed to do the same work as men, for example teaching, they were paid a good deal less; until an Act of Parliament was passed in 1882 a woman's property became her husband's as soon as she married. Moreover, women were not allowed to vote. This annoyed them more than anything. It proved that men believed women were not fit to help run the country.

Then, in 1903, Mrs. Emmeline Pankhurst and a group of determined ladies, formed the Women's Social and Polictical Union. Their aim was to win women the vote. They called themselves 'suffragettes' because the suffrage is the right to vote.

At first, the suffragettes tried to win over Parliament and the Government by peaceful means. They had no success, so they decided to use violence or, as they called it, 'militancy'. In October 1905 they planned to interrupt a Liberal Party meeting at the Free Trade Hall in Manchester. Sir Edward Grey, one of the most important of the Liberal leaders was going to speak. First of all, the suffragettes had to choose the question they were going to ask.

Funeral of Emily Davison Find out how she died.

Mrs. Pankhurst's daughter, Christabel wrote:

The question was to be painted on a banner in large letters. How should we word it? 'Will you give women suffrage?' – we rejected that form, for the word 'suffrage' suggested to some ignorant or jesting folk the idea of suffering. 'Let them suffer away!' – we had heard that taunt. We must find another wording and we did! It was so obvious and yet, strange to say, quite new. Our banners read:

> WILL YOU GIVE
> VOTES
> FOR WOMEN?

Thus was uttered for the first time the famous and victorious battle-cry: 'Votes for women!'
Unshackled

Suffragettes This picture was taken during an election. Why was it a good time for the women to press their claim?

1 What question did the suffragettes first think of using?
2 Why did they reject it?
3 What question did they choose?
4 Do you think the suffragettes' slogan was a good one? Give reasons for your answer.

The two suffragettes who were to interrupt the meeting were Annie Kenney and Christabel Pankhurst. Christabel describes what happened:

Annie rose first and asked: 'Will the Liberal Government give votes to women?' No answer came. I joined my voice to hers and our banner was unfurled, making clear what was our question. The effect was explosive! The meeting was aflame with excitement. There was some consultation among chairman and speakers and then the Chief Constable of Manchester, kindly and fatherly in manner, made his way to us and promised us an answer to our question after the vote of thanks had been made. We accepted his promise and we waited. The vote of thanks was carried. Sir Edward Grey rose to reply without one word in answer to our question! The bargain thus broken on his side, we were free to ask our question again: 'Will the Liberal Government give women the vote?' The answer came then – not in word, but in deed. Stewards rushed at us, aided by volunteers and accompanied by loud cries: 'Throw them out!' We were dragged from our seats resisting as strongly as we could and still calling out: 'Will the Liberal Government give women the vote?'

Outside we were in the grip of policemen. The matter must not, I knew, stay where it was. What we had done must be made an act of lasting importance. We must, in fact, bring the matter into Court, into prison. For simply disturbing the meeting I should not be imprisoned. I must use the sure means of getting arrested. I must 'assault the police'. But how was I to do it? I could not strike them, my arms were being held. I could not even stamp on their toes – they seemed able to prevent that. Yet I must bring myself under arrest. The vote depended upon it. Lectures on the law flashed to my mind. I could, even with all by limbs helpless, commit a technical assault, and so I found myself arrested and charged with 'spitting at a policeman'. It was not a real spit but only, shall we call it, a 'pout', a perfectly dry purse of the mouth. I could not *really* have done it, even to get the vote, I think. Anyhow, there was no need, my technical assault was enough. A kindly magistrate who had known Father, was not at all severe! But we gave him not the least chance or excuse to let us off. To prison we went.

Unshackled

1 What happened when Annie Kenney asked her question?
2 What did the suffragettes do then?
3 What happened in the meeting, as a result?
4 What promise did Sir Edward Grey break?
5 What happened when the suffragettes asked their question again?
6 How did Christabel make sure she was sent to prison?
7 Why did she want to go to prison, do you suppose?

In spite of demonstrations like this, the Government still refused to give way, so the suffragettes became more violent. Here is what happened on March 1st, 1912:

A band of women set out on such a window-breaking campaign in the principal streets of the West End, as London has never known. For a quarter of an hour or twenty minutes nothing was heard in the Strand, Cockspur Street, Downing Street, Piccadilly, Bow Street or Oxford Street, but the falling, shattered glass. Many of the finest shop fronts in the world had been destroyed and splinters of glass had been scattered over their valuable contents. The attack was begun practically simultaneously. It was one of the busiest periods of the day. Suddenly women, who a moment before had appeared to be on peaceful shopping expeditions, produced from bags or muffs, hammers, stones and sticks and began an attack on the nearest windows. Information was immediately sent to the police and all the reserve constables were hurried out.

The most daring incident of the day was the excursion of Mrs. Pankhurst and two other ladies to Downing Street. The police patrols in the street were taken completely by surprise. A large force of extra police immediately went to Downing Street. In spite of the efforts of the constables however, four other women caused further damage before they were arrested.

Daily Telegraph

1 Where did the suffragettes break windows?
2 What shows they were well organised?
3 What damage do you suppose the suffragettes did in Downing Street?

WOMAN SUFFRAGE

ANTI-SUFFRAGE LEAGUE

'There was an old dame in a huff;
"Women don't want the vote", she cried;– "Stuff!"
When they said– "But we *do*", she answered– "Pooh pooh!
I don't – and let that be enough!"'

What people is this cartoon attacking?

A suffragette who was in prison usually went on hunger strike. The prison authorities did not want her to die, for that would make her a martyr. Accordingly, they tried something which, until then, had only been used on patients in lunatic asylums who refused to eat. This was forcible feeding.

Here is a story about a suffragette, Lady Constance Lytton, who had a weak heart. She was arrested twice, first as herself and then, later, disguised as a mill girl with the false name Jane Warton. This is what happened the second time:

> No examination was made of her pulse or heart. As Lady Constance Lytton she had had a heart examination by two prison doctors and another who, as it seemed, had come from London. As a result, she was not forcibly fed, but released. As 'Jane Warton', the working woman, she had no heart examination and was forcibly fed. Four wardresses held her down, a fifth helped with the forcible feeding. The doctor offered the choice of a steel or a wooden gag, explaining that the steel gag would hurt. The prisoner was silent. After an effort with the wooden gag, the steel gag was used. Her jaws were forced painfully wide, the large tube pushed far down her throat and food very quickly poured down, but returned in a few seconds after, in a bout of sickness, while doctor and wardresses held down her retching body. Then they left her – no clean clothing could then be supplied, it seemed, and she lay as she was until the next morning. From the next cell she could hear the distressing sounds of the forcible feeding of Elsie Howey.
>
> The following day, Lady Constance was fed by force a second time. The suffering and sickness were this time worse than before. The same evening doctors and wardresses came again to the cell. Again the horror and the vomiting and now while the vomiting continued, so did the inpouring of food. After this third feeding, Lady Constance showed greater signs of illness than before, and the doctor called in the assistant medical officer to test her heart. He rapidly did so, and pronounced it a 'splendid heart'. At last, one morning, the Governor and doctor arrived at her cell. It was to tell her that she was released on medical grounds. The Press Association had heard a rumour that she was in Walton Gaol. The prison officials suspected that their mysterious prisoner was someone other than she professed to be.
>
> Lady Constance Lytton had proved her point: that the Liberal Government had a different standard of treatment for working women and for other women. When she was Lady Constance Lytton they found her to be suffering from a serious disease of the heart and unfit for forcible feeding. When she was 'Jane Warton', they did not even question the state of her heart and fed her by force.
>
> *Unshackled*

1. What happened when Lady Constance was in prison under her own name?
2. What did the prison authorities fail to do when she was pretending to be a mill girl?
3. How was Lady Constance fed?
4. How else did she suffer?
5. Why did she at last have a medical examination?
6. What did the assistant medical officer say?
7. Why was Lady Constance released?
8. What was the point she had proved?
9. Why was her action particularly brave?

One of the best known novelists of the time was Marie Corelli. This is what she said about the suffragettes:

> A great question is before the country. It is this: Shall we sacrifice our Womanhood to Politics? Surely the best and bravest of us will answer No! – ten thousand times no! Rather let us use every means in our power to prevent what would be nothing less than a national disaster. For Great Britain is already too rapidly losing many of the noble ideals which once made her the mistress of the world. Preachers of all creeds are reproaching women (and rightly too) for their neglect of their highest duties – for their frivolity, waste of time, waste of money and waste of love. And if the mothers of Britain give up their simple *womanliness* to take part in politics, then darker days are in store for the nation than can yet be imagined. For with women alone rests the Home, which is the foundation of Empire. When they desert this, their God-appointed centre, then things are tottering to a fall.
>
> 'Votes for Women!' is the shrill cry of a number of discontented ladies who seem to have missed the best of life. And it is well-nigh useless to repeat the plain truth that Woman was and is destined to make voters rather than to be one of them.
>
> Women have quite as good brains as men – they can become great artists, great writers, great scientists – that is if they choose to practice the self-denial which go with these careers. They might even become great musicians, if with depth of sentiment, **they** would also obtain self-control.
>
> But Woman always lacks **the grand** self-control which is the inward power of the **great musician**. She was born to be a creature of sweet impulses – of love – of tenderness – and these things are no doubt the true origin of music itself – music which she *inspires*, but cannot *create*. It is the same way – to my thinking – with politics. Woman's business is to *inspire* the work, and let her light 'shine through'.
>
> *Woman or – Suffragette?*

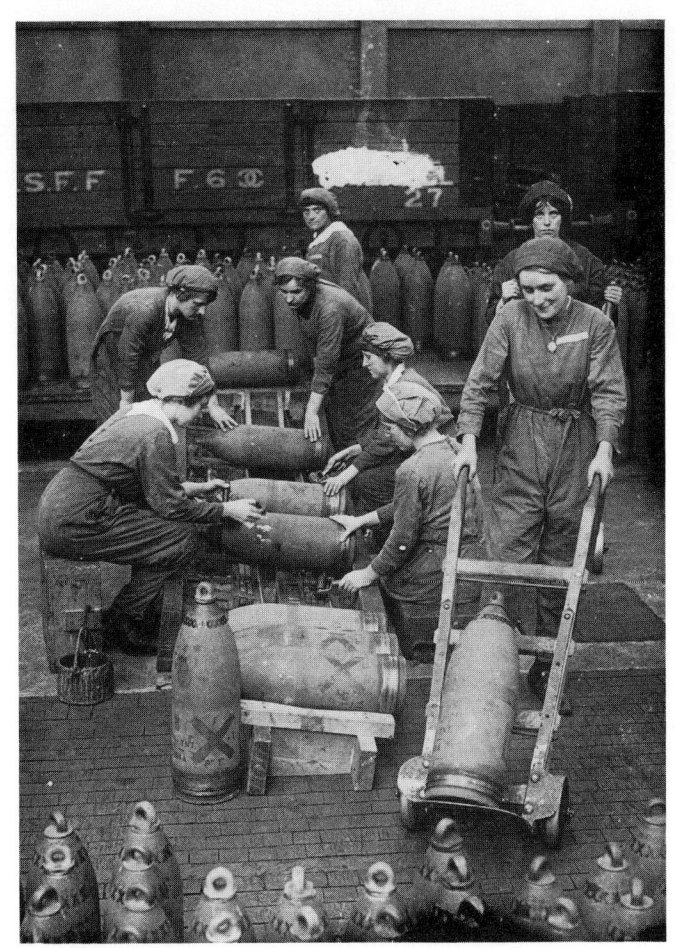

Women in munitions factory, during the First World War How did doing work like this help women to win the vote? (See page 130).

According to Marie Corelli:

1 Should women have the vote?
2 What are preachers accusing women of doing? Does she agree with the preachers?
3 What will happen if women take part in politics?
4 What is a woman's most important duty? Can you think of a saying which gives the same idea?
5 What is wrong with the suffragettes?
6 What can women do as well as men?
7 Why do women not make great musicians?
8 What can women do to help the writing of music?
9 What part can women play in politics?
10 How far do you agree with Marie Corelli? (Can you name a famous woman composer?)

The First World War began in 1914. Later, Christabel Pankhurst wrote:

> Mother and I declared support of our country. We declared an armistice with the Government and suspended militancy for the duration of the war. We offered our service to the country and called upon all our members to do likewise.
>
> To win votes for women a national victory was needed, for as Mother said, 'What would be the good of the vote without a country to vote in?'
>
> Some people were astonished. How, it was asked, could we support a Government that had been torturing women and had opposed the women's cause?
>
> The answer was that the country was our country. It belonged to us and not to the Government, and we had the right and privilege, as well as the duty, to serve and defend it.
>
> *Unshackled*

1 What did the suffragettes do when the war began?
2 Why did they take this action?
3 Why were people astonished?
4 What was Christabel Pankhurst's answer?

During the war, hundreds of thousands of women took the jobs of men who had joined the army. A lady who visited a munitions factory wrote:

> First of all we visit the 'danger buildings' in the Fuse Factory. The girls all wear, for protection, green muslin veils and gloves. They are making small pellets for the charging of shells, out of a high-explosive powder.
>
> In another room girls are handling a black powder for another part of the detonator, and because of the irritant nature of the powder, are wearing white bandages round the nose and mouth.
>
> There is great competition for these rooms the Superintendent says! The girls in them work on two shifts of $10\frac{1}{2}$ hours each, and would resent a change to a shorter shift.
>
> After the Fuse Factory we pass through the High Explosive Factory where 250 girls are at work fitting 18-pounder shells with high explosive.
>
> 'They are not as strong as the men' the Superintendent says, 'but what they lack in strength, they make up in spirit.' I talk to two educated women who turn out to be High School teachers from a town that has been several times visited by Zeppelins. 'We just felt we must come and help kill Germans,' they say quietly.
>
> *England's Effort*, Mrs. Humphry Ward

1 What work are the women doing in the factory?
2 Why is this work dangerous? Why is it unpleasant?

British nurses in France

3 According to the Superintendent:
   a In what way are the women in the factory not as good as the men?
   b How do they make up for this?
4 Why did the two teachers say they were working in the factory?

Women who were thirty years old or more were given the vote in 1918, even before the war ended, though it was not until 1928 that all women over the age of twenty-one had the same right to vote as men. Writing in 1973, J. B. Priestley said:

> The decision to take 'direct action' by attacks on property, by setting letter boxes and even houses on fire, by threatening politicians with horsewhips, by planting bombs, brings us close to our own times. For my part I think it was a mistake then, just as I think similar courses of action are a mistake now. To add to the horrible sum total of violence in this world will never improve it. Alive myself at the time, and with many older friends who were active supporters of the movement, I believe that constant and earnest persuasion did more for it than the sensational publicity the militants received. The opposition to the Women's Vote by a man like Asquith was political. He felt – and he was quite right – that female suffrage at that time would give the Tories a huge bonus. Though in general sympathy with the movement, I am certain it was really the First World War itself that made further opposition to the Women's Vote clearly ridiculous. When girls and women had been making munitions and driving heavy lorries, it was no use telling them any longer that God and Nature intended them only to make ginger puddings and darn socks.

The Militant Suffragettes – Introduction

Note: Asquith, a Liberal, had reason to be worried. Most women vote Conservative.

According to Priestley:
1 Why were the suffragettes wrong to use violence?
2 What was the better way?
3 Why were Liberals, like Asquith, against giving women the vote?
4 How did the First World War help the suffragettes?

Written Work
1 Imagine you are a suffragette. Say what you are doing to win the vote. Explain why you think you are right to behave in this way.
2 Now imagine you are against giving women the vote. Say what you think of suffragettes.

Research
1 Find out more about the suffragettes. Why was Emily Davison one of their special heroines?
2 What famous men supported the suffragettes?
3 What are the aims of the 'Women's Lib.' movement?

The General Strike

During the First World War, Britain needed a lot of coal. Miners earned good wages, far better than those of the soldiers fighting in the trenches. After the war, much less coal was burnt, its price fell, and the mine owners were losing money. They told the men that if they wanted to keep their jobs, they would have to work longer hours, for lower wages. The miners' answer was to go on strike. They said that if their employers did not have enough money for their wages, then the government must find it.

The miners asked the other workers to help them, so the Trades Union Congress (T.U.C.) called a General Strike. It began on May 4th, 1926.

Coal mining

Here first of all, is a description of work in a coal mine, written by George Orwell:

Most of the things one imagines in hell are there – heat, noise, confusion, darkness, foul air and, above all, unbearably cramped space. You see opposite you a shiny black wall three or four feet high. This is the coal face. Overhead is the smooth ceiling made by the rock from which the coal has been cut: underneath is the rock again, so that the gallery you are in is only as high as the seam of coal itself, probably not much more than a yard. You cannot see very far, because the fog of coal dust throws back the beam of your lamp, but you can see on either side of you the line of half-naked kneeling men, one to every four or five yards, driving their shovels under the fallen coal and flinging it swiftly over their left shoulders on to the conveyor belt. Down this belt a glittering river of coal races constantly – several tons every minute.

They are on the job for seven and a half hours, theoretically without a break, for there is no time 'off'. Actually they snatch a quarter of an hour or so at some time during the shift to eat the food they have brought with them, usually a hunk of bread and dripping and a bottle of cold tea.

The Road to Wigan Pier

1. In what ways was coal mining unpleasant?
2. Imagine you are a coal miner. What would you say if your employer asked you to work longer hours for less pay?

Here is an extract from a workers' news sheet, published on the first day of the strike:

Hold Tight – That's Right

Congratulations to the workers of Great Britain! Nothing finer has ever been seen than the completeness of their response to the call of the T.U.C.

The stoppage is complete. The wanton brutality of the Government and the coal-owners in their combined attempt to force a reduction of rates upon the already underpaid miners has met solid resistance of the whole class.

And the gallantry of the printing workers in silencing the lying capitalist press with their last-minute lies, made a splendid start to the greatest display of unity in British history.

This morning's issue of the *Morning Post* utters the lie that 'the Trades Union Congress has upset the entire country and challenges the King's Government.'

This is as false as hell. The country has been upset by the stubborn greed of the coal owners and by the decision of the Government to take their side.

This was a direct attack upon the living standards of the whole working class, and in resisting it the T.U.C. did no more than their duty.

The workers are defending their lives.

The boss class and its Government are the challengers.

The Government which has made this criminal bungle should be forced to resign.

The workers did not strike until they were forced. They will hold fast to the end.
EVERY MAN BEHIND THE MINERS.
NOT A PENNY OFF THE PAY: NOT A MINUTE ON THE DAY.
AN INJURY TO ONE IS AN INJURY TO ALL.
NO GOVERNMENT HAS THE RIGHT TO ORDER MEN AND WOMEN TO STARVE.

Workers' Bulletin, May 4th, 1926

Note: Newspapers like the *Daily Express* had prepared articles which were very critical of the General Strike, so their workers refused to print them.

According to the *Workers' Bulletin*:
1. How have the workers of Britain answered the strike call?
2. What lie did the *Morning Post* tell?
3. Who is **responsible** for the strike?
4. What should the government do?
5. What are the workers determined to do?

To help fight the strike, the Government published its own newspaper, the *British Gazette*. This table shows the numbers of copies sold:

May 5	232,000	May 8	836,000
May 6	507,000	May 10	1,127,000
May 7	655,000	May 11	1,801,000

(May 9 was a Sunday)

1. Draw a bar diagram to show how the sales of the *British Gazette* increased in the first week of the strike.

Here are some headlines from the *British Gazette*:

ORDER AND QUIET THROUGH THE LAND.

Growing Dissatisfaction Among The Strikers.

INCREASING NUMBERS OF MEN RETURNING TO WORK.

850 Omnibuses In The Streets Of London.

MORE AND MORE TRAINS.

1. What impression is the *British Gazette* trying to give?
2. How do these headlines contradict the articles in the *Workers' Bulletin*?

NEWCASTLE EDITION.

Official Strike News Bulletin.

The British Worker.

Published by The General Council of the Trades Union Congress.

NO. 2. WEDNESDAY, MAY 12TH, 1926. PRICE ONE PENNY.

Meditations of a Trade Unionist on Reading Mr. Baldwin's Latest Guarantees to Strike-Breakers.

So you will "guarantee" that all I'd lose
In Union benefits should be made up,
And you "might" keep your promise, though the woes
Of them that gave up everything to fight
And now are starving with their wives and kids
Make one a bit suspicious;
Still you "might"!

Also you've promised you'd protect my skin
And save my bones and make it safe for me
To walk about and work and earn my keep.
I'm not afraid for that. I know my mates —
They're decent, quiet chaps, not hooligans;
They wouldn't try to murder me,
Not they!

But could you make them treat me as a pal,
Or shield me from their cold, contemptuous eyes?
Could you restore the pride of comradeship?
Could you call back my ruined self-respect,
Give me protection from my bitter shame,
From self-contempt that drives out happiness?
Such guarantees are not in mortal power.
I'm sticking to my mates;
That's my reply.

TO ALL WORKERS

The General Council wishes again to impress upon all Trade Unionists that it is essential for them to be exemplary in conduct and to give no opportunity for police interference.

Pickets especially are asked to avoid obstruction and to confine themselves strictly to their legitimate duties.

ALL'S WELL!

The General Council's Message to Trade Union Members.

We have entered upon the second week of the general stoppage in support of the mine workers against the attack upon their standard of life by the coalowners.

Nothing could be more wonderful than the magnificent response of millions of workers to the call of their leaders

From every town and city in the country reports are pouring into the General Council headquarters stating that all ranks are solid, that the working men and women are resolute in their determination to resist the unjust attack upon the mining community.

The General Council desires to express their keen appreciation of the loyalty of the Trade Union members to whom the call was issued and by whom such a splendid response has been made.

They are especially desirous of commending the workers on their strict obedience to the instruction to avoid all conflict and to conduct themselves in an orderly manner. Their behaviour during the first week of the stoppage is a great example to the whole world.

The General Council's message at the opening of the second week is "Stand firm. Be loyal to instructions and Trust Your Leaders."

LORD BALFOUR ANSWERED.

Day by day in the Cabinet's newspaper, Mr. Churchill, acting as its super-editor, publishes articles by prominent public men. These are suspiciously like one another.

Monday's contribution was signed "Balfour," but the hand almost all through is the hand of Churchill, who is trying, still, to create panic by representing an industrial dispute about wages as an attempted revolution.

Lord Balfour must know perfectly well that the Trade Unions have no revolutionary, no political, aims. They are simply doing their utmost, in the only way open to them, to prevent the wages of an important body of workers from being driven down to a point which the mineowners themselves have admitted to be "miserable."

The reference to the Strike being directed by a "relatively small body of extremists" again betrays Mr. Churchill's hand. It is mere violent, headlong, foolish propaganda foolish because no sensible person will believe it. It is impossible that Lord Balfour can suppose Mr. Pugh, Mr. Thomas, Mr. Bevin, and other members of the General Council, who have always been moderate, reasonable men, to have been suddenly transformed into "extremists" as rash and reckless as Mr. Churchill himself.

(Continued on Page Two.)

PASS THIS ON OR POST IT UP.

Convoy of food leaving the docks Why are soldiers travelling on the lorries?

The Government had been expecting a General Strike and was ready for it. Here is something which happened in London:

> The London Docks were opened yesterday by a convoy of flour-laden lorries, and convoyed to Hyde Park. From there, their loads were sent to districts where supplies were shortest. The convoy of 104 lorries with its escort of 16 armoured cars, cavalry and mounted police, extended for some two miles, and was received everywhere with the greatest astonishment and enthusiasm. Two battalions of Guards had, on Friday morning, been marched down to take possession of the Docks, and on Friday evening 500 volunteers had gone to the Docks by another route. The Guards and volunteers were ready to help load the flour on the lorries by 8 o'clock on Saturday morning.
>
> All arrangements worked without a hitch, and about 11.30 the great convoy started under escort. There was no attempt whatever at interference, and as the news of its progress spread, large crowds of people – many of them women – collected to cheer and welcome the flour on its way. The sight was as popular as a Lord Mayor's procession.
>
> *B.B.C. Bulletin*, May 9th, 1926

1. What did the lorries carry from the docks?
2. How were the lorries protected? Why do you suppose this was done?
3. Who loaded the lorries at the docks?
4. How did the people of London greet the lorries? Why do you suppose this was?
5. How did the government make sure the people had this piece of news?

While some volunteers worked in the docks, others ran the railways. A young lady who went to London by train wrote to her parents:

> It is really fine to see how nice and good-tempered everybody is about the strike. When I arrived at Paddington there were no ordinary porters, but I met a very good-looking man, medical student he looked like, who seized my suit-cases. I wanted to get to Baker Street, so he and I explored passages with locked gates to try to find Praed Street: he knew nothing about it, apparently. Eventually he went outside and stood in the middle of the road and shouted 'Baker Street' to the first car that came along. And it stopped, and I got in with my luggage and went to Baker Street Station. There everybody carries your luggage for you, and is awfully nice. It is perfectly splendid to hear, instead of 'Arrer 'n'Uxbridge', a beautiful Oxford voice crying, 'Harrow and Uxbridge train.' Ticket collectors say, 'Thank you very much'. One guard of a train due to depart, a smartly dressed young man in plus fours, waved a green flag. Nothing happened. He waved again, and blew a whistle, then said

to the driver in hurt tones, 'I say, you might *go.*' It's all very jolly and such an improvement on the ordinary humdrum state of things.

1. What does the writer think of the volunteers who are looking after the stations and running the railways?
2. How did she get from Paddington to Baker Street?
3. What incidents showed that the volunteers were having problems?
4. What does the writer think about the strike?
5. Do you think most travellers would have agreed with her? Give reasons for your answers.

Here is a story about railway volunteers, from a trade union newsheet:

The train was manned by the usual volunteer personnel in sweaters and plus fours, and all went well, though very slowly, until Staddlethorpe junction was reached. Here the line divides into two branches, one leading to Selby, and the other to Saltmarshe and Goole.

The train stopped and the amateur driver was promised by the amateur signalmen that the junction points were set in the direction of Selby. A fresh start was made, but in the course of time a passenger looked through his window and was alarmed by the unfamiliar scenery. The train was again pulled up when it was found that it had, in fact, reached Saltmarshe. With a fine disregard for Board of Trade regulations for passenger trains, it was driven backwards to Staddlethorpe Junction to start its journey again.

Railway Strike-Committee Bulletin

1. What mistake did the volunteer railwaymen make?
2. How did they put their mistake right? What rule did they break?
3. Why do you suppose the Railway Strike Committee told this story?

As the Government was expecting trouble, it called for volunteers to be special constables. One of these was a retired colonel. He was asked to protect a lorry whose driver was also a volunteer:

I sat beside the driver and asked him if he had done much driving before. He replied that he hadn't. I didn't feel at all happy about the zig-zag course he was steering, and it was not long before my fears were realised. Suddenly we swerved across to the wrong side of the road, and collided with a Rolls Royce, ripping off one of the wheels. The driver of the Rolls Royce was naturally angry. A fight seemed likely and a crowd of idle strikers gathered round and began to take sides in the dispute.

We had been instructed what to do in the case of accidents, but hadn't been told how to handle hostile crowds. I came down from my perch, waved my truncheon and said, 'Stand back there.' The appeal had little effect, and I began to wonder what my next move should be. I became fully aware of my lack of training, and that what I had learnt in command of a regiment was of little use here. An ugly situation was developing, when a regular police sergeant appeared. As if by magic, he took control. He told the lorry driver to pull in to one side, and then buzz off, and proceeded to calm down the driver of the Rolls.

1. Why was the colonel nervous from the start?
2. What accident was there?
3. How did the colonel try to control the crowd?
4. Why was he unable to do so?
5. Who saved the situation? How?

Here is a message which the T.U.C. issued at the start of the strike:

Message To All Workers

The General Council of the Trades Union Congress wishes to stress the fact that this is an industrial dispute. It expects every member taking part to be exemplary in his conduct and not to give any opportunity for police interference. The outbreak of any disturbance would be very damaging to the prospects of a successful end to the dispute.

The British Worker, May 5th, 1926

How does the T.U.C. want strikers to behave? Why?

This is what happened to some railway passengers, in spite of the T.U.C.'s message:

The train arrived very late – a small engine and one carriage – and to our surprise we saw that many windows were broken. We were told that we would have to run the gauntlet of the strikers who had posted themselves on a pit heap near Annitsford Station. An old workman had the idea that if we stood above the windows, any glass would fall only at our feet. Accordingly two of us stood on the seat and held on to the luggage rack, while the workman lay down full length and placed his coat over his head. The carriage was duly raked from end to end, but we took no harm from it. Arrived at Morpeth, there was not a window left unbroken that side of the carriage.

1. What danger did the passengers run?
2. How did they protect themselves?
3. How badly was the train damaged?

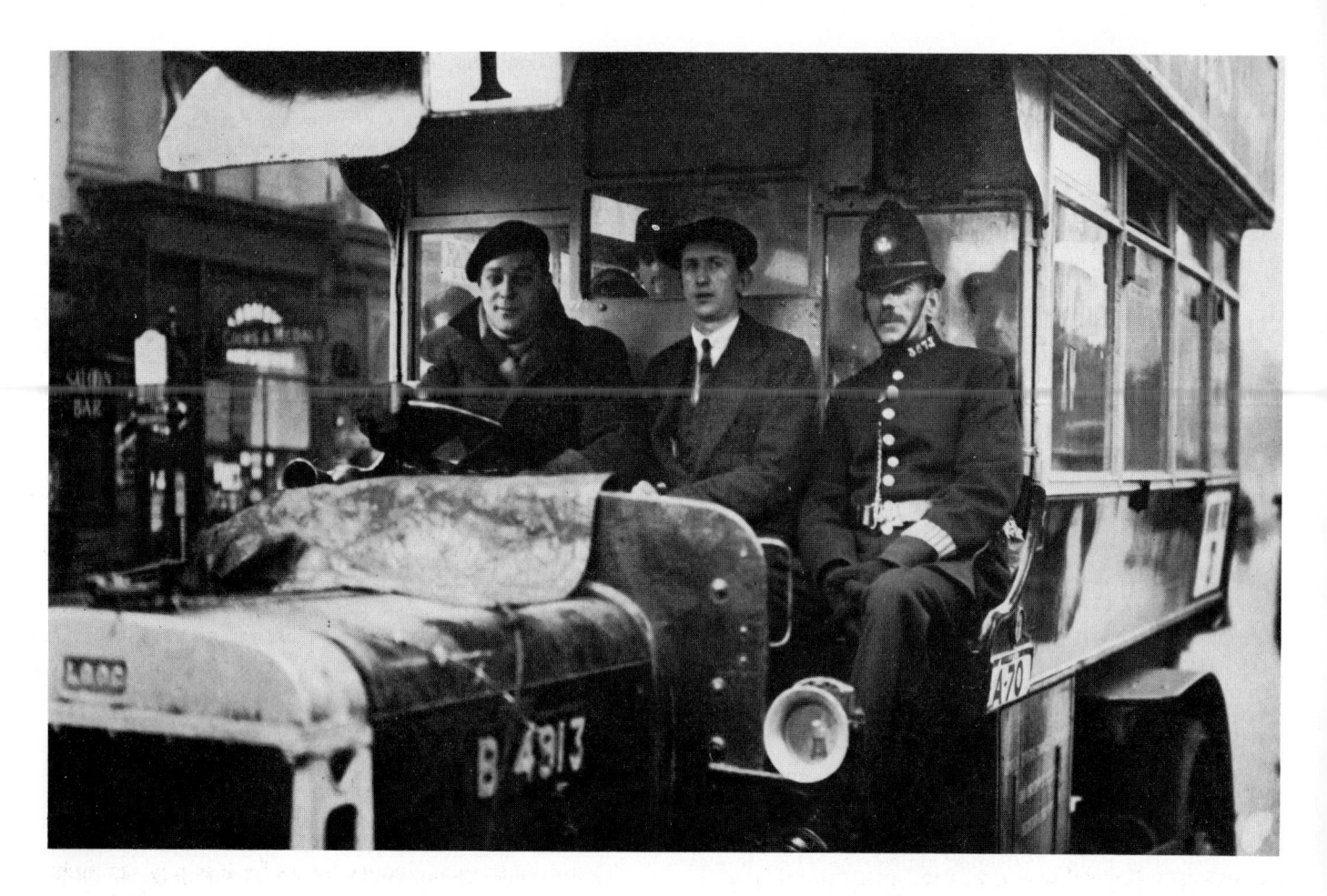

Volunteers drove the London buses. These are some of the things they wrote on their buses:

> 'A stone in the hand is worth two in the bus.'
> 'Try our Fresh Air Cure.'
> 'Keep your bricks, please. All windows broken.'
> 'I have no pane, dear mother, now.'
> 'I'm about done for, so they call me Mr. Cook.'

Note: Cook was the miners' leader.

1. What do these slogans suggest is happening to the buses?
2. What do these slogans tell you about the volunteers who wrote them?

Here is a newspaper report:

> There was a serious disturbance at Edenthorpe near Doncaster, yesterday, when 15 men were arrested and were later brought up at Doncaster West Riding Court, charged with interfering with transport.
>
> In court was disposed a large heap of stakes, lead piping, iron bars and large forks.
>
> A lorry that had been from Bradford to Grimsby for fish had to stop to fill up with petrol. About 200 men, all armed with sticks, iron forks, iron bars etc., then attacked the three men in charge of the vehicle.
>
> They set upon the three men and dragged them from the lorry. There were cries of, 'Burn it!' and 'Murder them!'
>
> All the 15 men were sentenced to three months imprisonment with hard labour.
>
> *Daily Chronicle*, May 13th, 1926

1. What was the lorry carrying?
2. How many men attacked it? Why do you suppose they did so?
3. How many men were arrested? How were they punished?

This extract was written by a *British Gazette* reporter who went to the West Riding of Yorkshire:

> I expected trouble in this district, but it has been entirely uneventful – a week spent in the midst of people who are sorely distressed at the upheaval, but are anxious to preserve order and to return, as soon as possible, to normal working conditions.
>
> I made various short tours of the coalfields during the week. I talked to miners and mine owners. On all sides the same story was to be heard: 'Everything quiet.' The pit ponies were brought above ground and were allowed to graze in quiet comfort – the only creatures who have

anything to gain by the strike: the men played football at the pitheads.

There were various slight outbreaks of ill-temper, but they were not serious. The people who overturned buses were mostly callow youths, glad of some escape from boredom: they cannot be regarded as typical of the general community.

I called daily on the superintendents of police, and the officer in charge of the local Territorials, who were standing by at the Drill Hall: on the officials at the Town Hall where volunteers were being enrolled. They replied unanimously, 'There is no trouble so far, and we do not expect it.'

The British Gazette, May 12th, 1926

Note: Territorials are part-time soldiers.

1. How, according to the writer, are the people feeling?
2. How are the miners behaving?
3. Who is doing best out of the strike?
4. What crimes have there been? Who was responsible?
5. What steps are the authorities taking against the strike?
6. What did the men in charge tell the writer?

The General Strike lasted only nine days. The main reason it collapsed was that the Government had prepared for it, while the T.U.C. had not. Most people went back to work, but the miners who had started it all, stayed on strike. In August, the *Daily Express* printed this report on the West Riding of Yorkshire:

Extraordinary scenes of intimidation have today prevented many hundreds of miners willing to work from going to the pits.

Crowds of miners and women lined the roads to various collieries. Any worker who appeared was booed, and his name and address taken. Workers were pulled off their bicycles and violently attacked as they rode to the pits, and one man was discovered lying in the roadway by a police patrol.

Terror has been caused among the wives and children by mobs going from house to house and ordering men not to go back to work.

Today, a man trying to go to work was chased by a crowd of men and women. He fell on his knees before them and begged for mercy, and was allowed to go home on promising the crowd that he would not try to work again.

Daily Express

1. How do strikers prevent men from going to work?
2. What does this tell you about the spirit of the strikers?

This is a report, also in the *Daily Express*, from the South Wales coalfield:

Everywhere sullen crowds of idle mine workers, unshaven and dishevelled, fill the narrow streets, while in the doorways of the endless rows of cottages their womenfolk sit for hours staring sadly into space.

The plight of the women and children is pitiful. I am told, for example, that the Rhondda Urban District Council will require at least £1,500 a week to supply milk to expectant mothers and to babies up to the age of twelve months, in place of the £150 which they are at present permitted to spend under the Ministry of Health regulations.

More than 40,000 applications for the relief of destitute persons have already been dealt with by the various stations set up by the board of guardians in the Pontypridd district alone. Twenty thousand of these applications were received in one day this week. The Feeding of Necessitous School Children Act has been brought into operation in the schools; the youngsters are lined up in food kitchens two or three times a day for their meals.

1. Who is suffering most from the strike?
2. What is being done to help?

In November 1926, the miners ended their strike. They had to work longer hours for less pay, as their employers wanted. Also many of the pits which had been closed during the strike did not open again, and their men were without jobs.

Written Work
1. Three volunteers, a railwayman, a bus driver, and a special constable meet after the strike. They talk about their experiences. Write what they say.
2. You are a coal miner. Give an account of your own strike and of the General Strike. Say how you felt when the General Strike began, and when it ended.

Research
1. Read more about the General Strike. Find out as many reasons as you can for its failure.
2. What action did the Government take against the Trade Unions when the strike was over?
3. Find out what you can about Stanley Baldwin, who was Prime Minister at the time of the General Strike.

The Falklands

On April 2nd 1982 the Argentinians captured the Falkland Islands. Immediately the British government sent a task force to recover them. Its commander was Rear Admiral Woodward. There was a fleet of 100 ships including the liner *Canberra* and the P & O Ferry *Norland*. They carried 3 Commando Brigade which was made up of Royal Marine Commandos and the Second and Third Battalions of the Parachute Regiment.

On May 26th, British ships sailed into San Carlos Water and began landing troops and supplies. It was from here on May 27th that the Second Battalion of the Parachute Regiment set out to take Darwin and Goose Green. They had a difficult, dangerous task. As you can see from the map, the two settlements lie on a narrow isthmus, and the Argentinians had dug trenches across Darwin Hill.

The officer in charge of 2 Para was Colonel H. Jones, known to his troops as 'H'. He had 450 men divided into four companies. His plan was to send 'C' Company to clear the way to the start line, which the battalion was to reach by the evening of May 27th. Soon after midnight on May 28th 'B' Company was to advance down the west side of the isthmus, outflanking Mount Darwin. 'A' Company was to advance down the east side of the isthmus and capture the Argentinian position on the hill itself. 'D' Company was to leapfrog 'B', while 'C' was to come forward in time for the attack on the Goose Green settlement. This was to take place in daylight so that there would be less chance of killing civilians.

With the battalion was a B.B.C. correspondent called Robert Fox. As the troops were preparing to move Colonel Jones asked him where he wanted to go. 'I don't know', said Fox. 'I've never been in anything like this before.' 'Neither have I', said the Colonel.

All went well until dawn, but by then the battalion was in trouble. 'B' Company ran into heavy fire from Boca House and could not advance. On Darwin Hill 'A' Company met heavy resistance from well-prepared positions. Then, on the west side, 'D' Company came to the rescue. It made its way along the beach and attacked Boca House from the rear. The Argentinians there surrendered. On the east side 'A' Company did manage to capture Darwin Hill, but only after a bloody battle in which Colonel Jones was killed.

The second-in-command of the battalion, Major Keeble, now took charge, and all four companies advanced on Goose Green. They had surrounded the main Argentinian forces, but Major Keeble was worried. Goose Green was heavily defended, and his men were exhausted. Rather than order an attack, he decided to give the Argentinians the chance to surrender. To his great relief they did.

The capture of Goose Green was a splendid victory for 2 Para. Nonetheless, like all battles, it had its share of strange incidents. In this section we will look at some of them.

Lt.-Colonel Herbert Jones On the left is the decoration he was given, posthumously, for the courage he showed at the battle of Goose Green. What is this medal?

A. The Death of Colonel Jones

It is unusual for commanding officers to be killed. This is because they have to stay out of the thick of the fighting if they are to direct their troops. Yet Colonel Jones, an excellent officer, was shot at a crucial moment. Sergeant Barry Norman was with the Colonel at the time. He told Robert Fox what happened:

> As we progressed towards the gorse 'A' Company came under heavy fire from the hills off to our right. We were pinned down quite heavy and the colonel decided Tac 1, his party, would move up to join 'A' Company and he would find out what the score was because he wasn't satisfied the battle was progressing as fast as he wished.

Colonel Jones reached the Headquarters of 'A' Company, with some difficulty, and discussed what to do with its commander, Major Farrar-Hockley. Sergeant Norman went on:

The guns could not be used because some friendly forces were too close to the enemy positions. We had to use the battalion mortars.

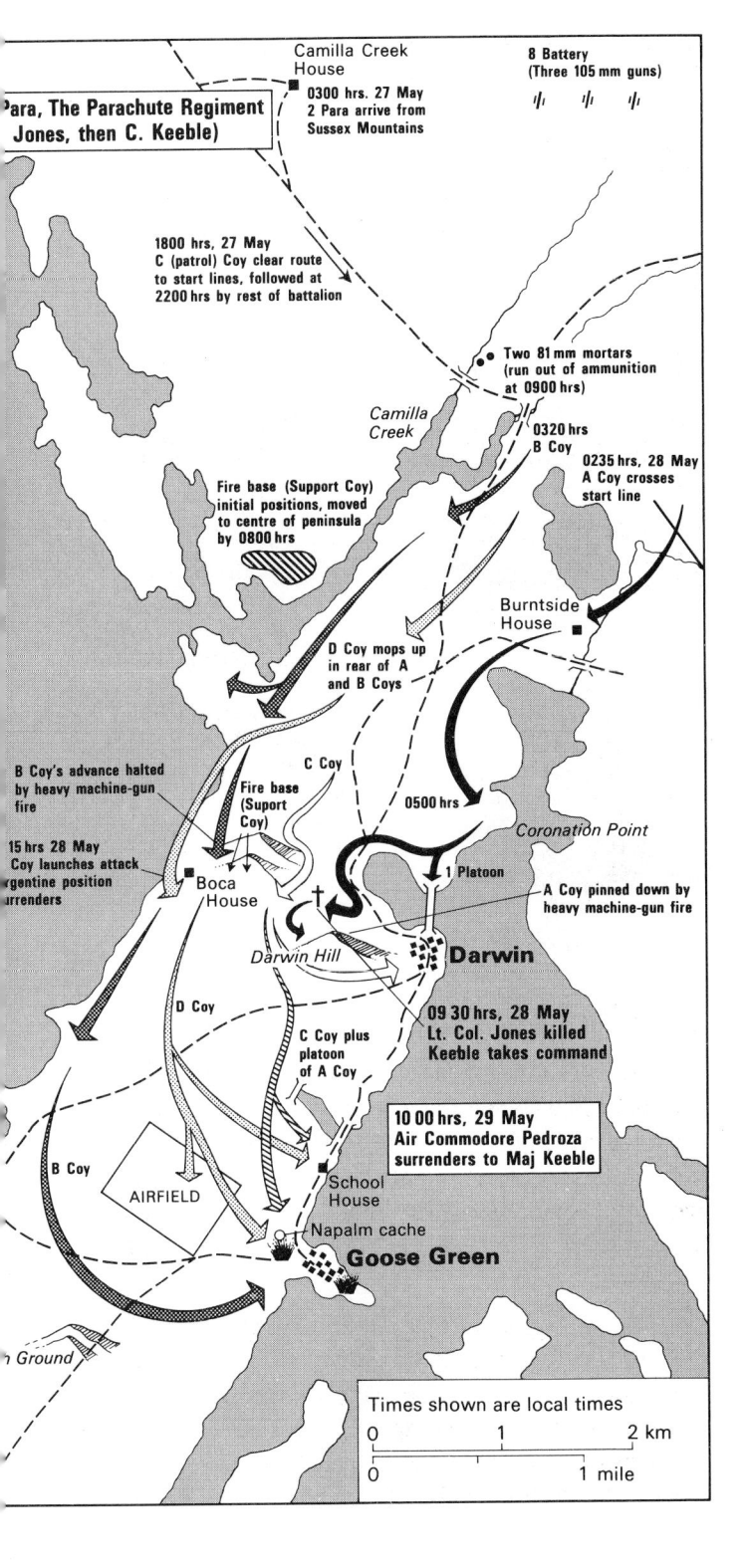

We used the battalion mortars, but then the Colonel decided we would attack across the top of the open hill and asked for mortar smoke, which we got. Once we got on the top, the smoke ran out: we'd run out of the mortar ammunition and we were caught there, about thirty of us, along the top of the hill, pinned down by quite heavy fire. In fact, Captain Dent, the second in command of 'A' Company, was killed in that part of the action. The Colonel then shouted out, 'Follow me' and turned to his right and ran down into the dead ground, which was on the right side of the hill, and headed towards the enemy position. I immediately followed and was followed by Corporal Beresford, others of Tac 1 and 'A' Company.

I was less than twenty metres behind him, but he got a bit away from me because he was a pretty fit bloke. He got round into a re-entrant and I went round to follow him, someone to my rear shouted: 'Watch out, there's an enemy position on the left.' I immediately looked left and saw an enemy trench, and as I noticed it, it opened fire on me. I hit the ground and I looked up and the Colonel was in between two enemy positions in complete dead ground.

I returned fire to the enemy trench, and the Colonel took his magazine off his submachine gun, checked it, reloaded it and proceeded up the hill towards the enemy position that we'd just noticed. As he got within three feet of the position, I shouted out: 'Watch your back'. But he took no notice and was shot in the back from a trench to the rear. I remained there for some considerable time, possibly for ten minutes – it felt for ever – pinned down by two enemy positions. Eventually two 66s were used on the enemy trenches and they surrendered. I believe it was Corporal Abols who fired the successful rocket of the two: all I heard was a bang at one end and even bigger bang at the other, and I was quite relieved that they surrendered.

Eyewitness Falklands

Notes: 1. Tac 1 was the 'tactical headquarters team', a small group whose duty it was to protect the Commanding Officer.
2. A re-entrant is a narrow valley closed at one end.
3. 66s are 66 mm rockets.

1 Why did Colonel Jones decide to join 'A' Company?
2 Why was it impossible to ask the artillery to bombard the enemy positions? What was used instead?
3 Where did Colonel Jones decide to attack?
4 Why were he and his men in danger very soon?
5 What did the Colonel shout? Where did he run?
6 What did Sergeant Norman see as he followed the Colonel?
7 How close did the Colonel get to the position he was attacking?
8 How was he killed?

9 How were the Argentinian positions finally destroyed?
10 Draw a sketch map to show **a**) the Argentinian position Colonel Jones was attacking, **b**) the Argentinian position from which he was killed, **c**) where Colonel Jones fell, **d**) where Sergeant Norman was at the time.

Why did Colonel Jones behave as he did? Robert Fox wrote:

> It has been argued that a battalion commander should not have been so far forward as 'H' was in the battle by Darwin Hill. It has also been said that a commander should not have led the kind of attack that 'H' did when he shouted to Sergeant Barry Norman, 'Follow me'. Who can say what was going through his head as he charged across that twenty-metre strip of ground to the enemy machine-gun position? All of us on the battlefield knew that he would not ask anyone to carry out an action that he would not do himself. Chris Keeble, his second-in-command, says that he had decided to go forward because he needed to see the battle for himself; his intelligence reports before the attacks started were now being proved to be so badly wrong about enemy positions and the strength of the Argentinian defences. When he discovered that 'A' Company was being held up, that artillery could not be used and there was no mortar smoke left to hide an attack, Chris Keeble thinks he took the calculation 'Do I use ten men now to do what it might take more than a hundred to do if we wait?' Sergeant Norman describes 'H's' reasoning for his charge at the enemy machine-guns in more simple terms. 'He was a very determined man and he said throughout all the actions and all the briefings that if we hit the Argentinian trenches hard, they would fold. He wasn't satisfied that the action was going as fast as he wanted: he was very impatient and wanted to go through as fast as possible. It was natural for him to say "Follow me" and in every exercise we've done with him, he's led from the front.'
>
> *Eyewitness Falklands*

British soldier inspects captured napalm bombs There was a grass air strip at Goose Green so the Argentinians used it as an air base. Napalm is a jelly which sticks to the skin of its victim and burns fiercely. Fortunately, the Argentinians did not use this dreadful weapon, though they had the bombs all ready and primed.

1. What criticisms have been made of Colonel Jones?
2. According to Major Keeble:
   a. Why did Colonel Jones come forward into the fighting?
   b. Why did he make the attack?
3. How did Sergeant Norman explain Colonel Jones's action?
4. Which explanation seems more likely to you, Major Keeble's, or Sergeant Norman's? Could they both be right?

B. The White Flag Incident

After the capture of Mount Darwin, 'C' and 'D' Companies advanced to the school house, just north of Goose Green. Later, the *Daily Telegraph* reported something that happened there:

> *White Flag Shooting By Argentines*
> At least one British officer was killed at Goose Green when Argentine soldiers waved a white flag and then opened fire on British troops, it was disclosed yesterday.
> Major Chris Keeble, who took command of the 2nd Battalion, Parachute Regiment, after Lt. Col. H. Jones was killed, was quoted in a dispatch from Jeremy Hands, I.T.N. reporter.
> He said the Argentines' action sickened him.
> 'The Argentines fought until they realised they were beaten. Then they showed the white flag. Then they fought a bit further,' he said.
> 'That's what sickened me, particularly when you look into the loss of one particular officer's life.'
> *Daily Telegraph*, Wednesday June 2nd, 1982

In his book, written after the war, Robert Fox said:

> It was here that one of the saddest incidents of the campaign took place. Argentinians in a trench facing 'D' Company hoisted a white flag. As Lieutenant Jim Barry got up to take the surrender, a British machine-gun opened fire to his right; immediately there was answering fire from an Argentinian position to his left, some distance away from the trench trying to surrender. Jim Barry was killed as he stood in the open. Those at the scene do not think that this was deliberate treachery, with the white flag being used as a decoy.
> Surrenders and negotiations are very difficult to manage while fighting is continuing. Jim Barry died because of a mistake, though the circumstances were not to be reported accurately for some time.
> *Eyewitness Falklands*

1. What trick did Major Keeble think the Argentinians had played?
2. How does Robert Fox explain the incident? Draw a sketch map to show a) where Lieut. Barry was killed b) the Argentinians who raised the white flag c) the British machine gun which opened fire d) the Argentinians who returned the fire, and killed Lieut. Barry.

C. The Surrender of the Argentinians

By nightfall on May 28th the British had surrounded Goose Green settlement. The following morning, Major Keeble sent two prisoners of war to the Argentinian commander with this message:

> *To* the Commander, Argentine Forces, Goose Green
> *From* the Commander, British Forces, Goose Green Area
> **MILITARY OPTIONS**
> We have sent a PoW to you under a White Flag of truce to convey the following military options:
> 1. That you surrender your force to us by leaving the township, forming up in a military manner, removing your helmets and laying down your weapons. You will give prior notice of this intention by returning the PoW under the White Flag, with him briefed as to the formalities, no later than 0830 hours local time.
> 2. You refuse in the first case to surrender and take the inevitable consequences. You will give prior notice of this intention by returning the PoW without his White Flag, although his neutrality will be respected, no later than 0830 hours local time.
> 3. In any event, and in accordance with the terms of the Geneva Conventions and the laws of war, you shall be held responsible for the fate of any civilians in Goose Green and we, in accordance with the laws, do give you prior notice of our intention to bombard Goose Green.
> Signed C. Keeble
> Commander, British Forces, Goose Green Area
> 29/5/82

1. What choices did Major Keeble give the Argentinians?
2. What did he say would happen if they took the second?

After some negotiations the Argentinians agreed to surrender. Robert Fox describes what happened after that:

> We crossed into a pasture and the Air Force men marched towards us to form up in an open square. The Air Force commander, Wilson Pedroso, said that he agreed to the surrender terms and then turned to harangue his men in one of the strangest ceremonies I have witnessed. I heard bits and pieces about pride in the fatherland and the cause of the Malvinas, but not much more. At the end there were shouts of 'Eviva' and a

British soldier inspects Argentinian weapons surrendered at Goose Green Many of the Argentinians had neglected their weapons, even allowing them to go rusty.

singularly tuneless rendering of the Argentinian national anthem. It sounded first like a dirge, then the chant of a doleful football crowd. At the end, the men threw down their arms, some with evident relief. The Air Vice-Commodore stepped forward, came to attention, saluted Chris Keeble and handed over his pistol and belt, saluted again and walked away.

At first we had mistaken the Air Force contingent for the entire military garrison remaining in Goose Green. There were about 250 Air Force personnel on parade. If there was the same number again of Army and special forces, it would be roughly the strength we had expected to find in the settlement, about 600 men at the most.

What Major Keeble's party saw next was one of the most amazing sights of the campaign. We saw the soldiers coming out of the houses and huts, first by platoons and then companies. There were first fifty, then a hundred, and then too many to count quickly. As they marched up the slope towards us we realised for the first time that the paratroopers had been fighting not a few companies of Argentinians as had been thought but at least two, and possible three battalions. About nine hundred to a thousand men formed up by companies.
Eyewitness Falklands

Note: 2 Para lost 17 men killed during the battle, the Argentinians perhaps as many as 200.

1. Describe how the men of the Argentinian Air Force surrendered.
2. How many of them were there?
3. How many men of the Argentinian Army did the British expect to see?
4. How many, in fact appeared?
5. By how many, roughly, did the Argentinians outnumber the British? (2 Para was 450 strong).

Two British journalists, Max Hastings and Simon Jenkins, described an incident after the surrender:

The paras now enjoyed their euphoric moment of victory. They were overwhelmed by the relief of being spared another battle. Keeble led his men into the settlement, and knocked on the door of the first house, where he found the settlement manager, Eric Goss, with his wife, 'Would you like a cup of tea?' asked Mrs. Goss.
Battle for the Falklands

Research
1. Find out why the Falklands war happened.
2. Read about other incidents in the war, especially the capture of Port Stanley.